SÍ SEÑOR

SÍ SEÑOR
My Liverpool Years

ROBERTO FIRMINO

QUERCUS

First published in Great Britain in 2023 by

QUERCUS

Quercus Editions Ltd
Carmelite House
50 Victoria Embankment
London EC4Y 0DZ

An Hachette UK company

A CIP catalogue record for this book is available
from the British Library

HB ISBN 978 1 52943 527 6
TPB ISBN 978 1 52943 564 1
Ebook ISBN 978 1 52943 566 5

PICTURE CREDITS
All images supplied courtesy of Roberto Firmino, except: 3 – Alex Livesey/Getty; 4 –
MUSTAFA ABUMUNES/Getty; 5 – Andrew Powell/Getty; 6 – Clive Brunskill/Getty; 7 – Plumb
images/Getty; 8 – John Powell/Getty; 9 – Silvio Eugênio da Silva; 10 – Camila Machado
Rodolfo; 11 – FK Pictures - Felippe Gonçalves, Katia Gonçalves; 16 – Oli Scarff/Getty; 17, 24 –
Rodan Can; 18 – Jan Kruger/Getty; 19 – Andrew Powell/Liverpool FC; 21 – Luciano Lopes de
Souza; 22 – Mark Paul Volante; 23 – FK Pictures - Felippe Gonçalves, Katia Gonçalves.

10 9 8 7 6 5 4 3 2 1

Typeset by CC Book Production
Printed and bound in Great Britain by Clays Ltd, Elcograf S.p.A.

Papers used by Quercus are from well-managed forests and other responsible sources.

God, Your works are wonderful, and I know it well.

Holy Spirit, my Guide, and Jesus, my Saviour,
thank you for such love.

My beloved wife, Larissa, who has always been
my faithful helper and never let go of my hands.
Valentina, Bella, Liz and Sophia, you are my fuel.
I hope to be a good example and warm your hearts.

I dedicate this book to you.
Without you, none of this would exist.

Contents

Contents

Preface

Obrigado

I never wanted to leave Liverpool Football Club.

I feel it's important to say that right from the start, so there's no doubt.

On 3 March 2023 I opened a new note on my phone and started writing a message to Jürgen Klopp, the Boss. I didn't want to face him and stumble over my words, so I wanted to prepare it, get it just right: 'I've talked to my family and made the decision not to stay at the club anymore. I believe my time here has come to an end. Thank you very much for everything.'

I also didn't want the Boss to insist that I stay, as had happened with my friend Philippe Coutinho years before. But he didn't insist. He already knew that moment was coming. I did too, which is why I said it. I didn't want this, never wanted to go, but I had to accept the inevitable. Discussions over a contract renewal had been dragging on and I finally understood that there weren't two paths for my choice: to stay or not to stay. There was only one. And someone needed the courage to make that decision, to actually say it.

So I did.

The final three months in Liverpool were filled with love, memories, and endless demonstrations of affection and respect from the club, staff, teammates and, above all, the fans. I was humbled by so much love and will be forever grateful.

I doubt there's a club in the world with fans as passionate or loyal as Liverpool's, no place as alive as Anfield. I'll always be a Red. I never imagined I would achieve so much at the club, become an idol or see my family and I fulfil all our dreams. It was the honour of my life to wear the red shirt of Liverpool Football Club.

I arrived in the city as one person and I left as another.

Liverpool changed me. I had changed too. My life can be divided into two parts, like the history of the world itself: Before Christ and After Christ. In 2019 my transformation began to take shape and I started embracing life in Christ.

Before that, I lived through a phase of discovery and rebellion. I wasn't the first Brazilian boy to rise from poverty to become a football idol, and I won't be the last either. Overnight, everything becomes easier and everything comes easily: money, luxury, cars, women; all you could ever wish for. You feel like you can do whatever you want. It happens so fast and it's not easy to control all of that, to manage it. Who are the real friends? Who can you trust? Who truly loves you? Who only loves your money and fame?

Thank God, I always had people by my side who helped me stay focused, kept me in line. I always wanted to be a football player, to succeed. I couldn't miss that opportunity.

The most important person, of course, was Larissa. My love, my passion, my safe haven, the woman of my life since the moment I first saw her in Florianópolis. It wasn't easy, I made mistakes, but in the end love triumphed. We got married in 2017, in my hometown, Maceió.

We already had two beautiful daughters: Valentina, born in Germany, and Bella, in England. They were sent by God and were a crucial bond in our love. At a different, more settled time in our lives, two more princesses arrived: Liz and Sophia. The four girls are our most precious gifts, an infinite love.

In 2018 Larissa was touched by Christ. In the same year, two essential players for our team and two essential couples for our lives arrived in the city of Liverpool: Alisson and Natália; Fabinho and Rebeca. They were important for Larissa's affirmation and my own encounter with God, which would happen soon afterwards, transforming me after a period of resistance and stubbornness. Life in Christ distanced me from drinking, parties and empty fun that leads nowhere. I started valuing much more what was already close to me, which, before, I couldn't see: true friends, family.

In the following pages I'll tell you the story of the two Bobby Firminos. There's a constant they both share, something that didn't change: the smile. Sure, it became a little whiter and brighter, I know, but it has always been with me. It has always been my main way of expressing myself. I was an extremely shy, quiet boy of few words, so it was often my smile that saw me through, that opened doors, that won the love of many people.

The other way I expressed myself, of course, was on the field, doing what I love: playing football. I'm blessed because the Lord empowered me with the talent necessary to make people happy, to bring joy and emotion to their lives, to make them smile too.

From the terrace of my apartment in my dear city, Maceió, in the north-east of Brazil, where I began putting this book together, looking back on my life, on eight special years at Anfield, I see a beautiful blue sea. Always beautiful. From the ninth floor, with all the comfort you could have, comfort I could only dream of when I was a boy, I see a fishing boat passing by with the red colours and the emblem of CRB, Clube de Regatas Brasil, my father's favourite team and the club where my transformation began – from a boy playing with friends in the street to a real football player playing in front of thousands.

In Maceió the two major teams are CRB and CSA (Centro Sportivo Alagoano): red and blue. Does that remind you of another city, another pair of rivals? The city of Liverpool Football Club, deep in my heart now, and Everton, our eternal rivals. Reds and blues, just like in Maceió. Some things remain the same, always.

Liverpool was home for eight years. It's where three of my four daughters were born and it's the club that allowed me to fulfil the dream of playing in a World Cup with the yellow shirt of the Brazilian national team, the ultimate goal for any child, any football player from my country.

You've heard me speak very little over these years. There have been few interviews or off-field events. I battle shyness every day of my life. If speaking in public in my own language is already difficult for me, you can imagine how much harder it is to give an interview in English. You know that it would be impossible for me to write the story of my life in English. This book is a collaborative work, with the help of God and many people crucial to my development as a person and as a player. This book wouldn't exist without their involvement, just like Liverpool's success, all those trophies – Premier League, FA Cup, League Cup, Community Shield, European Super Cup, European Cup and

World Cup – wouldn't exist without everyone, without a massive collective effort, on and off the field.

Not all heroes wear capes; some are called Dad. My father, José, was my childhood hero, an inspiration and an example. A generous, serious, honest man dedicated to family.

My mother, Maria Cícera, shaped my character. When I thought I knew everything about life, she would give me a lesson in how things really were. A woman of strong personality and a soft heart, always present in my childhood, she suffered when I left home at just 16, but she knew that my purpose was greater and she fought for it alongside me.

My sister, Marcella, came to light up the house. At first, the little 'Bebeto', as they called me in the neighbourhood, would get angry because he had 'lost' the TV – football had been replaced by cartoons. And also because I had to carry her heavy bag of nappies back and forth. When I left home, she was only six, and I'm grateful that she was the companion she was to our parents.

Besides my family, I can't forget about the essential people in my journey. My lifelong friend Cesinha Lucena, from our youth days at CRB to our daily interaction during the glorious years in Liverpool, has been a loyal companion who I knew would always be with me, in good times and bad.

To my fellow brother in Christ, Isaias Saad, my pastors

Jairo and Keila, and my entire faith family from Manah Church, I extend my heartfelt gratitude. You have been and continue to be instruments of God in my life. Thank you for showing me love, true love, while many were just massaging my ego.

I also want to thank João and Lina, wonderful Portuguese people from Madeira, who have been by my side all these years, taking care of me and my family with a lot of love.

And Sven Kampmann, the physiotherapist who has been with me since 2015, helping to keep the 'racehorse' ready to run, fit for the fight. Hendrick Meyer, César Thier and my friend Júnior, better known as JJ, who assisted in keeping the train on track in Germany. As well as all the doctors, physios and trainers who stood by me in the most complicated times, during injuries.

I want to thank the Boss, my dear coach Jürgen Klopp, who trusted me from day one – and all the guys who were part of his coaching staff over the years. The guys from Liverpool's scouting department: Michael Edwards, David Fallows, Barry Hunter, Andy Sayer and Fernando Troiani, who pushed for my signing to be approved by the club's management. Also Mike Gordon from Fenway Sports Group, who supported my arrival at Liverpool.

Many coaches and scouts believed in me throughout my journey. Guilherme Farias and Toninho Almeida, the first to see me at CRB, believed in a 14-year-old Roberto when others didn't. Bilu and Dr Marcellus were responsible for my dramatic departure from Maceió to Florianópolis. Later, Hemerson Maria, was an essential coach for my development at Figueirense. Márcio Araújo, was the first to give me a chance among the professionals, Renê Weber promoted me to the first team at Figueirense, and Márcio Goiano effectively gave me the minutes and opportunities to play when I was just 18.

A big thank you to all the players who played alongside me, in all the clubs I went through. At Liverpool I was welcomed with open arms by Lucas Leiva and Philippe Coutinho, groomsmen at my wedding. With them, Alberto Moreno, Allan Souza, and their wives, we shared great and warm moments in England. These are friendships that will last forever.

The professional journey I've travelled had meaning because Christian Rapp and Roger Wittmann took care of it with love and responsibility. Together with Nenê Zini and Eduardo Uram, they formed the group of representatives who supported me and guided me.

And last but certainly not least, a super special thank you to Julio Gomes, the author of this book, who skilfully translated my feelings, who became emotional, excited and even saddened with every detail. His curiosity was boundless and he journeyed alongside me in this story, sparing no effort to ensure that no detail was forgotten. Julio was consistently supported by his friend, mentor and editor Sid Lowe, two football and life-story enthusiasts.

My country is a great breeding ground for football talents. It's also a place where many people, many children, go through hardships they shouldn't have to endure. Possibly, one thing is connected to the other. There's a direct link between the lack of opportunities and the abundance of talent in Brazilian football. It's up to me, with God's guidance, to try to help the children in my hometown and my beloved state of Alagoas to find better opportunities, and that's what I'm doing.

Many ask me what the most memorable moment of my eight years in Liverpool was. It's not easy to answer. Maybe a goal? Maybe an assist? Maybe a victory or a title? We'll embark on this journey to perhaps discover together.

Among the many goals and all the affection I was given, one of my most unforgettable moments was the last. On 20 May 2023 I played my final game at Anfield; an opportunity to bid farewell to the fans, that day will stay in my memory and the memory of my family forever. My father, mother and sister were there, as well as my wife Larissa and our four daughters: Valentina, Bella, Liz and Sophia. They won't forget.

The fans never let me walk alone, serenading me with a beautiful song they had created in my honour. '*Sí, Señor*' is the song I can forever call mine, one they sang with pride and passion. I felt embraced and loved by all.

Now, let me tell you about the moments I experienced in red: who the Roberto Firmino was that arrived in Liverpool hungry for titles, young and immature ... and who the Roberto Firmino is who found Jesus and – yes, sir – left the club as the highest-scoring Brazilian in the history of English football.

Chapter 1

Sí, Señor!

What if I told you it was a dentist who changed my career and gave me the push I needed to become a football player?

Yes, I know. It sounds strange. And I also know you're all thinking about my smile now, all those perfect white, sparkling teeth. I'll tell those stories in detail – about the dentist from Maceió and how I got my smile – but, don't worry, this isn't a book about teeth. This is the true story of a poor Brazilian boy who became an idol for the greatest football club in the world – and feels humbled and honoured by it.

Let's begin at the beginning, shall we? Actually, better to start with my eight years at Liverpool, the best years of my life, and how they marked me forever, how they transformed me; with the glory, the trophies and Klopp, the man who took us there; with Anfield, my home.

I arrived at a club that was a giant in England, respected for its history – but one that was currently, in the eyes of the world, not on the same level as other giants. Not yet, at least: we would change that. Those were the years of Spanish domination in Europe, with Barcelona and Madrid. Domestically, Chelsea had just won the league, but the English titles were more or less being won consecutively by our Manchester neighbours, United and City.

But we were coming.

I had enjoyed four extraordinary seasons at Hoffenheim in the Bundesliga, four and a half years that helped me grow as a player, as a person, and which led me to the Brazilian national team. While still playing for Hoffenheim, I was called up for the 2015 Copa América, and that European summer transfer window was to define my future. At the time, I had attracted the attention of Bayern Munich, the powerhouse of German football, Manchester City, who had been winning Premier League titles, and Liverpool. The Lord guided me to the perfect place.

Liverpool fans well remember what had just happened and what would happen next, but for those who are reading it here for the first time, some context is needed. Just over a year before my signing, at the end of the 2013–14 season, Liverpool lost the Premier League title in a way that broke their fans' hearts. They were leading the league, closing in on a first title in a quarter of a century, but dropped points in two of the last three games. The incredible goalscorer was Luis Suárez, the great captain was Steven Gerrard, and the manager was Brendan Rodgers. In the following season, 2014–15, without Suárez, things didn't go so well and Liverpool finished sixth in the Premier League after being eliminated in the group stage of the UEFA Champions League.

I mention this because it's important to know where they were and to talk about Rodgers, the manager when I was approached and signed by Liverpool that summer of 2015. In addition to Suárez, Gerrard had also left. It was undoubtedly a moment of transition and rebuilding for the club. And, truth be told, things didn't exactly go well with Rodgers at the start of my first season. It took me a few years to realize that I wasn't signed by Rodgers but rather by Liverpool's scouting and recruiting department.

Everything changed in October of that year when a guy named Mr Jürgen Norbert Klopp arrived in Liverpool. I have to give him his full title, although I confess I had to look it up. I just called him 'Boss'.

My story with Klopp existed even before we met in Liverpool. When I was playing for Hoffenheim, Borussia Dortmund had approached the club and wanted to sign me. I knew the importance of Dortmund, of course: in my early years in the Bundesliga they had been champions twice and runners-up twice. They were finalists in the 2013 Champions

League, losing the all-German final to Bayern Munich. They were always there, so the invitation to play for them was something to be considered. I always listened carefully to what my representatives said in moments like these. Roger Wittmann and Christian Rapp, both from the agency Rogon, have managed my career since I left Brazil. Nenê Zini and Eduardo Uram facilitated the deal that took me to Germany, along with Rogon. This is a relationship built on trust. They presented me with options and made recommendations based on solid arguments – which I almost always followed. On that occasion, they believed it was better to wait for the opportunity to make a direct leap to the Premier League, instead of spending another three years in Germany.

There had been contact from English clubs. However, it would be necessary to wait a bit in order to get a work permit from the British government, as I had never been called up for the Brazilian national team before.

I love football and I watched it all the time, from the Brazilian championship to the Chinese and Japanese leagues. Any league, really. Of course, I knew the strength of English clubs and how competitive the league was. It was already leaving all other European leagues behind. So, if my representatives thought it was better to wait, then we could wait. And look how wise and good God is: I would be chosen to play for Brazil later in 2014, and then for the Copa América in 2015, which opened Premier League doors to me. God ended up putting me in the path of Jürgen Klopp, who had already shown the desire to sign me for his team in Germany. This time, he didn't need to: as it turned out, they had done it for him. By the time he arrived in Liverpool, I was there waiting for him. This was England, a different club and a different context, but it worked.

But at the time, things weren't working at Anfield. When a club decides to change the manager in the middle of the season, it's clear that things are not going well. Eight games into the 2015–16 season, we were only tenth in the league. The owners decided to end Brendan Rodgers' contract. Honestly, I can't say I was upset, as I wasn't getting many opportunities, and I was being played completely out of position. The great news of Klopp's arrival came a few days later.

What can I say about him? I feel blessed to have had the opportunity to have lived and shared so many moments with Jürgen Klopp and the team that came with him – a team that would undergo changes over the years. Eight glorious, unforgettable years.

Together, we conquered the Premier League, a title that had eluded Liverpool for 30 years. And, to be honest, we should have won one or two more. We won a UEFA Champions League and reached three other European finals – two in the Champions League and one in the UEFA Europa League. We won the FA Cup. We won the League Cup. We won the

Community Shield. We won the UEFA Super Cup. We won the FIFA Club World Cup, a title that the club had never won before.

We won it all!

Wow.

As I read this, just looking back on that list I get emotional. When I go beyond the medals to the memories and the men I shared that time with, even more so. It's impossible not to remember the great moments, the joys and sorrows, everything we went through together; the transformation. Me, the Boss, my teammates, and all the people who have worked or still work in the great family that is Liverpool Football Club.

Klopp is a special manager for several reasons. First and foremost, he is so charismatic and very passionate about what he does. When he speaks, you stop to listen. He is witty, powerful and yet there's a lightness to the way he communicates. There's an irresistible positive energy surrounding him that's contagious – it's like he fills the room.

What I like most about him is how he knows how to handle a group of players. And it's all year round. He manages to have the players on his side, keeping each one of us up there, always 100 per cent motivated, ready and keen to win games, to achieve.

Think about the guy who doesn't play. A club like Liverpool is entirely made up of skilled players. There's not a bad footballer there. All of them represent their national teams. They were signed for a lot of money, or came up through the club academy, overcoming barriers on their way to the first team. And all of them want to play, without exception – every game, every minute. There's no football player who's content sitting on the bench or getting a few minutes here and there. Anyone saying that would be lying! We're all competitors, and the first competition is internal.

Striking the right balance presents a monumental challenge for the manager: to be respected while keeping the players – all of the players – happy and motivated. It's not always possible. I won't deny that I struggled with this badly in my last two seasons, when I frequented the bench more than I would have liked and got annoyed with the Boss. I've seen it from both sides and I know where I would rather be. Of course, there may have been one exception or another over the years: no leader is unanimously accepted. But Klopp is good with the group, even for that guy who doesn't get as many minutes as he'd like. The guy on the bench, the squad player, is kept engaged; he wants to win, to help the team that he still feels part of. We're all focused on the same goal, in it together.

One of Klopp's keys to maintaining unity was by encouraging exclusive moments for us, the players. Sometimes that would mean a dinner; other times a trip to somewhere around the world. This used to happen once or twice a season. These gatherings were meant to help us clear our minds from the exhausting and stressful daily routine of games and training; to talk about other matters and build bonds – friendship. The coaching staff never attended; this was a moment for the players.

Another important tool in Klopp's bag was his motivational speeches. During pre-season there was always a meeting with him and the players in a hotel, and Klopp used to bring someone to talk to us, to inspire and motivate us for the entire season.

I remember a specific one, in 2019, when he brought a big-wave surfer, German Sebastian Steudtner, to talk to us. A few years after our meeting, this guy ended up having his record for surfing the biggest wave in history recognized by Guinness World Records. He surfed a wave of 26.21 metres in Nazaré, Portugal – a wave the size of a building. It's absurd! The record is still his. I like to think we brought Sebastian a bit of luck. He brought us luck, that's for sure. Sebastian shared stories about the great challenges he faced and the methods he used to control anxiety, fear and the mind. He talked about when he fell from a giant wave and, to escape death, he knew that, rather than fighting or panicking, he needed to stay calm and control his breathing until he could finally resurface. In a competitive football season, we go through similar experiences. It feels like you're going to die, going to lose, and in those moments of anguish, it's crucial to stay calm and rediscover focus and direction.

There were other inspiring tales over the years, delivered by people from all walks of life. That's when the Boss would speak up or show a video, and he had this amazing ability to get you to empathize, to motivate you. Man, you would leave the team talk wanting to play immediately. You would want to help, to train, to move, to play, to win titles. At that moment, you felt like nothing could stop you, nothing could stand in your way all year. It's challenging to stay attentive, focused and motivated for eight or nine months, but the Boss had a way.

Klopp also keeps the players at the top of their physical and mental game through daily work and conversation. He's an open guy, someone you feel free to knock on the door of his office at Melwood or AXA, Liverpool's training grounds old and new. Come in, have a chat. Talk about anything. You can tell him how you really feel. He gives you the freedom to speak your mind. Of course, in the end, he makes the decisions he needs to make and believes are best for the club and the team. It's not possible to please everyone all the time. There were certainly players who might not have felt this freedom – I can only speak for myself – but I always felt it, from the first day.

Klopp has always been a reserved person outside the club. He doesn't visit players' homes or invite them to his house. Of course, he was always present and had a great time with us at club celebrations or other official events. But apart from that, no, you wouldn't see him. He is great to relate to, but only within the work environment, without crossing the line.

In training, especially in the early years, he was the kind of coach who participated in everything: stopping drills, correcting positioning, giving lectures. Especially so on the day before games. Sometimes he could sense that we lacked a bit of focus, or that we had lost concentration for a moment, however brief. Maybe we would concede a goal from a set piece. He would stop everything and say loudly, 'Let's wake up, guys, tomorrow is a big game!'

Mind you, in my last two years, I saw him mellow a bit.

I wasn't one of his favourite targets, thankfully. I vaguely remember one time he entered the dressing room and asked, 'Bobby, were you on the field today?' But perhaps I didn't understand what he said correctly. Not fully understanding the language has its advantages! And there was one telling off I remember vividly, something that happened during the coronavirus pandemic. Let's just say it was a haircut that did it, not a lack of intensity in training.

Roberto Firmino and Jürgen Klopp formed a great partnership because we share non-negotiable principles. We are people who like to work collectively, not individually. There are no personal interests. We willingly gave that up for the greater good, the collective. We see ourselves as pieces of a machine. Important pieces, sure, and it's crucial that everyone feels important. But we know full well that for everything to work, the other pieces also need to be fitted and functioning.

Perhaps what unites us is also the German mentality of working tirelessly. Klopp is German by birth and upbringing; I'm not, but Germany taught me and shaped me. I had no choice: I had to embrace their mentality when I went there, and it was good for me. Without it, I would never have succeeded in Europe.

I was only 19 when I left Florianópolis, in the south of Brazil, to play for Hoffenheim. A kid with so much still to learn, I had never played a first division match, not even in Brazil, and suddenly I found myself in a completely different country, with more intense and tougher football than anything I had experienced before. It's easy to understand why some Brazilian players return home almost as soon as they arrive in Europe.

I don't judge. There are obstacles that are truly difficult to overcome. But I knew what I wanted. I arrived in Germany in the winter of 2011 with a weak, fragile body, simply unable to compete. It was snowing, snowing a lot. I had never seen snow in my life. Back home, the average temperature never drops below 20°c; in Hoffenheim it would regularly drop below freezing. I lived in Sinsheim, a small town of 35,000 inhabitants, where there wasn't much to do besides train hard. The nearest big city was Stuttgart, an hour away. Stuttgart, hometown of my friend Mr Klopp.

I struggled at the beginning, studying German with Professor Raquel five times a week, taking hits during training. All too aware of the need to gain muscle mass, I worked hard, using all the tools provided by the club. I used my salary to set up a gym at home. Initially, no one at the club knew about it. I did it all with the help of a guy named Hendrick Meyer, who was assigned by my representatives to assist me in adapting to a new country with such a different climate and a complicated language. Another crucial person was César Thier, a former goalkeeper who worked on the club's coaching staff. Meyer and Thier were Brazilian-Germans, angels sent by God.

Somehow, Hoffenheim noticed my efforts and appreciated my perseverance. They were patient and invested a tremendous amount of time, care and attention in me. I wanted to become an athlete more than anything and I wouldn't waste the opportunity. This is an example of what the German mentality means. Work, work, work. That's Klopp's mentality. I love that guy.

I'll say it again: I love that guy.

Eight years is a long time, though, and the work does get tiresome. In my last couple of seasons at Anfield, I noticed that some players were mentally and physically exhausted. Maybe that was part of the club's attempts to rejuvenate the squad.

Klopp and the coaching staff noticed that and in my last year, the 2022–23 season, they gave us more time off. They also saw that the routine of travel–hotel–game was getting a bit much. We would stay in a hotel together even for home games, which not every team does. Locked up, all you can do is wait, or maybe go for a stroll on the morning of the game. It's tiring, I won't deny it. But it was a special time, perfect, and I will always remember it through the wonderful song the fans came up with for me. You'll know the one – but did you know that it was Klopp himself who 'ordered' the song? Just another reason to love and admire him.

Until the end of the 2017–18 season, our fans had a few chants with my name in, but they weren't proper songs like the greatest players in the club's history have. Just *'Bobby Firmino, Bobby Firmino.'* Something simple like that. And then, in May 2018, before the Champions League final against Real Madrid in Kyiv, Jürgen Klopp gave an interview to Liverpool's official TV channel, talking about the songs the fans sang and how he enjoyed watching internet videos of the fans' creations. Which was when he made the request: 'There's no song for Bobby Firmino. They only sing his name; that's not a song. Hello?! He really deserves a song. I want a song for Bobby!'

The Boss's request is an order. Yes, sir!

I wasn't aware of the origin of the song that would mark my career and my life so much. A friend passed me the text of a blog written by a Liverpool fan, explaining how the verses of the song originated in a bar in Belgrade, the capital of Serbia, on the eve of our match against Red Star, in the group stage of the Champions League. That game was in November 2018, six months after the coach's 'order' to the fans. The rest is history.

It goes like this:

> There's something that the Kop wants you to know
> The best in the world his name is
> Bobby Firmino
> Our number nine
> Give him the ball and he'll score every time
> *Sí, Señor*
> Pass the ball to Bobby and he'll score

They say the Kop can suck the ball into the net. I don't doubt it: they carry everyone; embrace you. I don't remember exactly when I first heard the song, but, to be honest, the first time I heard it I didn't think of it as such a big deal. My mistake was a big one. Today I recognize its importance and appreciate it so much. It's very gratifying to have a song that's so special; it's a tribute that moves my whole family.

The rhythm is wonderful and when you hear 'Sí, Señor', the song gets stuck in your head all day long. I catch myself alone, at home or in the car or anywhere, moving my lips and singing, '*Síííí, Señor, pass the ball to Bobby and he will score.*' My dear friend Sadio Mané has also said that he does the same thing at his house; he prefers the song the fans made for me over his own! I love the song for Mané too, by the way.

I also had a second song sung by the Liverpool fans. But this one only lasted for one game, thank God, and although many thought it was funny – and I could see why too – it was also a reason to be ashamed. I didn't feel comfortable hearing it.

At the end of 2016 I was arrested by the Liverpool police for driving under the influence of alcohol. I'll tell you this story later; I'll tell you about the drinking too. For now, it's enough to recall that, after spending a night in a cell, we had training the next day (Christmas Eve), then a game against Stoke City at Anfield and Klopp played me despite what had happened. I had an outstanding game. I was the Man of the Match; we won 4–1 and I scored.

The fans are quite witty. At the end of the match, they sang something like, '*Bobby Firmino, he drinks when he wants.*' They don't miss an opportunity. I laughed and then the other players made fun of me in the dressing room. They told me to drink as much as I wanted because it worked. It's a joke, of course: experiencing prison is not something I am proud of, and nor is driving under the influence.

Luckily, the song didn't catch on; it was just for one match. Happily, '*Sí, Señor!*' did.

There's a bit of debate, though, even among the fans themselves: '*Sim, Senhor*' in Portuguese, my native language? Or '*Sí, Señor*' in Spanish? They're practically the same, right? The languages are similar. I don't mind the '*Sí, Señor*'; it's still a song with a Latin rhythm and I really like Spanish culture. They can sing '*Sí, Señor*' or '*Sim, Senhor*'; I'm happy either way. I would love to think they might keep singing it at Anfield, even though I'm no longer there.

I've been asked if it's possible to pay attention to what's being sung in the stands during a football match. Of course, it is! The fans are like the 12th player for us: genuine participants. Of course we're paying attention to the game, focusing on football, but we're not impervious to the stands; we're human beings. When the fans sing and support, it pushes you. It inspires and motivates you to run harder, maybe reach a ball you wouldn't have reached. Thousands of people singing your name brings out the best in you, driving you to give everything – everything.

It's inevitable, *sí, señor*!

Chapter 2

Ball on the Roof

The real problem was that blasted dog. He definitely had it in for me. Every time I passed by that corner, the stray dog would come after me, trying to bite me. It might seem like he just wanted to play or take the ball for himself, but it wasn't quite like that. It wasn't about the ball. It was personal. I would always run away – it was the only solution – but he wouldn't give up and would chase after me. I don't think I ever faced a defender like him. He got me twice. He got me good and I ended up with a bite on my calf. The other time, it was on my thigh. I had to get a shot, some rabies vaccine.

Apart from that formidable opponent, I can't complain about my childhood. If it were possible, I would ask God to allow me to relive the entire thing, as if I were watching a movie. I miss it, miss it a lot.

We never had much at home, never had luxuries. But

we never lacked food, at least that's how I remember it. We never went hungry, even though poverty surrounded my beloved neighbourhood of Trapiche and permeated my family's daily life.

Trapiche da Barra is a flat region in Maceió, between the sea and Mundaú Lagoon, which flows into the Atlantic. It's a poor area, but within a ten-minute drive are the grand waterfront buildings of the city's wealthiest people. This is a characteristic of many Brazilian north-eastern capitals: rich and poor separated by just a couple of miles. The north-east overall is the poorest region in Brazil, marked by similar social disparities. Unlike other Brazilian capitals, such as the two largest, São Paulo and Rio de Janeiro, the cities in the north-east strive to find their place in the sun, and struggle to attract businesses and foster social and technological development. It is a region that encompasses nine states – including my own, Alagoas – and where you'll find some of the most spectacular beaches in the world. But it's also where the '*Sertão*' is – a vast area marked by droughts, hunger and a lack of opportunities. The people of the north-east are hardworking and resilient, and I am very proud to be from this part of Brazil.

Trapiche, in Maceió, is essentially made up of small, single-storey houses, many of them with exposed bricks. The streets are narrow and potholed, with houses interspersed by small local shops. One of them, a store next to my home, is where I used to shop for my mother. Many times, I didn't have money – I didn't even bring any. The shopkeeper would let us pay on credit, settling the bill at the end of the week. Today, that same store is still there, but with different paint on the wall, a different name, and with bars on the windows and door. People no longer enter but simply request what they want, and the purchases and payments are made through the bars, possibly a result of many thefts.

It has always been a dangerous neighbourhood. My mother didn't like me going out of the house – and I always did – because she was afraid of the company I kept. In the homes across the street reggae music played all night and the smell of marijuana was always in the air. Drugs were rampant in the neighbourhood, alcohol flowed freely in the bars, and week after week we would see fights and shootings. I have seen dead bodies and corpses lying in the street. As a young boy, you get used to this recurring scene, and that's a problem: violence becomes normalized and assimilated as part of the local landscape. By adolescence, I knew all the guys involved with drugs. They were friends from another phase of my life; I knew each one by name. They would offer weed to me, but I never used it, and my stance was respected. They didn't bother me.

From my street, where I played football, I could see the Rei Pelé Stadium, the largest in Maceió (where both CRB and CSA play). It was the view I cherished the most. Of course, any child who grows up with a ball at their feet and sees the stadium every day, out beyond the canal, dreams of scoring a goal on that field.

My father was a street vendor, carrying a huge weight on his back. He sold soft drinks, beer and mineral water in front of the nightclubs in Maceió; heavy stuff filling the ice-filled cooler he lugged about. He didn't spend much time at home, because we needed him to provide for us. He only stopped working because I had to ask him to, when I was already in Germany and could help my parents financially.

He and my mother met because they lived across from each other in Trapiche. My mother says she was very close friends with my father's sisters, my aunts. They named their first son Roberto Firmino in honor of my grandfather. In my childhood, my nickname in the neighbourhood was Bebeto – a common name adopted because I was slim and fast like the star of Brazil's 1994 World Cup team.

My father used to take me to watch CRB games, walking the 15 minutes or so to the Rei Pelé Stadium together, to the end of the street, across the little bridge over the *valetão*, and there it was. The bridge was always in poor condition. I've seen people fall from it and that's not pretty: the *valetão* is an open sewage channel that runs through there. It required careful crossing to take that shortcut to the Rei Pelé.

Nowadays, no more than 20,000 people can enter the stadium. But at its inauguration in 1970, during a match between the Alagoas state team and Santos, the attendance was almost 45,000. Pelé scored two goals. By the way, it is the only stadium in my country with the name 'Rei Pelé', an honour bestowed to the greatest of them all in his lifetime, shortly after Brazil's triumphant 1970 World Cup.

I remember my father being proud when I started playing in CRB's youth academy, wearing the jersey of his beloved team. But I didn't just support CRB: I also supported Corinthians, a major club from São Paulo, who won the Brazilian championship in 1998 and 1999. Those were some of my earliest football memories. It's very common in the north-east region of Brazil for a child to support their local team as well as a team from São Paulo or Rio de Janeiro.

I watched a lot of football during my childhood, along with listening to music. My father has always been crazy about music. He would leave the radio on at home, with the volume turned right up. I grew up in that environment and developed a taste for it. My father particularly liked a very famous singer in Brazil, perhaps the most famous of all, called Roberto Carlos – not to be confused with the legendary left-back – and listened to Paulo Sérgio, who sang romantic songs.

I had a great sense of rhythm, and I even played percussion in *pagode* gatherings, a typically Brazilian style of music beloved by players. To this day, there is always music playing in my house. When I underwent my conversion and started living in Christ, I wanted to learn how to play the piano to perform hymns, so started taking classes. I believe that if I hadn't become a professional football player, I would have tried to pursue a career as a singer. Despite my affinity for music, what I truly loved in my childhood was playing football. It was all I could think about, my passion.

When I return to my neighbourhood, Trapiche, today, everything looks small: small houses, narrow streets, small grocery stores, alleyway upon alleyway. When I was a child, everything seemed so big. People would put chairs in front of their houses and spend time talking, watching the world go by. The streets have been paved now and new buildings have gone up. In my time, it was all dirt and mud, the setting for my friends and me to spend the whole day playing. There was no well-maintained grass, properly watered before a match. We played around the potholes, on a completely uneven terrain, and with almost no rules. This kind of setting is crucial to understanding why Brazil is this eternal powerhouse in football, an endless generator of talents. I played under the scorching midday sun, in unbelievable heat and in the dirt. You have to adapt to keep the ball, to stay on the team, to play. There aren't many opportunities or choices available for a boy from Trapiche; there are few ways out. Football is often one; in fact, there isn't really a Plan B. This fact alone creates a winning mentality in a child. It toughens us up.

My mother, Maria Cícera, is called 'Dona Ciça' by everyone in the neighbourhood. She says that I was a mischievous, restless boy; that when I started taking my first steps, I would knock down everything in my path. I grew up and continued to be clumsy, to the point that my mom's friends asked her not to bring me along when she visited them. I never stopped for a minute, either. At seven years old, she says all I did was play football around the neighbourhood. I would spend hours kicking a ball against the wall of my house. Once, twice, ten times, a thousand times. I would hit other people's doors, break windows on the street, knock down birdcages with the birds inside. According to my mother, some annoyed neighbours even cut the football in half and left it at our doorstep to put an end to the game and the noise. That was the only way they could take a nap in the afternoon.

My mom says that I would escape from home at six in the morning to play. When I didn't show up at the time agreed with my group of four or five friends, the other kids would throw stones at the roof to wake me up: a signal to leave the house and go play football.

'I started locking the gate, but it was useless,' Dona Ciça says.

It was useless, Mom, because I would jump over the wall.

Or I would find where the keys were hidden. There was no stopping me. I would only come back home to eat.

Sometimes.

Breakfast was couscous, sometimes cassava and sausages. We never ran out of rice and beans for lunch, mixed with chicken. It was always chicken. In the afternoon I would have biscuits and drink chocolate milk. The menu didn't change much throughout my childhood and adolescence.

The house where I lived still belongs to my parents and is rented out. It's nicely painted, all white, and the roof now connects to an iron gate, so it's no longer possible to jump over the low wooden gate like I did in my childhood. I pass by and see a motorcycle parked right in front. What other lives are inside? What do the people who live where I grew up do?

I remember throwing stones on the roofs of other houses to call my friends for football as well. And throwing stones at the mango trees to knock down the mangoes we would then eat. I remember the games that kids played: flying kites, playing marbles, spinning wooden tops. I remember the clay pitches scattered around the neighbourhoods of Maceió where we played with our local team, Flamenguinho, or Little Flamengo. Around the age of seven or eight, I joined the team, my kit so big and baggy it drowned me. We would get on the regular bus with our coach, André; a bunch of kids causing a ruckus and heading towards fun and a dream. Every weekend, we would play in a different field. And they were big fields, despite our young age. I was good with the ball! Every Brazilian child wants to be a football player and that was my dream to be able to help my family.

I also remember the 40-minute walks to spend Sundays at Sobral Beach with my mother and playing football there in the sand. The beach, you can be sure, is another huge factor in why so many talented Brazilian footballers emerge. The temperature doesn't vary much in Maceió and other north-eastern capitals. It's hot all year round, only the amount of rain changes. There isn't a single day of the year without groups of children or adults gathering to play football along the Brazilian coast. Playing football on the beach is delightful.

The school I attended is still there, 300 metres away from my old house. But to get there, you had to cross a busy avenue. It was very dangerous, with constant accidents. Whenever I return to Maceió I pass through my neighbourhood and the places where I grew up. We should never forget where we come from and value what we have.

Maria Rita Lyra de Almeida State School has a tall metal structure, with a roof that resembles a mountain – a huge metal V-shape. Once, our ball ended up there, and I had no doubt. Aged eight or nine, and very brave and fearless, I climbed the wall, got up on the rooftop and reached the base of the next level, where there was a kind of makeshift ladder stretching towards the sky. I made it to the top and got the ball.

Great.

And now, how was I going to get down?

News spread quickly back then, even without cell phones. My mother showed up. I don't know if she was more angry or more worried, but she was definitely both. She was scared because I was so high up. Stuck on the roof, way out of reach, racking my brain to find a way down the smooth, sheer metal slope. I don't remember exactly how I did it, but I managed to come down somehow. And I got told off, big time. My mother was a warrior, but she worried so much about her children.

There was another time, however, when she couldn't prevent the worst from happening. While playing football with my friends, I got my foot caught in the drain where the sewage flows. There was a large hole; the drain in the street was in front of a small bar where the guys played pool and video games – I think that bar doesn't exist anymore. I was playing there with my friends and the ball had fallen in. I tried to get it, of course. I slipped and cut my leg. That happened two or three times but that day was the worst: the cut was deep, bleeding a lot, and I could see something white. The bone was visible, or at least that's what I thought it was beneath the blood, and I almost passed out. I was scared that I would never be able to play football with my friends again. They carried me to a taxi. We went to the hospital and I received ten stitches. I still have the scar.

The other school I started attending when I was around ten years old was called Professor Tarcísio de Jesus State School, 140 metres away from where we lived, just around the corner to the right. I enjoyed studying, I was disciplined, but the reality for the many poor children in Brazil is that education takes a back seat, and certainly if they are trying to make it in football. Either because the child can't keep up, or because they need to help their parents or take care of their siblings at home, or . . . because they have to play football.

Today, a sports court has been built in the school. Before, there was just a small, uneven patch of ground, which I called the 'little field'. Two columns held up the school's roof and they were our goalposts. Our Maracanã.

Just a few metres from the school was my friend Neto's house. We were always together. I was around 12 or 13 years old, and I would play a lot of dominos and checkers with him. Further along was the yellow house of another friend of mine; now it's a sugarcane juice stand. Our group of friends would gather in front of his house and go out to play and kick the ball around on some field in the neigh-bourhood. Then it was all dirt, mud and clay. Today, it's almost all concrete.

Another person present in my childhood and adolescence was my cousin Zequinha, son of Uncle Marcinho, my mother's brother. We didn't live so close, so we would mainly meet on weekends. We would take long walks to visit the family, and I would get annoyed because I had to carry heavy bags with nappies and baby stuff – my sister Marcella had been born by this point.

At Tarcísio de Jesus, a school football team was formed that was more than just a team. The teachers wanted to help us understand the importance of behaving better and working as a team. That's when I discovered the spirit of solidarity which would mark my style years later in professional football. One teacher, Ari Santiago, recalls that I was always the first to go to the school office to ask for the ball during the break between classes – always with a smile on my face. He says I was shy and that was my way of expressing myself. My trademark long before now. I was already involved in other teams formed in the neighbourhood as well, and my Uncle Marcinho would often take me to the kick-abouts he played in. Little by little, he started getting me to play, right there in the middle of the adults.

When I was 14, my mother did something that changed my path, turning football from just a game played at school and in the street with friends into something more serious. She recalls that one day she was sitting on the doorstep, talking with friends, when I came rushing in wearing the

CRB shirt. One of my mother's friends asked if I played football and suggested that she take me for a trial at CRB.

My father's team and mine as well? Yes, please.

My uncle knew some people at the club and arranged it. My mother and I took the bus and went there one Wednesday. It was a 40-minute journey and it wasn't easy to contain my excitement. When we arrived, my mother looked for a man named Guilherme Farias, coach of the youth team, who was waiting for us. Guilherme tells the story like this: 'The team had gathered and I was there with them when Roberto's mother came, asking for the boy to have a trial. I took him to this small field. He'd only touched the ball three times when I said, "Boy, get your documents ready."' And that's how my years as a player for CRB began.

I would love God to allow me to relive all these memories. Today's Firmino would love to see little Roberto running after the ball, going to the beach, skipping classes to play, playing with friends, causing mischief, and, of course, running away from that blasted dog. I see little Firmino when I watch kids playing football here and when we do evangelical missions in the state of Alagoas. I started helping impoverished communities when I arrived at Hoffenheim and my financial situation changed. The first thing every player always does is buy a house for his father and mother, moving them to a better place. It's not about denying our roots, it's about escaping certain issues, like urban violence, and providing physical comfort. Initially, I helped people we knew and the neighbourhood and schools with toys and food donations.

Today, with the help of pastors, we carry out missions in poor communities in Maceió and Alagoas, bringing food, the word of Jesus, and some hope to these children. We always want to do more and more and more. There's a simple reason why: I will never cease to be a boy from Maceió, I will never stop visiting Trapiche. I feel proud to know that I'm an inspiration to the children in my neighbourhood, my city, my state. Becoming a football player isn't easy, and what I always try to convey to them is the importance of fighting, striving and taking the right paths. God willing, one of them can become what I have become. Today, many of those children want to be Firmino. When I was little, I wanted to be Ronaldinho.

Chapter 3

No Look

Of all the goals I scored for Brazil, the one that gets remembered best, the one that I always felt really made people take notice of me, is the one I didn't even see. It was 2019, the final group game on the way to winning the Copa América at home, and we were playing Peru in São Paulo. We were a goal up when their goalkeeper, Pedro Gallese, tried to send the ball up field, but I had gone to close him down. The ball rebounded off me, looped up over him, hit the bar and bounced back perfectly onto my chest. Gallese had got back to face me again but I stepped around him and rolled the ball into the net. It was a goal that was very much mine: the combination of belief, work and talent. And, above all, the fact that when I put the ball in, I turned my head and looked the other way. As it hit the net, I didn't see it: my eyes were trained instead on the teammates who would come to embrace me. It wasn't the first time I had scored a no-look goal, which had become a little trademark, my thing; it wasn't even the first time for Brazil. I had done it just four games into my international career in a friendly against Chile at the Emirates in 2015, taking Danilo's pass, dribbling round the keeper and tapping it into the net while turning my gaze.

If that one had gone a little unnoticed, if not many people seemed to realize that I had looked the other way as I put the ball into Claudio Bravo's net and there wasn't much fuss, 2019 was different. After all, it was the Copa América, in Brazil: the kind of game everyone watches, even those who don't follow football so closely. I always felt many unsuspecting people learned who Roberto Firmino was on 22 June 2019. Goals like that changed my status in the eyes of the public – and even among my Brazilian teammates. In that moment, I gained credibility, respect among players of tremendous quality. They couldn't believe I had done it – it's not like I only did it when the game was safe – and they loved it. In the dressing room they kept congratulating me: 'You've got to be kidding, scoring a goal like that!' They thought it was inspired, which it was – and by one man in particular. Here was my homage to my hero.

I wore the Brazil shirt 55 times. Actually, I wore it far more than that. I will always remember getting my first, aged ten – not least because it wasn't *quite* right. It probably wasn't easy for my mom that day. She went through a lot of trouble to buy me a national team shirt for the 2002 World Cup where Brazil would become champions for the fifth time – and the last time for quite a while. She came home all excited, telling me she had bought Ronaldinho's jersey, but she didn't get it at all. My idol wasn't *that* Ronaldinho. My idol was the *other* Ronaldinho. The Gaúcho. Ronaldo, the Phenomenon, was also called Ronaldinho in Brazil and, confused, she had got me his shirt by mistake.

It's not that I didn't like Ronaldo. Of course, I did! Everyone loved him. I was fortunate enough to meet him one day and thank him for everything he did. He was a true great, top scorer at that World Cup, having come back from the tragedy of the 1998 final and the horrendous knee injury he had suffered since. Nineteen ninety-eight is my first World Cup memory – I was six and I still recall the tears after losing the final to France, with Zinedine Zidane scoring twice – but the memories of 2002 are more vivid, like it was yesterday. Because that tournament was played in Japan and South Korea, games were broadcast in the middle of the night in Brazil. I remember the streets painted, Brazilian flags everywhere. My country lives and breathes the World Cup – always has and, I hope, always will. My dad would wake me up to watch the matches. Sometimes, we'd watch the games on our TV at home, or we'd go to my grandma's next door.

Led by Ronaldo, Rivaldo and Ronaldinho, that team is

etched into history and my memory, immortalized for all of us. They were all brilliant, but the one I truly loved was Ronaldinho. His free-kick against England in the 2002 World Cup quarter-finals was the most memorable goal of my childhood. Some might doubt it, but I fully believe him when he says it was deliberate, that he was aiming at the goal, over David Seaman. That was perfection, a work of genius.

I loved watching him for his style, his skill, his charisma and the smile on his face – and as I grew up, and my dream of playing football took shape, I tried to incorporate everything I saw from Ronaldinho into my own style. In 2005 and 2006 he was by far the best football player in the world, collecting individual accolades and titles with Barcelona. Many of Barça's matches, whether in the Champions League or La Liga, were broadcast on free-to-air TV in Brazil, and I didn't miss a single one. Whatever else I was doing could wait. I hadn't yet been discovered, but I dreamed of being like him.

When I think of Ronaldinho, a lot of words spring to mind. The main one, though, is 'magic'. And right after that comes 'humility' – truly inspiring qualities that influence any boy with a ball at his feet. The magic materializes in moments that transport you; humility manifested itself in the way he carried himself on the pitch. Most players, when an opponent hits them hard, might fight back. Ronaldinho would just smile and get back up. He always had the last laugh and he knew it.

That infectious smile – magic and humility coming together – doesn't go unnoticed by any child. Anyone who dreamed of playing football during Ronaldinho's golden era wanted to play like him, dribble like him, smile like him, *be* like him. He was the purest expression of Brazilian joy. He didn't curse, didn't complain, didn't fight. He always stayed calm with opponents, referees, even journalists. Above all, he enjoyed it. It was impossible not to love him and, instinctively, I copied everything he did.

Such influence illustrates why being a footballer is a challenge for many players, especially the younger ones. We have a tremendous responsibility because kids all around the world watch us and copy every gesture we make on the field – the good and the bad. Ronaldinho expressed himself through his moves and his smile. And for me, shy as I've always been, my smile was my way of getting things done. I had the smile already; I just needed the moves. They would come in due time.

The artistry of Ronaldinho's game always inspired me. So many of the beautiful moves and passes I made wearing the Liverpool shirt started there: watching him on the field fired my imagination. I wanted to do everything just like him. Nutmegs, dribbles, runs, brilliant passes, incredible technical skills . . . and, of course, those passes where he'd twist his neck and look the other way. It was his signature move, the final flourish. If he did a nutmeg, a chip, or pulled off a fancy dribble, it was like he had to round it off with a no-look pass, even if it was short – just as a way of marking the moment. Google it and there are endless compilations of Ronaldinho's no-look passes in all the shirts he wore. I know: I did it. I was addicted to YouTube. I practised all sorts of tricks, but that was the skill that most moved me, so I watched it over and over and practised and practised.

It's not an easy skill to put into practice, because the game goes so fast, but I managed to copy that and, dare I say, improve on it. The Bobby Firmino no-look goal is the evolution of the Ronaldinho no-look pass. It became my trademark . . . and maybe even my obsession. It's not that I planned them as such – you can't decide in advance to do something like that – I just wanted to emulate Ronaldinho. It took a little youthful craziness, too, in order to come up with and execute something like that. But I couldn't help it. My first time in a competitive game was on 30 August 2014. I was only 22, but it was my fifth season with Hoffenheim: it was the second game of the season against Werder Bremen away and I remember it as if it were happening right now. A lofted ball into the area from Sebastian Rudy allowed me to dart in from the left wing (where I was playing) and get there ahead of the keeper. I took the ball from him and it bounced in front of me, the goal wide open. Now, how can I explain this? There's no explanation. In that moment, the decision to shoot one way, while, simultaneously, turning my head the other without looking at the ball, just popped into my mind. It was like Ronaldinho himself had done it. He did no-look passes; now I had scored a no-look goal – and it was going to become my thing.

I did it against Chile and Peru, and I did it with Liverpool too. The first time was in my third season, against Sevilla in the Champions League in 2017. As always, the goal came from a situation where I found myself with an open goal – I was crazy, sure, but never quite crazy enough to attempt it any other way. Mané advanced on the left, shot across goal and the goalkeeper parried. I picked up the rebound inside the penalty area and all I had to do was tap it into the net. So why not do it with style? Ball in the net, eyes the other way. The following year I did it twice more: against West Ham and then against Arsenal, when I scored my first hat-trick in a red shirt.

The third goal that day was a penalty, which reminds me: in 2020, the Croatian Andrej Kramarić scored a spectacular penalty, shooting to one side while looking the other way. It was a no-look penalty! He played for Hoffenheim, my former team, and they thrashed Borussia Dortmund. Even though the match was already decided, it still takes a lot of courage to pull that off. After the game, he tagged me on Instagram, challenging me to do the same. I thought it was really cool because it was clear that I had become associated with no-look goals globally and was an inspiration for others, just as Ronaldinho Gaúcho had been for me. A few years later, in 2023, Lucas Ocampos, then playing for Sevilla, converted a no-look penalty in the Europa League final. And in the shootout! Talent combined with madness.

I didn't take many penalties at Liverpool – in fact, I had the responsibility taken away from me – so I never got the chance to take up Kramarić's challenge. One day, I will. I want to score a no-look penalty. It won't be planned, but one day maybe it will pop into my mind at just the right time. Confidence is everything; when you're confident, you can do anything. And usually without thinking: the flashy moves I made on the field, like back-heel passes or stopping the ball with one foot and playing it with the other, were pure instinct, the talent the Lord gave me.

It's important to say that I never scored a no-look goal or did a move – whether it was a back-heel or a flick – with the intention of belittling any opponent. With one exception: when I nutmegged Lautaro Martínez during Brazil versus Argentina in the semi-final of the 2019 Copa América.

If you've scored a great goal, you've got to have a great celebration too – something that's *yours*. And, thinking about it, the two things are not so different: moments of inspiration and creativity, for all that you can plan, only really appear spontaneously. When it all comes off, it's wonderful. My cele-brations became almost as memorable as the goals themselves. There was the gunslinger. There were the capoeira moves, unleashing flying kicks into the air. And there were those moments when I would point to my ear because I wanted to hear the crowd explode with me, or to answer a few critics here and there. There's nothing like the emotion of hearing Anfield roar with you. There was also the time I ran to hug Jürgen Klopp at Leicester. I never went towards the opposi-tion's fans, never taunted rivals, never provoked anyone and always shared the celebrations with teammates. But that day at the King Power Stadium, I admit, I was delivering a mes-sage to the coach on the other bench, a reminder to Brendan Rodgers that he hadn't believed in me like the Boss did.

Probably the best was the Pirate, where I covered my eye after I scored against PSG, despite barely being able to see anything, having damaged it in the days building up to the game. There was also the Angry Bobby celebration after a spectacular long-range shot that secured victory for our team away at Stoke in 2018. That one, and one I got against Arsenal the same year, were probably the most beautiful goals I scored in the Liverpool shirt. Not that I was in it for long – that day I got a yellow card for taking my shirt off, which happened quite a bit. I even read somewhere that I got more yellows for that than anyone else in the Premier League. (I don't know if that's true, but I can believe it.) And that's even taking into account all the times I threatened to take my shirt off, but managed to hold back. Players know they're not allowed to; that if you do there's a card coming. We can't say we haven't been warned. But sometimes you can't help it. Besides, if the goal is especially beautiful (like the one against Stoke) or important (like in the Club World Cup final against Flamengo), then it's worth it.

Taking your shirt off is one thing; this was something else. I think I only ever regretted one goal celebration. It was in a Champions League playoff game against Hoffenheim, my former team. We had won the first leg 2–1 in Germany, on what was a special night, returning to my old home. There were reunions and I was treated very well; I felt respect and nostalgia for everything I had experienced there and held so dear. When it came to the second leg at Anfield, we won 4–2 and I got the fourth with the tie already decided. Usually, players don't celebrate goals against their former club, but I didn't even think about it. I wish I had. Hoffenheim had been so good to me and I could have lived without that celebration. With time, I hope the fans, who always treated me so well, aren't upset.

The thing is, it wasn't just the fact that I celebrated; it was the way I did it. It was nothing to do with my former club; I just wanted to imitate a celebration that Ronaldinho Gaúcho – who else? – had done in the past when he played for Flamengo and Atlético Mineiro. It was a Brazilian funk dance move where he lowered his shorts to his knees, his loose shirt maintaining his modesty, and that day I did the same. It didn't really work as well and, while some people found it funny, I wouldn't advise it. Taking off my shirt? My wife could forgive that. But taking off my shorts? That was different and I never did it again. This is what I mean about being responsible and remembering always – always – that kids are watching and might want to copy you; that there are people who have welcomed you along the way to whom you owe a lot and must always show respect. All I was trying to do was pay homage to the man I had tried to copy, but I had got it wrong.

Despite all that, I've never actually met Ronaldinho. One day, I hope I can. He's a very special guy: my inspiration, the player I wanted to be, whose number 10 shirt I wanted to wear, even if I ended up wearing number 9 at Liverpool and started life as a number 5.

Chapter 4

Wrong Name, Wrong Number

The first proper football match I ever played lasted only three minutes. I stepped onto the field as a number 5, took up my position in deep midfield, missed two easy passes and the coach took me straight off again.

That all too brief episode shows just how cruel football can be. Many kids fall by the wayside, are unable to endure such experiences without the necessary support. You have to be a fighter before you become a player.

At 14 years old I earned a spot to play for CRB, the red team from Maceió, my father's team, my beloved team, whose matches I watched at the Rei Pelé Stadium – the one I could see from my street in the Trapiche neighbourhood.

It was like a dream. I had been playing football since I was very young, but always in completely amateur settings:

school or the neighbourhood team. Now I was a player for CRB, the city's biggest club, no longer the street corner or local team, and the idea of genuinely becoming a professional footballer, and helping my family, began to form in my mind.

I remained that shy kid who didn't speak much. Hardly at all, in fact. My communication during training was through the ball at my feet. I didn't complain about anything, didn't ask for anything. I just listened and did my best to execute the orders given. The facilities at CRB were basic, typical of what you find all over Brazil, especially in the northeast. There's not much money, still less for youth football. Everyone makes do in order to play, to prove themselves and try to make it in the profession. I had a family structure that ensured there was food on the table every day and I could take the bus to get to training, and slowly but surely, studies took a back seat.

Many talents fail. Either because parents don't want their children to stop studying – and, in reality, football kind of forces you into that situation – or because the family needs those kids helping out at home. Often, young players are already working. It's a shame that it's like this; it would be great if there were more protection for kids and their dreams; if they had more chances to show what they're capable of.

Coach Guilherme needed a defensive midfielder, a number

5, and that's how I played for CRB's youth team for two years, from 14 to 16. The beginning wasn't easy at all; lasting that long didn't look likely. The first time I went out with the team for a match was in a place in Alagoas called Messias. There was an A team and a B team among the youth squads at CRB, and I had just arrived, so I was in the B team at the start of the game. Three minutes and two bad passes later, it was over. It was a very tough moment and I saw that even the other kids found it strange. But I didn't say anything; my shyness was a genuine barrier. There wasn't much to say anyway, just keep moving forward.

The chance to do so came quickly. That same Saturday, there were more games and I got another opportunity. This time, I scored from a free-kick, played well, and CRB's B team – mine! – ended up winning the cup in Messias. The summary of the day is the summary of what a football player's life can be like. Highs and lows can be separated by just days. Or, in my case, minutes.

As the training sessions progressed, I earned my place and gained the trust of the coach and the other kids. We went to the club every Monday, Wednesday and Friday afternoons after school. Mondays were for physical training, running on the sand at Pajuçara Beach. Wednesdays and Fridays were my favourite days, the days for playing with the ball.

It was there that I met César Lucena, Cesinha, a great friend who's been crucial in my life to this day. He's the brother I never had. He was a full-back and, as one of the boys who had been at the club the longest, he knew a lot of people. On top of that he's outgoing, strikes up conversations, forges friendships and becomes a focal point in creating team spirit. Cesinha and I hit it off right away, because we took the same bus home from training and we'd chat together. He was the talkative one, I just listened and laughed.

We spent two years of camaraderie in CRB's youth team, sharing many experiences. We lost touch a bit when my career took me away from Maceió and he didn't continue with football – although we'd occasionally talk on MSN Messenger. His family had a different situation from mine; his mother didn't like to see studies taking a back seat. There were two championship finals he couldn't play in because he had repeated a year in school. Years later, when I had already become a professional, I reached out to Cesinha in Maceió. I wanted to invite him to be a part of my journey. He couldn't come initially because he was studying business administration in Maceió and starting his professional life, but he did visit me a few times in Florianópolis and Hoffenheim, to witness my career growth up close.

That plan of being together only materialized when I made the move from Germany to England, and Cesinha started living in Liverpool. Besides being a great friend, he provided emotional support for my family and helped with logistical aspects, sorting out everyday issues and needs. Cesinha was in the stands for all of Liverpool's matches, both home and away, and he was also someone to discuss games with at home, what was working, or not, for me. It's always good to hear the opinion of someone who wants to help, knows football, and isn't so deeply involved with the team from within.

Back at CRB, Cesinha and some other boys were part of a group that made life a nightmare for newcomers. Anyone who arrived for a trial had to overcome the barriers they put in their way. 'A new full-back? Cesinha plays full-back. Let's go after that kid! A new defensive midfielder? That's Roberto's position. Let's make him suffer.' I didn't take part in any of that, I just had fun. There are many barriers for a kid to overcome before becoming a football player. There's the trial, the struggle for a spot in the team, the internal competition – so many things that can go wrong.

I gradually earned my place by playing and learning in midfield. Depending on the team's needs, Coach Guilherme would place me in different positions. I even played as a right-back once and occasionally as a centre-back. I was a quality defender. I'd win the ball and start a move. I enjoyed giving nutmegs, pulling off tricks. I liked to dribble and deliver good passes. Many times, the coach would get mad at my audacity.

Looking back today, I'm convinced that those two years

playing as a defensive midfielder were crucial in turning me into what I became when I arrived in European professional football. In football in the past, attackers attacked, defenders defended. In today's football, that distinction just doesn't hold, it doesn't exist. Every attacker needs to know how to defend, is obliged to close spaces and passing lanes, engage in combat, win back the ball. Finding space in such a physical, fast game is very challenging. You have to play at high speed and, preferably, win the ball back in the attacking half, to be closer to the goal and facing vulnerable defences. That was the ethos for eight years at Liverpool. Our team had a lot of intensity and was ferocious in the pursuit of ball recovery and acceleration. Which suited me. Jürgen Klopp mentioned a few times that the attacking trio that played together at Liverpool from 2017 to 2022 – Salah, Mané and Firmino – combined offensive creativity, speed and finishing with the desire to defend. I was the false 9. Also, perhaps, a false 10. And definitely a false 5. For me, it was only natural to put into practice what I did during adolescence for two years: pressing opponents to win the ball back. Many of these tackles turned into scoring chances for our team, assists for Mané and Salah.

At 16 I moved up to CRB's youth team and started being taught by another coach, Toninho Almeida. Right from the start, Toninho told me that he saw quality in my game and it didn't make sense for me to be in defence. I started playing sometimes as a number 8, sometimes as a number 10. Now, I could finally do what my idol, Ronaldinho Gaúcho, did: sprints, passes, flashy moves, goals. My physical build also helped; I was a tall, strong kid who knew how to use that to my advantage.

Toninho, a former player, worked with me after training sessions and taught me much of what was necessary for a midfielder. I practised skills, finishing, sprints with and without the ball. That's when I started to truly shine and attract attention. Training sessions had become daily; a different level of responsibility. I'm very grateful to Toninho for recognizing the best position for me and for helping me develop so much as a player. We trained in the Pajuçara neighbourhood, where the old CRB training centre was located. There was a big field there where the professionals trained and smaller fields – part dirt, part grass – on either side. There I improved with every match, every week, every month.

When I was 15 or 16 I met Dr Marcellus Portella, a dentist who supported the club and provided free care to some of the boys at CRB. Remember at the beginning of this book I mentioned how a dentist changed the course of my career? That was Marcellus. He approached me one Monday having seen me doing a fitness session at Pajuçara Beach with a torn boot. My toes were poking out of the end and he joked,

'Is it the fashion to have your toes sticking out like that?'
I said it was torn. He asked me my shoe size.

'41.' (Probably 9 in the UK.)

'I'll get you a new one tomorrow,' he said.

And he did.

The next day, Dr Marcellus gave me a brand-new red and white Mizuno boot in the box, right there at CRB. I had been using an old Puma boot, which a veteran player called Marcos Alagoano had given to me when he got a new pair. I'd had it for a while, so it was worn out, falling apart. Now, the club's dentist had gifted me something better. Marcellus always used to come watch our practices and games, often staying around and chatting with the boys. He later told me that, during that time, he tried to alert the people at CRB about my talent, asking them to take a special look at me. He says he was ignored.

Others *had* seen something in me, though. By the time I was 16 there were already people approaching my mother, offering to become my agent. She was very afraid of all that; I think she was scared of the possibility of someone taking her son away or not guiding him properly. My progression didn't slow. I got called up for the under-20s and a few games at the Rei Pelé Stadium, as a kind of warm-up or undercard before first team matches. This was quite common in Brazil at that time, but is rarely seen now. Kids get to experience a full (well, filling) stadium, get accustomed to the pressure, the weight of playing in front of a packed house.

One day, Marcellus came to talk to me after practice. He was someone I trusted, who had already helped me and whom I had known for a long time. He told me that CRB was getting too small for me and that we needed to come up with a plan to take me somewhere else. The way I was playing at the time showed I was clearly destined for greater things. Many of the videos of my performances at a young age were only recorded because Dr Marcellus decided to invest in them. He paid someone to film CRB's youth games and compiled the footage to create a DVD of my highlights.

For a kid, it's really hard to figure out who's who in such moments. Of course, financial interests are everywhere; nobody does anything just out of kindness. I understood that by now it was necessary to introduce Dr Marcellus to my mother. I told him I would let him know when my mother was at home so he could come pick me up. That day, I went to a public phone to call him and within minutes Dr Marcellus showed up at the gate. I remember the conversation between him and my mother. She was defensive and wanted nothing to do with it. 'Who is it?!' she yelled. She didn't even open the door for him. They talked through the fence that separated my house from the street in Trapiche, but that first contact broke the ice. My mother gave in and it was decided that I would be under Dr Marcellus's care when it came to football.

The time had come to make a decision. As I progressed on the field, things started happening much faster. I played for CRB's under-20s against ASA from Arapiraca, our state rivals. I was only 16 and I scored an incredible goal from outside the penalty area. Everyone went wild. Few could have imagined that would be my last match for them.

CRB had changed their position. They had not offered me a contract before, but now they decided it was a good idea to tie me to the club. I wasn't so sure. I could see that this was happening a lot: young players would find themselves trapped and their careers would be compromised. Marcellus kept telling me not to sign anything, not even toilet paper. A few days after that match with the under-20s, some CRB directors tried to force the issue. They took me into a room, closed the door and told me I had to sign a contract. I resisted, but they kept insisting. Luckily, Toninho, the youth team coach, saw what was happening and saw me crying, desperate. He picked up the phone and called Dr Marcellus to tell him what was going on. I'll never forget that. Toninho faced serious consequences for what he did, but he defended me anyway. Some at CRB were furious and he lost his job as the youth team coach, was demoted to a minor position in the club. It was a very tense situation. Dr Marcellus arrived at the club furious, and Toninho had to hold him back to prevent a fight breaking out right there and then. I was extremely nervous and upset. I left the club without signing anything and declared that I would never return. And I never did. My dad seemed sad; he wanted to see his kid playing for CRB.

And now what? What would be the next steps? Dr Marcellus saved me from signing a contract with CRB that likely would have been detrimental to my career; Dr Marcellus, too, had seen other young players tied to their clubs. He didn't want me stuck with a lengthy, binding contract when I could be somewhere bigger. But he wasn't an agent, he didn't have contacts or connections. To make matters worse, I had sustained an injury, a three-centimetre tear in my adductor muscle.

The city's newspaper reported that a dentist had stolen the young promise from CRB. The club was desperately trying to reach me, calling my house and my family. Dr Marcellus funded my treatment at a physiotherapy clinic in Maceió. He would pick me up at home in the morning, take me to the clinic and then, in the evening, pick me up again for a hydrotherapy session. But what about when I recovered? Where would I play? Toninho, once again, was the one who helped us. He got in touch with a guy named Bilu, another significant figure in my career.

Bilu was a professional player born in Maceió who had played for both CSA and CRB. He had just finished his contract with Atlético Mineiro at the end of 2007 and was recovering from surgery in São Paulo FC's medical department, Refis, while waiting for an opportunity at a new club.

When Bilu returned to Maceió, he was impressed by my highlights DVD and agreed to meet with us. So Toninho, Dr Marcellus and I went to Bilu's mother's house for a meeting. The first time we met, he said he would try to help, and that he had contacts at São Paulo FC, where he had received his treatment. Bilu was friendly with Milton Cruz, who was then a permanent member of São Paulo FC's coaching staff and very close to the club's president. Whenever a head coach was fired at São Paulo, Milton Cruz would take over the position temporarily. He was an influential figure within the club, which at that time was the most powerful club in Brazil; they had recently won the Club World Cup (against Liverpool!) and were aiming for their third consecutive Brazilian championship title. What young player wouldn't want to play there?

A few days later I was boarding an airplane for the first time in my life. The destination? The largest city in the country, the gigantic São Paulo. It all happened incredibly fast. Within days I was out of CRB and on my way to another city for a trial with a giant. On board were me, Dr Marcellus and Luiz Fernando, another boy who stood out as a defender at CRB, but who ultimately didn't become a professional.

São Paulo FC has a training centre within the city limits, where the first team trains, and another massive one in a nearby city called Cotia where the youth teams train. When we arrived, we were greeted by a man named Geraldo Oliveira, who was the youth team manager but wasn't aware that Bilu had arranged the trial. There had been a communication breakdown between Bilu's contact in the senior team and the youth team staff. What I remember most was the cold. It was June. Winter in São Paulo doesn't compare to Liverpool's winter, but I came from Maceió, a city where it never gets cold; in comparison Cotia was bone-chilling.

Geraldo decided to welcome us in, but there were no available spaces in the athletes' dormitory, only a house next to the training centre, on top of a hill, from where you could see all the fields. It was a whole new world for me, but real chances didn't come. My time there was brief. São Paulo already had highly promising players in their youth team, like Lucas Moura, who would later play for Tottenham, and Oscar, who ended up at Chelsea. I hadn't arrived there during a trial period so all I could do was train, wait and hope. I stayed in that house with some boys around my age; I went in quiet and came out silent. The sessions during the week were mostly focused on physical aspects, with only two involving the ball. So I wasn't properly evaluated or able to showcase what I had to offer.

Bilu told me that years later, after my breakthrough at Liverpool, Milton Cruz contacted him to ask if that Firmino from Maceió was the boy who had spent a week in Cotia.

'That's him,' Bilu said.

'I can't believe it,' murmured Milton Cruz on the other end of the line.

It was me, all right. In the end, many potentially great players slip through the fingers of clubs in Brazil, the country with an endless supply of raw talent. But God knows what He's doing and His plan for me was different. After spending a few days in São Paulo, Bilu managed to arrange a trial for me at Figueirense, the club where he had played two years before and had good connections. Figueirense is a traditional team from Florianópolis, the capital of the state of Santa Catarina. Over 3,000 kilometres separated Maceió from Floripa (Florianópolis), the city where I would live for the next three years.

And so began a long period without returning home and I went the whole time without seeing my mother, father and sister. It was a necessary sacrifice to pursue my dream.

Dr Marcellus stayed close to my mother and kept her updated about what was happening in Florianópolis. He would go and see her, sitting there on the curb in front of her house, telling her not to worry about me. He reassured her that it was all going to be worth it in the end. My mother cried a lot and the doctor would say, 'Dona Ciça, your son's flying high. He won't come back. But he will make it to the top, you'll see. I won't rest until I see Roberto wearing the Brazil shirt.' He used to say the same to me, even back when I was still at CRB.

As for everyone in Maceió, they kept saying: 'That dentist is crazy.'

The Figueirense youth team coach was a guy named Hemerson Maria, an acquaintance of Bilu, who had mentioned that they were looking for a midfielder and that they could send me there for a trial. I arrived in Florianópolis on a Tuesday. There was a fitness session in the morning and small-sided practice games in the afternoon. I was determined not to let the opportunity slip past me. Figueirense had a strong youth team, having won the state championship three times in a row, and I wanted to be part of it. In that practice I scored with two bicycle kicks in less than 15 minutes – the first one, a classic; the second, even more beautiful. I controlled the ball with my chest, chipped it over the defender's head, and then completed it with another bicycle kick. Hemerson Maria later recalled everyone just staring at each other wondering what was happening. Who was that kid? He shared what I hadn't seen on that day: 'I told the other lads right away, "Let's head back to the stadium; I'm taking this kid straight to Erasmo Damiani [the youth teams' coordinator]. We're going to tell him he's approved." I kept looking back the whole way to check he hadn't run away! I already knew a phenomenon was right there among us.'

The next day, there was full training and I tore it up again. I remember it vividly: I dribbled and dribbled, again and again. They tried to take me down, but just couldn't. This was the chance I had been waiting for, the one I missed at São Paulo, and I had to seize it no matter what. I was inspired. Much later, once I was more integrated into Figueirense and we had become great friends, the other players admitted that they had wanted to break my legs during that first training session where I was destroying them all. Every club has its cliques and its competition, especially in the youth teams, and a new guy is always seen as a threat; all the more so if he's doing that.

There's a paradox here. Football is a team sport and that's a hallmark of my game, but during a trial, you have to be individualistic, do everything you can to stand out. During the practice game, my first at Figueirense, I managed to be both individualistic and a team player at the same time. I controlled the game, committed fouls, suffered fouls – it was a complete performance. Everything was perfect. After the first week of training, Hemerson Maria came to tell me that I was officially approved and that we would be working on a contract for me to stay with Figueirense. I was ecstatic to hear the news. He asked me my name again.

'Roberto.'

He was surprised. 'Wait, I've been calling you "Alberto" all week, kid! Why didn't you tell me that wasn't your name?'

There you have it. He had been calling me the wrong thing all week, but I didn't have the courage to correct him. If I was shy before, you can imagine how it was in a new city, a new club, with people I didn't know. He didn't know my name, but he knew enough. I had passed the test.

Chapter 5

Across the Ocean

The first time I came to Europe, I got deported. I was 17, had never left Brazil and had flown halfway around the world on my own for a trial at Olympique Marseilles, but I didn't set foot in the country let alone kick a ball. I didn't even get out of the airport. My phone was taken off me and I was unable to talk to anyone. I was locked in a room for five or six hours, terrified and in tears, then put on a plane and sent back across the Atlantic in the other direction, all those hopes in pieces.

It was 2009, my second year at Figueirense, where I was a junior who had participated in the Copa São Paulo, the most famous, respected and watched youth tournament in the country – a sign that I was performing well. I wasn't a full professional, didn't have a representative and wasn't contemplating going to Europe – my dream was to move to a major city and play for one of the big clubs in Brazil – but an agent connected to Figueirense named Maeda had managed to arrange a trial for me in France.

I was still under age, not yet 18, and I remember my mom desperately didn't want me to go. But Dr Marcellus, the dentist from Maceió who was still looking out for me, somehow convinced her that this was an opportunity we couldn't turn down. Bilu gathered together all the necessary documents and permission slips, and I packed my bags. Alone, I boarded an Iberia flight heading to Spain, where I would then get a connecting flight to Marseille. At that time – and I didn't know any of this, of course – immigration into Spain was at its height. Under pressure from the rest of Europe, it was tightening its border controls. They were deporting lots of people arriving in Madrid on flights from South America. And that meant me.

I got stopped on the way in, with no idea why. When the immigration officer arrived, speaking rapidly in Spanish, I couldn't work out what was happening. I was carrying an invitation letter from Olympique Marseille, proof that I had reason to be there. The officer talked to me and asked questions, but I was nervous, didn't understand anything, and was terrible at communicating. I just pointed to my passport and the letter: 'Passport and letter, *señor*. Passport and letter. Please, look: passport and letter.' It wasn't enough to convince the Spanish police. Two minutes later they took me to a room with a bunch of other people in the same situation and informed me that I would be sent back to Brazil that very day. There was only water and a few bananas for dozens of people. No one talked to me or offered help. We were just abandoned, in an incredibly helpless situation, thousands of miles away from our homes. I didn't know if I was under arrest or not, if I would stay under arrest or not. I felt like I was in a horror movie. Today, I think about how many people who have no intention of causing harm have their dreams shattered by moments like these.

I had taken a cell phone with me, but the police had confiscated it. They let me make a call. I only knew one number by heart: Dr Marcellus's. I don't know if there was any other number written down somewhere, from the club or the agent, but I was too nervous to think about options. I was already a shy kid who didn't talk much. Tense and desperate, I couldn't explain anything, couldn't convince them. I just cried and cried and cried.

My mother was crying too. Dr Marcellus rushed to her place upon my call. Me on one end of the line, her on the other, speaking into Dr Marcellus's cell phone. Me on one side of the Atlantic, her on the other. Imagine the feeling of a mother receiving a call from her child in another country, saying he's been detained and not knowing what's happening. Maybe it was irresponsible to send a boy like me, underage, alone, to another country. No less irresponsible were the immigration officers who ignored the invitation letter; they didn't check its authenticity, didn't call anyone and didn't explain anything. It's horrendous to think that I wasn't the first and wouldn't be the last boy dreaming of playing football to get into such trouble.

I felt like I was in jail. The hours passed like days. I sat on the floor of that room with no window, or meals, for I don't know how long. At some point, maybe after five or six hours, a police officer called me. They put me on a plane. I was deported back to Brazil. It wasn't the best way to start a professional career.

A few months later, I was back – which isn't to say that my problems were over. Despite what had happened at Madrid airport, I didn't hesitate to board a plane again and give it a second try, so determined was I to make it. This time Figueirense, who desperately needed to raise money, were better organized and Maeda came along to support me and avoid the risk of being deported again. This time we did make it to Marseille, where I spent a month training with the under-20s. I stayed in Olympique's accommodation and shared a room with another player who I can't honestly say I remember. I had a dictionary with me and learned the very basics of French, like how to count to ten. I learned my new name too: Robertô, with the accent *('Robert-o')*.

Although I couldn't communicate well, the memories I do have of that time are fond ones. I got to explore the city and Maeda would meet up with me from time to time to take me out for dinner. The French seemed to like me and I even got to train a few times with the first team. There was a Brazilian player in the senior Olympique team, Brandão, who had some success in Europe and played as a forward, but we never got a chance to talk. More importantly, I never got the chance to stay. I'm not really sure what happened. What I was told was that the French club didn't match the amount Figueirense wanted. Either way, it was time to begin again, back in Brazil.

Opportunities eventually opened with Figueirense's first team and my life would change completely. Football is full of moments like these and I often think about how many talented boys fall by the wayside. I also think about the luck that some people have, that things happen for them at the right time, with the right people. As I always say, God brings us together for a reason. If I had stayed in Marseille, how would my career have developed? I might not have met many of the people who were important in my life. I might never have worn the Liverpool shirt. Maybe, then, this was supposed to be.

And, in truth, heading back wasn't such a big deal for me. I had become happy there. Floripa is a beautiful place: an island with wonderful beaches from end to end, lagoons, sand dunes and a vibrant tourism scene. The club's headquarters, though, were on the other side of the Hercílio Luz Bridge, on the mainland of the city, the most populous part. I had arrived after the failed attempt to play for São Paulo and had made a great first impression. After my trial at Figueirense, the director of football, João Batista Abelha, contacted Bilu to say that I had been approved and they wanted me to stay. We signed my first amateur contract, where I received an allowance of around 250 or 300 Brazilian reais a month, which was about £100 at the time. I lived in the club's dormitory, which was literally beneath the stands of the Orlando Scarpelli Stadium. It was a long corridor with rooms side by side. In my room, there were four bunk beds. I lived with a bunch of guys I didn't know and at first I didn't talk to anyone. We had three meals a day there and each morning a bus would take us to the training ground, a 30-minute drive away.

The structure the club provided was more comfortable than the life I'd had in Maceió, but, to start with, it just wasn't home. You're a stranger, you don't know anyone. I used the allowance to buy some personal hygiene items and then spent it on phone calls and the internet to speak to my mother. I opened a bank account for the first time and sent the rest of the money back to her to help with the bills. Sometimes she asked me to come back, but I didn't. I even stayed behind during New Year 2008 because there was an important competition coming up. I was so determined to make it that I wouldn't back down. When I was out on the pitch I didn't need to think about any of those difficulties. Besides, my smile was helping: little by little, the ice was broken, and the boys adopted me and became my family. They made fun of my accent, typical of north-eastern Brazil, but it didn't bother me. Things were getting better all the time. In southern Brazil, the cold could be much more prevalent than in Maceió, my hometown, where I used to walk around in vest tops and flip-flops. But that had to change. I was so shy that I didn't even have the courage to talk to store attendants, so the boys would call them over for me and help me pick out clothes to try on. The boys loved me and I loved everything I was experiencing, especially on the pitch, where I was flying. There was a reason why Olympique had been interested, even if it didn't eventually come off. I had even been given the shirt I always wanted. No more number 5, like in the beginning at CRB, not now. I had been handed the number 10.

Just like Ronaldinho.

Not that following my idol was always the best idea. By now, coach Hemerson Maria knew my name was Roberto, not Alberto. My relationship with him at Figueirense began with the two bicycle-kick goals I scored in that very first tryout, went through that confusion of names, and ended with a great friendship. He was my mentor; I was his apprentice. He was the one who assigned me the number

10 shirt for the youth team. When he gave me advice, I listened. He played a pivotal role in my development as a player, offering tactical and positional guidance that stayed with me for life. He never needed to waste a single minute with me to demand punctuality, dedication or commitment. But he did give me a talking to once about being too flashy, which served as a warning that I heeded. I can still hear him saying, 'You'll end up hunted down and they'll ruin your career, boy.'

I was, of course, a huge fan of Ronaldinho Gaúcho and wanted to emulate everything he did, including the no-look plays that were a constant in my game, even during practice. Hemerson called me aside and said I was overdoing it, that I didn't need it, not all the time. 'You'll get yourself into trouble with opponents, it'll irritate them, and you'll become a target,' he warned. 'It's a skill to use sparingly, to occasionally trick the opponent, really make a difference, not something to use everywhere.' I listened to him, as I always did, and started using the skill more judiciously. Like, only when scoring goals for Liverpool, Hoffenheim, or the national team . . .

Hemerson was impressed when, at the end of my first year, I decided not to return home to see my family in Maceió. At that point, I didn't have any money. And I had my eye on the Copa São Paulo de Juniores, that prestigious youth tournament in Brazil, which takes place every

January. Many of Brazil's football legends emerged from there. I scored two goals in the Copa São Paulo in 2009 and another one in 2010. I was working hard and starting to really stand out. Despite being just 17, I played with the under-20 team – that's when the unsuccessful attempts to join Olympique Marseille happened – and I was progressing so well that on 24 October 2009 the head coach of Figueirense's senior team, Márcio Araújo, called me up. He was short on players for a match against Ponte Preta in Série B of the Brazilian championship and had asked Hemerson Maria for help. Hermerson recommended me, saying I already had the physique and attributes needed for the first team. I came on for my first minutes as a professional player at half-time at the Orlando Scarpelli Stadium. I was nervous, but, even though we lost, I was involved in some nice moves and think I played well.

In January 2010, having given up my break to stay in Floripa to keep working, the new head coach, Renê Weber, decided to include me in the senior squad, although it wasn't until March, under a third different coach, Márcio Goiano, that I began to get minutes with the senior team – first in the Santa Catarina State Championship, then in Série B.

My first goal as a professional came on 3 March 2010: a thunderous shot from outside the box in a 5–3 victory for Figueirense against Brusque. Exactly 13 years later to the day, 3 March, I would be heading into Jürgen Klopp's

office to read my farewell message to Liverpool. Life is full
of coincidences.

I scored four goals in the Santa Catarina State Championship and eight more in Série B, helping Figueirense return
to the top tier of Brazilian football – including some goals
from outside the area and others with my head. My reper-
toire was already extensive despite my young age.

One of the most special goals was against Portuguesa in
May 2010. I hadn't seen my mother in over a year. Since
my arrival in Florianópolis I had only been back to Maceió
once, in early 2009, but that day she came to visit me and
watched the match at the stadium. That's when it hit her
that her son had really become a professional footballer.

The game was level and I scored the winning goal in the
second half. A poor pass from a Portuguesa defender gave
me an easy opportunity. I intercepted the ball and shot,
beating the goalkeeper. After the game I went to the stands
to give my shirt to Dona Ciça as a gift. The first thing that
she said was the shirt was very wet and cold, and she was
concerned that I might get ill. A mother is always a mother.

By this time I was receiving a slightly higher allowance
from Figueirense and was able to live in an apartment,
no longer in the club's dorms under the stands. Life was
different now. Along with the goals and the spotlight came
expectation. In the team, I was competing with Fernandes,
who was a Figueirense idol and beloved by a section of the

fans. Sometimes some of the crowd would get on my case when I made a mistake, especially if it happened when I was attempting something flash.

I had listened carefully to Hemerson Maria back in the early days, carried that lesson with me, and tried to choose the right moments to make spectacular moves, dribbles or complicated passes. But that didn't mean stopping entirely. From when I was young, some Figueirense fans would criticize me every time I made a mistake. I never got intimidated. I kept trying and trying.

Hemerson Maria told me about a game he attended in the stands, where a fan kept cursing me relentlessly. I wasn't allowed a single mistake. Hemerson stood up, turned around and yelled at the guy, 'Support this lad here, damn it! Soon you'll never see him here again, you'll only see him playing on ESPN!' In the end, he was right, as the German and English leagues were exclusive to cable TV in Brazil for a long time. This happens a lot in Brazil: some fans are more demanding of the youth academy players than of those who come from outside.

Despite the aborted mission to Marseilles, by 2010 news had spread that there was a talented kid on the scene. Many of the club's players were represented by Eduardo Uram and Nenê Zini, active and influential football agents in the Brazilian market. Some of the players, including the experienced defender Roger Carvalho, who was my friend, told me that having a good agent in football was important. They said it would open doors for me; that only then could I play for a big club. I didn't understand anything about the subject – it was never my thing – but they convinced me to listen to Uram and Zini's proposal.

One night, I had dinner with Nenê Zini at a fancy Japanese restaurant in a hotel in the city. He presented their financial and career management proposal. These guys were true professionals and I liked what I saw. My plan had always been to play for a big team in Brazil, but they believed my potential could take me even higher. I was convinced, and signed a contract with Nenê and Uram. They sent a DVD with my highlights and goals to the Rogon agency and Christian Rapp quickly fell in love with my game. There had been a possibility of moving me to the German market midway through the year, but the deal with Hoffenheim only came through at the end of the Brazilian season – during the European winter transfer window. Once the deal was done, I received a sum of money that allowed me to buy a new house for my parents and move them from Trapiche to a better neighbourhood in Maceió.

After finishing Série B as national runners-up, our promotion mission accomplished, it was time to pack my bags and head to Germany. First for the medical exams, then for the Bundesliga restart after the winter break. When I went to Germany, everything that had happened in Madrid came flooding back. The transfer to Hoffenheim had been agreed and I travelled for the medical in November 2010. When I landed at Frankfurt airport, the immigration officers took one look at my passport and guess what? There was that huge DEPORTED stamp I had received as a gift from the Spanish. Muchas gracias.

The Germans became suspicious. I had been kicked out when trying to enter Spain, and now I was trying to enter Europe through Germany? What kind of story was that? Would the drama repeat itself?

This time I wasn't afraid; I was confident. This time the immigration officers took the letter I was carrying seriously, the one from Hoffenheim. Everything was well explained. Luckily, there was someone assigned by Rogon to take care of me by the name of Hendrick Meyer and he was waiting for me in arrivals. Born in Brazil, Meyer had German parents and spoke the language perfectly. He was my life-line, a guy who would help me for many years, starting on that very first day. When the police called him he was there to confirm that the letter and its contents were true. Immigration cleared me and I headed out into the snow.

That was a bit of a shock. I had never seen snow in my life. I arrived at Hoffenheim in November 2010, just after turning 19, and had landed right in the depths of the German winter. Sometimes people forget how young footballers are when they set out on these journeys. Without

Meyer, I hate to think how much more difficult it would have been. How cold I would have been. How cold I would have been, too.

Before we met in person, we had communicated through Blackberry Messenger and Meyer warned me that it would be cold when I arrived in Germany. It's not that I didn't believe him. I did, but I was from the north-east of Brazil; I had no idea what *real* cold felt like. The only long-sleeved top I had packed was a thin one and the temperature when I arrived was, I don't know, maybe -15°c. Meyer stopped by the Rogon office and picked up a coat for me, but even that wasn't enough. On that first night, we went to a Hoffenheim game and I was freezing. Although I didn't say a word, Meyer noticed so he set off to get me one of those full-body Hoffenheim coats, like managers wear. We could have fit three Robertos inside, but at least now I was protected.

I don't know what would have become of me in Hoffenheim without Meyer's support and without César Thier, a former Brazilian goalkeeper who had also settled in Germany and worked as a goalkeeping coach at the club. He was my translator and became a kind of older brother to me, essential in helping me get to know the club and the German work culture. He also tried to get me out of the problems I created myself.

I didn't need to stay in a hotel for an extended period like many players do. I arrived and already had a house to live in, the home where midfielder Luiz Gustavo lived before being transferred to Bayern Munich. It even had all the Brazilian TV channels already installed. Which was great, but, with the time difference and my habit of watching Brazilian football games, in addition to lengthy chats with friends, I often went to bed very late. I've always had a hard time getting out of bed in the morning; I can sleep even with the alarm blaring at maximum volume. So César used to come to my house to literally wake me up and take me to the club. I got several fines for being late.

I could pay them, at least. There was no doubt anymore that I would be a professional football player. I had the kind of security I could have only dreamed of before: my problems were no longer financial. Hoffenheim had bought me for a few million Euros. I had a good salary, more money than I had ever seen in my life. I could go shopping and get a car.

The start there was tough, though. For the first six months, I trained but hardly played. I didn't know why and, quite honestly, it wound me up. I got increasingly angry and frustrated. We Brazilians don't accept sitting on the bench, but I was stubborn and I wasn't going to let another European opportunity pass me by, so I waited, worked and kept my mouth shut. Some players drown in situations like this, others rush back home. I wasn't going to let that be me.

The challenge was to prove that I could survive that massive transition in my life. The cold was intense and playing football isn't nice when the ball feels like a block of ice. Despite being tall and having a physique that helped me stand out in my youth, I was too skinny and fragile for this new reality in Germany. During training, there were sceptical looks. 'Who's this guy? What Brazilian did they bring?' Nobody had heard of me and, let's face it, I came from the second division in Brazil; I was far from being a star. The level of play was much higher and physically it was completely different. I got bumped and jostled from all sides. I struggled even to stay on my feet during training. There was only one solution: dedication. I would show them who I was: I had done it before and I would do it again.

Hoffenheim were patient with me. They had bet on my talent and also realized that, despite some delays here and there, I was a very dedicated guy. The training sessions were extremely tough and the physical aspect was a big change. There was the frustration at not being a starter right away too, that common characteristic of Brazilian players. We always think we're the best and that we should be playing – and that's even more so the case when you take into account the drive of a 19-year-old kid. There's a delicate balance to strike there: that kind of attitude can be seen either as the confidence every kid needs, or the arrogance he doesn't. You need to ensure that you're not seen as the latter. You also need to be aware of your shortcomings.

I knew immediately that I needed to get stronger to withstand the highly physical training sessions. Until I improved in that aspect, I wouldn't play, no matter how talented I was. I was always the last to leave the club daily, making the most of the facilities provided by Hoffenheim – the gym, ice baths, everything – always with a big smile on my face. I did all I could to learn the language too, taking five private lessons a week. In no time I had the basics needed for on-field communication: 'Pass . . . go back . . . attack . . . forward . . . backward . . .' All that came quickly; the language of the pitch, of the ball, is the first thing you learn. What took me by surprise, as well as the physicality, was the speed and intensity of the game: the ball zipping across the shorter grass in Germany; the referees letting the game flow, not blowing the whistle for every last thing, like in Série B in Brazil.

I made my debut on 26 February 2011 in a match against Mainz. By the end of the season I'd scored my first goal, against Eintracht Frankfurt, and earned my first starts. The club rewarded my efforts, recognizing that I was ready to play, and planned the next season with me as a key player.

However, there was one setback. In mid-2011 I was called up to play in the FIFA Under-20 World Cup with the Brazilian national team, but Hoffenheim wouldn't release me. I was furious; it was a childhood dream of mine to play for Brazil and I didn't want to miss that opportunity. But there was no way around it. The club's management believed that I was an important part of the team and couldn't afford to lose me for the entire pre-season and the early rounds of the Bundesliga.

I would have to be patient. It would take three more years before I joined the national team – and then it would be the senior side. I understood – from the club's perspective, that was undoubtedly the best decision to make – and I prepared myself as best I could for my first full season in Europe, 2011–12. They did their part too, helping my development.

In addition to Meyer and César, another important figure around this time was Júnior, or JJ, a friend from Maceió who lived with me in Östringen, a small town near Hoffenheim (I'd moved from one small town, Sinsheim, to another). There was also the Dutch winger Ryan Babel, who helped me a lot in my early days in Germany – he arrived at Hoffenheim the same winter as me, from, of all places, Liverpool. He used to talk to me a lot, give me advice – a very nice guy. Then there was Nenê Zini, who was the connection I had with Brazil, and who frequently visited to check how things were going. I spoke very little, almost never, in fact, but having the support of one of my agents was important; it gave me security and we developed a good personal relationship. I made it clear to Nenê that I had no intention of returning to Brazil. My place was in Europe now and I wanted to keep fighting for a future there.

Life was about to change and not just on the pitch. At the end of 2012, by which point I had completed two years in Germany, I returned to Brazil for the end-of-year festivities and a short holiday. I went to Florianópolis. My friends from adolescence and football were in the south of Brazil; it was where the most beautiful women were; a place I loved going on holiday. I had been invited to a party to bid farewell to Bruno Alves, who was leaving Figueirense on loan at the end of that season.

And that's where I fell in love. It was there that I laid eyes on Larissa for the first time. She says to this day that our love was something that had to be built over years. I guarantee that for me it was love at first sight. I looked at her and I couldn't take my eyes off her. She was avoiding my gaze, not giving me much attention. Until I mustered up the courage to speak to her. I confess, I found the courage thanks to alcohol. Only with a little bit of alcohol in my system could I approach someone to dance with me. I went up to Larissa with the best intentions, but she immediately cut me off: 'Look, don't waste your time on me. I'm not going to be with you. You can ask someone else to dance.' It was going to be tough. I didn't want to ask anyone else to dance; I wanted to dance with her. I persisted a bit and she gave me a small opening. She asked what perfume I was wearing; it smelt good. There was hope! It was Yves Saint-Laurent; I still remember it. To my frustration, though, nothing happened between us.

I went to Maceió for two or three days to spend Christmas with my family and all I could think about was that girl I had met.

Florianópolis is Larissa's hometown, where she lived with her parents and a brother. She was a mature girl for her age and was responsible for managing her father's restaurant's finances. Larissa had come out of a four-and-a-half-year relationship with another guy, which, from what she tells me, was abusive. When she finally got out, she decided to enjoy life.

Larissa's father, Maurino, nicknamed Kuta, still has the restaurant where she used to work. It's near Ressacada, the stadium where Figueirense's big rivals Avaí play. The restaurant is a meeting point for fans, and even players and executives, so it's natural that my father-in-law is an Avaí supporter. But one of Larissa's friends started dating a Figueirense player and that's how she got involved with the crowd from my former club, attending barbecues and parties, and that's how we first met.

I returned to Floripa after Christmas and our mutual friends had organized another gathering, followed by a late-night barbecue. I couldn't miss the chance to see Larissa again. It was one of those situations where friends were trying to set up a couple. We all went to a supermarket to buy meat for the barbecue and I was left alone in the car with Larissa. That's when our first kiss happened. A bit unexpected for her; entirely planned for me.

It was all very intense. In the following days, more parties and meetings took place, until one day we were at Jurerê Beach, one of the most popular in Florianópolis, but Larissa decided to leave because her father was upset that his daughter was at a party with some footballer he didn't even know – he wanted her to come home. I tried to bluff: 'Look, are you going to leave me here alone with all these women?' I wasn't interested in any other women, just her. It was just a silly speech and it backfired. Larissa replied, 'You do whatever you want. You're the one who's going to lose out, not me.' She turned and left. I was out of luck. What was I going to do there? I went back home. This girl was tough; she wasn't like plenty of others who easily threw themselves at football players. She was special.

We spent a few days together and all I wanted was to see her. But it was time for me to go back to Germany. I used to drink a lot during that time – morning, noon and night. During vacations, I didn't hold back. I went to one last party in the early morning before my flight, drank again, and called Larissa, asking her to meet me at the airport. 'I'm not leaving here without seeing you one more time!'

She came to the airport to meet me. Time ran away from me and I missed the flight.

Now what? Where was I going to go? We made a risky decision. We went to Larissa's house, which wasn't far from the airport and which meant meeting my future in-laws: her father, Kuta, who wasn't very fond of that football-playing kid; and her mother, Marilete. Then there was me: slightly drunk and sleep-deprived. Years later, Kuta told me that the only thing he remembered about that morning was that I couldn't stop smiling. That big grin, showing all my teeth – the old ones, of course.

Somehow, we convinced Larissa's parents to let her go with me to the house I had rented in Jurerê and stay the night, which was incredible, unforgettable. The next day, I caught a flight back to Germany. I had to pay a fine for being late for the team's return, but it was worth it.

All I could think about that January in 2013 was Larissa. All I wanted was to see her again. So I suggested she come and visit me. She was worried about how to do it, how to pay. And I said, 'Forget about it; I'll send you the ticket.' So, in February Larissa and one of her friends came to visit. It was the first time in her life that she had been on a plane and left Florianópolis. Quite an adventure, I must say.

When she arrived at my home in Östringen, it had an incredible impact. The pantry was empty. How did JJ and I, who lived together, survive without food? That was a good question. I don't know how JJ did it. But I basically had my meals at the club. In the first few months in Germany, my eating habits had been a complete disaster. Lots of late-night pizza, restaurants and junk food. When you're 20 or 21, you're not too concerned about it and your body can handle it, but in Germany I quickly learned that nutrition would be one of the keys for me to make it in competitive football and have a long career. We started a programme to gain muscle mass, strength and stability, so I ate a lot at the club: breakfast and lunch. And I even brought food back for dinner. I started paying close attention to my diet, avoiding junk and sugar. I also learned about the importance of sleep for a professional athlete – while it took me a little while to put that particular lesson into practice, my obsession with eating well and later taking the right supplements was something I carried with me throughout my career.

So, when Larissa arrived, there was nothing at home. The cupboards were bare. By the time I returned from training that day, Larissa had been to the supermarket, stocked up the house, and even made a beautiful *penne à la bolognese* for all of us. The next day, it was *filet à parmigiana*. Out of nowhere, we had good food at home. I don't think I'd had home-cooked food since I lived with my mother. Those were wonderful days, full of connection, partnership, and love.

Larissa returned to Brazil, then came back to Germany to visit me again in May, but things were confusing emotionally. I was becoming interested in other girls too. My head turned, my world was changing fast – and I didn't have the maturity for a committed relationship.

Maybe it didn't help that in the meantime Hoffenheim's season had been terrible, and we'd had to play in the playoffs to avoid relegation from the Bundesliga. Fortunately, we won both matches against Kaiserslautern, with me scoring two goals in the first leg away, averting disaster.

Relieved, at the end of the season I went back to Florianópolis for another holiday. In my mind, I was single with no commitment to Larissa. I made the mistake, which I see clearly now, of pursuing and even going out with girls who were part of her circle of friends. One night, we were at the same club, and I took Larissa's arm and said, 'Tonight, you're leaving with me.' She removed my hand and emphatically said, 'No.'

It was what we might call a dilemma. I wanted to be with her, but not just with her. I was 21 years old, immature. I wasn't the only guy in the world to be in such a situation, confused, but what I really wanted during those tumultuous days back in Brazil was for her to come to Germany with me. Eventually, she did. I imagine things were confusing in Larissa's head too. She also wanted to be with me, but was afraid of taking the wrong step with a football player who didn't know what he wanted in life.

I did everything I could to please her and convinced her to stay with me in a different country, far from her home, a long way from her parents – and her job back in Brazil. My father-in-law didn't like it at all. He asked Larissa to come back, at least to properly hand over her responsibilities at the restaurant. So she returned to Floripa, helped her father get organized, packed her bags and came to live with me in Germany. We officially started dating. We were two kids, full of passion and the desire to get to know each other.

That new season, 2013–14, marked my explosion into European football. I scored 22 goals and provided 16 assists, was named the season's best newcomer by ESPN, who broadcast the Bundesliga in Brazil and presented me with a trophy. Increasingly, I caught the attention of big clubs in Europe, as well as the Brazilian media. It was a special year. In the middle of 2014 the World Cup would be held in Brazil for the first time in 64 years. The Seleção is always the Seleção, but that was *our* World Cup, a very different event from the others. In April Luiz Felipe Scolari, the Brazil national team coach at the time, made a trip to Europe to watch games and passed through Hoffenheim to see the club's training facilities – but we all knew he was there to watch me. We had coffee, he talked to me briefly, nothing too deep. 'Wow, he knows I exist,' I thought. Even better, he was keeping an eye on me. That filled me with hope, making me think that my first call-up could be a reality, that I might even be the surprise inclusion in the World Cup squad. I was on fire at Hoffenheim, after all. I was playing as a number 10, rather than out wide, and this really helped my game.

In the end, Scolari didn't want to take a risk. My first call-up didn't come until after the World Cup – when the new coach Dunga picked me in October.

But there was something else happening in my life. At the turn of 2013 into 2014, I decided that Larissa and I should have a child. It hadn't even been six months since we had been together, and we were just two kids, but I felt we needed a baby to fill our home. I've always liked children and they like me; that was enough.

I didn't think about the responsibility, the reality. Other players had babies young and it was fine. I thought there would be people helping and my life wouldn't need to change much. I didn't have the maturity to understand the sacrifices; it was all desire, an idea I hadn't thought through. Larissa was a little shocked at first but she eventually agreed to the adventure and, in April, we discovered she was pregnant. In June, I proposed. Valentina, our first daughter, was born on 27 November 2014, just a few days after I played my first two games for the Brazilian national team. Valentina is one of the loves of my life. And if it wasn't for her, her very existence, maybe my relationship with Larissa wouldn't have gone beyond 2014 either.

I knew I wanted to have children and marry Larissa from the moment I first saw her in Florianópolis. But life is full of temptations that become obstacles, which can be insurmountable – or not. For a football player, especially a famous one, finding women who are interested in some kind of relationship isn't the hardest thing in the world. In my case, all it took was a little drink to lose my shyness and do foolish things.

I was very happy to be a father. But the fact is, the boy from Maceió who hardly spoke and just wanted to play football was already living his life's real dream. The hard truth is that back then playing for Brazil alongside other great football stars, my idols captivated me more, moved me more, than being a father or getting married.

Chapter 6

A Night in a Cell

I still think to this day that the police officer was an Everton supporter. How rude he was. I wonder: if he had been a Liverpool fan, would he have treated me differently? But, look, ultimately he was only doing his job. Just because I was famous and brought joy to many people in the city didn't mean I could be driving under the influence of alcohol with a car full of people. It was tremendously irresponsible.

The result? I ended up spending a night in a cell at a Liverpool police station. I lost my driver's licence – and suffered intense embarrassment, deep shame. It was a mistake never to be repeated.

The cell was tiny. It had a small window with bars. I was so drunk that there was nothing to do but lie down and sleep on that stone bed with its thin mattress. What made it tough was that, in the middle of the night, they put a noisy drug addict in the adjacent cell. I told him to be quiet. 'I want to sleep, mate! Some silence, please!' I must have slept for about two or three hours until the Liverpool support staff arrived to get me out of there, before the photographers showed up.

Embarrassment doesn't even begin to describe what that was like. It was a harsh lesson, one I learned immediately. I would never let that happen again. I learned my lesson and fortunately, no one got hurt. Today, I don't even drink anymore.

Meyer always used to tell me in Germany, 'There's one mistake you must never make under any circumstances: drinking and driving.' It's a mistake you can't make primarily to avoid putting anyone's life at risk. That's obvious. But Meyer also used to mention it because he knew that the laws and authorities in Germany and England were very strict, more so than elsewhere. Plus, I was a public figure. Such a slip up would undoubtedly end up in the newspapers and tarnish my image.

And that's exactly what happened. It was late 2016, close to Christmas, and the drinking binge occurred on my fourth anniversary with Larissa. We went out with many friends to a Brazilian restaurant that later turned into a kind of a nightclub. At the time, we were staying at a hotel in the centre of Liverpool. On the way back, I missed the hotel entrance and drove about 50 metres on the wrong side of the road to find somewhere to turn around. At the end of those 50 metres were the police. Their car was completely dark. Suddenly, the lights came on, and the sirens blared. And I already knew I was in trouble. I got out of my Porsche and walked towards their vehicle, thinking I could sort things out just because I was Roberto Firmino, with a brand new charming smile.

The officer put me in their car and asked me to take a breathalyzer test. I tried to fool him. I attempted to blow in a way that wouldn't reveal my state, concealing it with my hand in front of my mouth. You know how embarrassingly you behave sometimes when you're under the influence of alcohol, right? It would have been impossible to deceive that officer. And I'm sure he was an Everton fan.

Larissa tried calling Meyer about 40 times to get us out of the mess, but that night our guardian angel didn't answer. I don't know if there was much he could have done. The officer was genuinely angry and determined to take me to the police station – rightfully so. Larissa then called my Brazilian teammate, Lucas Leiva. She didn't talk to me for many days after all that, she was so angry. Lucas told me they sat parked up outside the police station in the middle of the night until someone from the club came to help me. Lucas didn't want to go into the police station and draw even more attention to what was happening, so he stayed in the car with his wife, Ariana, and Larissa, who was crying the whole time. In any case, police protocol meant I wasn't coming out until the effect of the alcohol wore off. It was a pretty tense situation for everyone.

I left the police station at six in the morning and had training at ten, even on Christmas Eve. I nailed it in training, despite the hangover. Lucas said I was on fire that day. Klopp called me into his office, asked what had happened. We had a calm conversation. He said he wouldn't drop me from the next game, but I'd get fined.

On 27 December we thrashed Stoke, I scored a goal and was the Man of the Match. That's when Liverpool fans' sense of humour came out, singing the song that went something like: '*Bobby Firmino, he drinks when he wants!*'

In addition to sleeping in the police cell, I had to appear in court. As Meyer had warned all those years before, the case ended up in the newspapers. It was bad anyway; it could have been worse. Fortunately, Meyer helped me dress appropriately for the appearance. I had planned to wear a suit from a famous Italian brand, with a lion on the back, which was quite flashy. He and Christian suggested I change my attire: a Liverpool suit, no expensive watch; it was time to show humility and respect in court. I was found guilty, lost my licence and paid a hefty fine.

The fine could have been heavier than it was. The court understood that we had been in a stressful situation. We were only staying in the hotel in the centre of Liverpool because, for the third time that year, my home had been burgled.

When I first arrived in Liverpool, I lived in a wonderful apartment with a view of the docks. Larissa wasn't there at the time, but Meyer and my physiotherapist, Sven, were with me, travelling back and forth to Germany and splitting their time between helping me and being with their families. I loved the apartment; we did a lot of things on foot, went to restaurants in central Liverpool, and more. But there was an opportunity to move into a larger house and even put a Ferrari in the garage. I always wanted to have a Ferrari! Besides, Larissa was back with our baby, Valentina. I wanted more space and a garden. I had been warned that the house had been burgled before. It was possibly targeted by thieves because it was known that there was always some rich football player living there. But I didn't pay much attention. After all, I was from Brazil. I was from Trapiche. I wasn't going to be afraid of burglars in England. I decided to take the opportunity and moved into the house, located in the Mossley Hill area. It was a high-end residence, but without many security features.

The first break-in was in May 2016, a few months after we'd moved there. We noticed that one of the cars was all messed up, things were missing. We didn't even lock the cars because they were inside the property, behind the walls. We went to check the security camera footage and saw a hooded guy jumping over the wall and stealing various items we had left inside the cars. Larissa was pregnant with Bella, our second daughter, and naturally that scared us. A week later Liverpool had the Europa League final against Sevilla in Switzerland and Larissa was going with me on the trip. We were afraid, so we left Valentina, who was just a year-and-a-half old at the time, at Lucas Leiva's house with his kids and caregivers. There was a club security guard there, assigned to ensure everything would be fine while we were out of town.

When we returned from the final, we were told that our house had been broken into again. This time, there were two burglars. The security system triggered the alarm and the police arrived quickly, but the thieves managed to escape, albeit without stealing anything.

Then came the third break-in, the robbery on 22 December. It was a Thursday night, and we all went out to dinner at a restaurant with Valentina and Bella, who was only four months old. Meanwhile, four hooded men broke into the house, smashed a window with a baseball bat, ignored the alarm and in three minutes caused considerable damage. The police arrived within five minutes, but that speed was in vain because this was the work of professionals who knew exactly where the valuable items were and what they could steal. At the time, we estimated the losses at around £200,000. We decided to terminate the contract and leave that house in January. We couldn't live there anymore with the feeling of insecurity; Larissa couldn't even sleep there anymore. That's when we moved to Formby, a slightly more remote location away from everything, but one that gave us more peace of mind.

The night after the December robbery, while we were all in the hotel because the police needed to examine the house for their investigation, we had a prearranged commitment to celebrate our anniversary. It was unavoidable because we were meeting friends who had come from Brazil to see us. I mixed drinks and ended up getting detained for driving in that state.

Alcohol had been a part of my life since childhood. My parents used to drink and excessive alcohol consumption is something that's ingrained in Brazilian society, normalized. Parents drink in front of their children; there's almost a kind of encouragement for young teenagers to get into this lifestyle. In my case, alcohol was a way to overcome shyness. I didn't have a favourite drink. The preference was to get cheerful, loosen up, find the courage to talk to girls and have fun.

During my time at Hoffenheim money was no longer a problem in my life – or at least that's how I saw things. After games, we had the habit of going for a night out and enjoying our free time. One place where many Hoffenheim guys gathered was a nightclub in Sinsheim called Kinki

Palace. Other times, we would go out to nearby cities. I didn't hold back on the drink, especially after victories, and Larissa would join me too. Those were my rebellious years, when I felt like I was above good and evil. I was a famous footballer, I was untouchable.

In that sense, the first Brazil call-up in 2014 messed with my head even more, opening up a whole new world. We went to play friendlies in Istanbul and Vienna, and in my second game, against Austria, I scored a fantastic goal from outside the box. The next call-up came in March 2015, a few months later, and I started, scored and provided an assist in a 3–1 win in France. Three days later I scored a no-look goal against Chile, earning the respect of my teammates and proving that I was a great player, one who didn't shy away from nights of celebration.

I was in a groove, a world away from the home life of a man who would have to take care of a baby that was on the way. Instead, it was a new world: exciting and full of temptation. And, in late 2014, right after Valentina's birth, things were really bad between Larissa and me. Larissa discovered inappropriate text exchanges on my phone and only stayed because the baby didn't have a passport yet. More than once, she packed her bags to leave. We argued. The next day I regretted it. But a few days later I would do it all over again. I risked everything I had for a wild night.

Our relationship was strained; trust was shattered. I didn't want her to leave, but I didn't make an effort for her to stay. After the passion of the first year, I was really in a different place, a different moment. The only thing that kept Larissa in Germany, in practice, was the impossibility of going back to Brazil with Valentina. Love was losing the battle.

My first season playing with the national team, 2014–15, wasn't as good as the previous year had been at Hoffenheim, but the fact that I had been called up allowed my agents to make the leap from the Bundesliga to the Premier League. I was in Chile, at the Copa América, when I signed the contract with Liverpool. Now, I was an even richer, even more famous guy, worth millions. It was a huge change, but Larissa, who was in Florianópolis with Valentina, only found out through the media. I met her after the tournament, but my mind was elsewhere: parties, alcohol, enjoying the fame. This was my first holiday period in Brazil after becoming a national team player. I really was a star now. At that moment, it was over. Our relationship was finished. I went to my in-laws' house, said goodbye to Valentina, took a plane and reported to Liverpool. My head was all over the place. So was my behaviour. A few weeks later, in August, I asked Larissa to bring Valentina to England. She stayed there for four days, but I put her up in a hotel, not in my apartment. The conversations were already revolving around child support, what I would pay. I didn't see or treat Larissa as my fiancée; she was only my daughter's mother.

The beginning was difficult at Liverpool in footballing terms too. Things weren't working out in the first few months under Brendan Rodgers' leadership. To make matters worse, I cracked a rib, which kept me out of action, isolated from everyone. I began to feel lonely so decided it was time to bring Larissa and Valentina back – as if it were always my decision to make and their obligation to comply.

Larissa was already rebuilding her life in Florianópolis with her father's financial support. But she agreed to come back again in October, around my 24th birthday. This time, I didn't book a hotel. I wanted her to stay with me. I insisted that she come with all her belongings, stay, and we could go back to living our lives together.

Now, however, she didn't want to. She was insecure, unhappy with my moments of rebellion. At this point in our lives, Ariana and Ainê were instrumental because they made Larissa feel welcome in the city. She began to consider the possibility of giving our relationship another chance. Having two friends made a big difference, and she could envisage a more family-oriented Roberto Firmino in that scenario.

But things remained unstable in the following months. In day-to-day life, I liked being close to the family, meeting up with Brazilian couples, training, playing. Klopp was appointed Liverpool's coach and things were improving for me. My mind didn't have as much time to think about nonsense. After all, my life was football. But during holiday periods and national team duty, at parties or whenever alcohol was involved, I didn't want that married life. I wanted to enjoy myself. Yet to grow up, I didn't give my own family the respect they deserved.

Larissa became pregnant again around the turn of 2015, 2016. And as the due date of our second daughter approached, I panicked again. Doubts and temptations were everywhere. I did little to help build that family life.

Bella, our second daughter, was born in August 2016 and things finally started changing properly. Having a child is a gift from God, a blessing, a tremendous responsibility. It was no longer one, but two perfect girls. It was time to assume my role as a man and I decided to propose to Larissa again. I had done it before, but those had been empty words. Among friends, I said I never wanted to get married – not to Larissa or anyone else. Now, with two daughters, I was determined to make amends, to do it right, for real this time. I meant it now.

I could sense the confusion in her head and the distrust in her heart. When things were good between us, everything was fine. At other times, I threw it all away – only to regret it later. In October 2016 I was called up for the first time by the new national team coach, Tite, and played a World Cup qualifier against Bolivia in Natal in which I scored, and it was there that I asked for Larissa's hand in marriage again. She didn't know whether to trust me, because I had done the same thing two years earlier. There were still many barriers I needed to overcome to be a man worthy of that family. One of them was alcohol, because it was when I drank that I made mistakes.

A football player needs to be very careful about the paths he takes and the places he frequents. Those who go to nightclubs often end up drinking, using drugs, being exposed to many things, susceptible to problems. They can get involved in a controversy, a fight might break out, their image can be ruined, lasting damage can be done. A professional's body is their only tool; it needs to be taken care of, looked after, if you want it to last, if you want to play for over a decade.

My change began after those events in the second half of 2016: Bella's birth, the renewed proposal and the night I spent in a cell. The transformation was slow and uneven, as was the shift in my attitude towards my family, but it was underway. From the night of my arrest, I started drinking less, not overindulging as often. I hired a driver.

On 20 June 2017 we finally got married in Maceió. It

was a grand and unforgettable celebration in my hometown. We'd had many ups and downs over the years – many mistakes were made, there were many slip-ups – but as Larissa likes to say about that night: 'Love won.'

Chapter 7

False 9

On Boxing Day 2019 there would be no capoeira moves, no eye patches and no gunslinging. That day, I had planned a different goal celebration. Considerably simpler, I would say: designed to show my gratitude to the man who believed in me – right in the face of the man who didn't. That day, in Leicester, my plan was to score and celebrate the goal with Klopp. Because I knew that Brendan Rodgers was standing just a few metres away.

It was the end of 2019, we had just returned from Qatar with the Club World Cup in our baggage, I had found Jesus in my heart and I was brimming with confidence. Liverpool were flying, chasing the club's first league title in 30 years, and were top of the table. Leicester were second. I could hardly have been more motivated. Except that I could: this was also my chance to send a message. We played brilliantly, delivering the kind of performance that led many to believe that this time we really were going to win the league. We won 4–0, extended our lead at the top and I scored twice. When the second went in, I ran straight to the touchline. It was nothing personal against Rodgers – I wish him all the best – but things just hadn't worked out between us. He didn't believe in me. So I ran to Jürgen Klopp, the coach who really did; the man who had changed my life. And then I gave him a great big bear hug.

In my eight years at Anfield I became so identified with Klopp that it felt almost like my entire Liverpool career had been played under him. I fitted in so well with what he wanted that some assume he was the one who signed me, that it had been plain sailing from the start.

It wasn't.

When I joined Liverpool in 2015 it was the first time I had arrived at a club with any kind of status. I wasn't an unknown quantity anymore, as I had been during the trials in Brazil and France, or even when I turned up in Germany. I was already an international, I was financially stable and I was a father now, even at just 23. I was a different Roberto Firmino. But I had arrived in Liverpool alone. Larissa, my fiancée, and I were going through a crisis, and she decided not to come to England. Instead, she went from Germany straight back to Brazil with our baby daughter, Valentina.

I signed the contract with Liverpool while I was in Chile, competing in the Copa América with the Brazilian national team. I hadn't yet completed the medical and was feeling some pain. Christian and Roger, my agents, decided to send a physiotherapist to work with me in Brazil during the short break. They were very concerned about the medical and also the demands that would come in the Premier League. More concerned, it seemed, than me. The physiotherapist was a German named Sven Kampmann, who I had left stuck in a hotel in Florianópolis for three days without him being able to find me. I wasn't responding to messages, unconvinced that I really needed his help. In the end, I gave in and met with him, and Sven has been with me ever since. Thankfully, he didn't give up on me. From Floripa we went together to Liverpool. Having a personal physio-therapist is vital for elite players these days – practically obligatory – and we had physiotherapy and strengthening sessions four times a week.

In those first three months Sven and Meyer spent more time with me in England than at their own home. No one was as demanding with me as I was with myself. At the end of each game, I made a habit of reviewing the full 90 minutes, watching my movements and identifying mis-takes. Often I felt embarrassed watching the errors back, but it was necessary to get it right next time, to improve, to be a better player. I would also always check with the coaches how many kilometres I had covered. Generally, I ran around 12 to 13 kilometres when I played the full 90 minutes. If I saw a number below that, around 10 or 11 kilometres covered, it bothered me, and I would try to run more and make more effort in the next game. When I had first arrived in Germany, I went a month without playing because my body wasn't ready. I started going to the gym, using a hyperbaric chamber, gathering all the information I could. I became a workaholic, the last to leave training every day, and I carried that attitude with me to Liverpool.

Still, there was no guarantee of success. I was placed in a wonderful apartment in the centre of Liverpool, with a beautiful view of the docks and the sunset. It turned into a true bachelor pad. The guys, Sven and Meyer, helped me with shopping, and we spent a good part of the days playing PlayStation. Sometimes, we walked to restaurants and I started to realize I needed to manage my reputation. I was already recognized on the street, even if I didn't play much. It was all new. Liverpool isn't exactly a huge city, but compared to Hoffenheim, it's another story. The club is also a different world. When you step into the dressing room for the first time, you realize just how high the level is, how intense the competition for places will be. And no one is there to make things happen for you. You need to fight for your space and recognition. Nothing you did before counts now.

The first days at the club were lonely because the group was on a pre-season tour in Asia, and the training centre at

Melwood was undergoing some renovations. The Liverpool I arrived at had a mix of veterans – players like Jordan Henderson and Lucas Leiva, who were taking on the leadership of the side after Steven Gerrard's departure – and younger footballers eager to prove themselves, and when the squad returned, I was fortunate to encounter two guys who would become so important in my life: Lucas Leiva, as I mentioned above, and Philippe Coutinho. Another important guy I quickly identified with was Dejan Lovren. Croats are similar to Brazilians: extroverts, cheerful, easy to get along with and befriend. Lucas had been at Liverpool for ages, he knew everything about the club and the city. He welcomed me with open arms, going well beyond the call of duty. I could never have asked for a warmer reception, a true friend's welcome.

He couldn't help me with everything, though. On the pitch, I had a terrible start that left me wondering how this was going to work out. I rarely played as a starter and when I did it was as a winger, with Christian Benteke playing through the middle. I remember games against Manchester United and Arsenal where I played on the right side of midfield, with the responsibility to defend more than play; I spent so much of my time dropping so deep and so wide I was practically a full-back. I was a long way from the parts of the pitch where I could truly make an impact. It was clear that the coach, Brendan Rodgers, didn't know how to use me. I don't think he understood my style of play – I definitely never understood his plans for me.

Maybe that was because he didn't really have any. What I didn't know, at least not at that point, was that he hadn't wanted me in the first place. The person who signed me didn't bother to tell me this tiny detail. When I finally found that out, it all made sense. It took me long enough: would you believe me if I said that I only discovered that four years later? Just in time for that Boxing Day fixture in 2019 when Liverpool travelled to the King Power Stadium to face Leicester City, managed by Brendan Rodgers. A few weeks before that fixture, I had come across an article that told the whole story. Rodgers wanted to sign Benteke to be Liverpool's number 9. Bringing me in was nothing to do with him; it was a decision taken solely by Liverpool's scouting and recruiting department.

The club decided to bring both of us in and let the competition for a place play out on the pitch. Which was all well and good, but it was the coach who selected the team, not the scouting department. Let's just say I started at a disadvantage. When I read that article years later, I had a feeling of, 'Ah, now I understand: that's why I was played out of position . . . that's why things weren't working.'

Rodgers treated me well, or at least that's how it seemed. He always smiled, spoke to me in Spanish – even though my Spanish wasn't great – and called me *amigo*. When it came to games though, he hardly recognized me. *Amigo*, indeed.

Luckily, I didn't have to put up with it for long. By October he had been sacked. Although I had been an expensive signing who clearly wasn't delivering under Rodgers, much as I was unhappy, I had nothing to do with his departure. I picked up a rib injury and spent some time out; I wasn't on the pitch during the final few games before his dismissal, which came after a draw in the Merseyside derby against Everton. I kept my frustration to myself, as always. Maybe if that situation had gone on for a few more months, it could have become a problem, but soon Jürgen Klopp took over and he had other ideas; that was a totally different story.

Just how different, I had decided to show them at Leicester . . . my way.

'It was Bobby here, Bobby there, Bobby everywhere.' I love it when I hear Jürgen Klopp talk about his initial plan to build Liverpool's team.

The Boss arrived just a few months after I had landed in the city and we connected immediately: there was chemistry there from the start. I was a man of few words, but I understood German well, much better than English, as, obviously, I had lived there for four and a half years.

During my Hoffenheim years, Klopp was the coach of Borussia Dortmund – the last team to challenge Bayern

Munich's long-standing dominance in the Bundesliga. He had caught my attention in Germany long before we met in person. In games against Dortmund, he'd always stand still in the middle of the pitch during the warm-up, arms crossed, observing the opposition's movements even before the game started. That always seemed strange to me. He would stare at the other team's players, which was intimidating. He continued to do this at Liverpool, but thankfully now I was on his side. That guy was genuinely scary! I admired him and it turned out he admired me too. At the end of the 2013–14 season he'd tried to sign me, but the figures didn't add up during negotiations between the clubs, and my agents felt it was better to wait another year to make the leap directly to England rather than commit to a bigger deal in Germany. I trusted them and it turned out perfectly. Better than even they could have anticipated.

So Klopp and I would get to work together, after all. The Boss says that when he saw that I was going to Liverpool, he wondered why other European giants hadn't chased me, clubs with even more money. Why hadn't they made a greater effort to sign a man he considered an extraordinary player? Back then, Liverpool weren't a leading contender for the most important trophies. Maybe Klopp – and the guys from Liverpool's scouting department – saw things in me that others hadn't.

Throughout my career – whether in youth teams, or at

Figueirense, then later Hoffenheim – I had always produced better results playing as a number 10. I liked to play with the freedom to create, set up passages of play and nice moves, and get forward to score goals. In Germany I gained a lot of tactical knowledge and learned to play in a high-intensity, fast-paced, high-pressure football environment, adding defensive tasks and spatial awareness to my game. At the beginning of my time at Liverpool, however, Rodgers preferred to put me on the wings, sometimes even on the right, marking the opposing full-back. No matter how hard I tried – and I did try – it didn't work. It wasn't the best way to use me.

When the Boss arrived at Liverpool, I was undergoing treatment because I had cracked that rib in a League Cup game after an awkward fall. He came to talk to me and said he was excited for the opportunity to work together. I was very happy and motivated immediately. Of course, there was a question mark next to my name. Not in my view, but I understand that there were doubts in the minds of some people within the club and among fans. Not in the minds of the players, though, and certainly not in the mind of the coach. My friend Lucas Leiva says that Klopp's arrival was the 'perfect match' and the other players noticed it immediately. They saw that I had talent but was being used out of position, and no one understood why.

I asked Lucas, a guy who had years of experience at

the club, to tell us what he saw during those first months, and about the initial meeting between Klopp and me. This is what he said: 'We could see that, in Klopp's vision, the team would be "Roberto and ten others". Your character- istics fitted perfectly with what the new coach wanted. I remember we had a training camp in Tenerife, Spain, and I noticed, talking to Klopp, that he was completely in love with you. When he arrived, he asked the captains, the leaders, how we liked to play. He needed to understand how the more experienced guys could adapt and create a working philosophy. We wanted to play with more people in the middle at that time. You were adapting. You were at ease playing as a number 9 and as a number 10, switching between the two positions, and you had a great sense of when to start pressing. We could see that straight away. You were the one who initiated the press without the ball, which Klopp considered so important. You became the central piece of the team, connecting everything, and becoming essential in boosting and improving other players.'

Things started to click. If my off-field life with Larissa was going through moments of doubt and instability, on the field I was a plane ascending steadily, no turbulence. All I wanted was to play football and Klopp helped me do that, changing everything. I couldn't have the broad perspective that Lucas and other guys had: I hadn't been there long enough and didn't see the shift in the same way. Today, it's easier to look back and see how everything was built; easier to identify each brick placed in its proper place; every moment lived until we reached glory.

My dear captain, Jordan Henderson, also says that the Boss talked about me to the other players in the dressing room, telling them, 'You don't know how good this guy is.' With the German's arrival, my football took off.

By the way, let me take this opportunity to say how much I love Jordan. He's the typical pain in the backside when he's on the field. He talks all the time, shouts all the time, demands the ball, speaks up constantly – and if you do something wrong, he lets you know about it. There were occasional moments when other players didn't like it and when that happened Jordan always reacted well: he knew how to manage each team mate. I remember Alisson speaking up one time and the occasion when Philippe Coutinho turned to him and said, 'Stop yelling at me!' He did.

I liked his way. For me, Henderson was a great motivator. He could be annoying *and* push the team at the same time. I learned a lot from him, from his style of leadership. I look up to players like him.

At the time the team played through the middle more. We didn't have fast, open wingers – Mané and Salah would arrive in each of the two following seasons – so Coutinho and I combined in a more narrow formation, adjusting to each other's movements, that false 9 role already starting to emerge. The chemistry we had on and off the pitch from the Brazil team helped; we understood each other almost without a word. He would drift to the left and I would play more centrally, but there would be movement; we alternated positions and duties. We were two number 10s in the middle of the field.

My first Premier League game as a starter under Klopp was against Chelsea at Stamford Bridge: the Premier League champions were a strong team, full of Brazilians. I played up front, ahead of Coutinho and Adam Lallana, but I moved all over the field, appeared in all the attacking areas, as the Boss had asked. In one instance, on the right, I received the ball and set it up for Coutinho, who was arriving from deeper. He cut to his left and placed it beautifully into the corner. That was the first of many assists in a Liverpool shirt; it was also the birth of Bobby Firmino as a 'false 9', even though I was wearing 11. I was a forward who didn't stay waiting for the ball in the area; I wasn't a target man and my focus wasn't goals; I was more about creation than finishing. I floated off the front, dropping into areas outside the box.

In the next game, a Europa League match in Russia against Rubin Kazan, with Coutinho out I played as a number 10 behind Christian Benteke. Again, I provided an assist, receiving the ball in midfield and setting up young Jordan Ibe for the winner. This was an early indication of the way it was going to be with me and, when I played my first big, big game a few weeks later, that was confirmed. In my fourth start under Klopp we thrashed Manchester City 4–1 away: 21 November 2015 will be forever etched in my memory because I scored the first of my 111 goals in a Liverpool shirt – but that is not to say I was a striker. Again, I played as a sort of false 9, moving through the attack with Coutinho and Emre Can to the left of me, Lallana and James Milner to the right, and provided more than I scored.

For the first goal, I exchanged a one-two with Coutinho on the left, playing him in to finish only for Eliaquim Mangala to score an own goal in trying to clear. For the second, I provided an assist to Coutinho. For the third, he received a beautiful back-heel pass from Can and returned the favour. Two on one against the goalkeeper, Coutinho simply rolled it to me to score my first for Liverpool.

I'm here recalling the details of these early games because it was clear from the very beginning that I would be the man the Boss wanted me to be, not 'just' a striker. Even before Mané and Salah arrived, the figure of the false 9 was a thing.

I like to participate, be in contact with the ball, get involved in the game. I've never liked being stuck in one part of the field. Klopp knew this from seeing me in Germany. I had the quality to shoot from outside the area – I had scored many goals that way – and I was also strong in the air inside the box. I had developed that during my time in Figueirense's youth teams when I trained relentlessly, finishing endless crosses with my head. Of my 111 goals in a Liverpool shirt, 25 were headers. I had the attributes to be a true number 9 as well. But Klopp and I wanted something more.

At Liverpool, I added that heading ability to the defensive part of my game, helping out at the back. Peter Krawietz, who had worked with Klopp since their Mainz days, was the guy who showed us everything about set pieces. He also prepared the videos for the upcoming games; he was a keen observer of our team and the opposition. I learned a lot from Pete and improved with his guidance. Another guy who had been with Klopp since the beginning of his career was Željko Buvač. The Boss considered himself the heart of the coaching staff, Pete was the eye and Željko was the brain. Klopp's right-hand man, Željko was the one who actively participated in training, organizing everything and leading sessions.

His departure in 2018 was a bit strange for all of us; nobody understood what happened. To this day, we don't know and we haven't heard from Željko. The rumours at the time were that they had clashed over some signing. Honestly, I never asked the Boss about it.

Klopp has always worked closely with the members of the coaching staff. It was a team effort. They would often stop training sessions, show us videos, tactical systems and movements on the chalkboard, then correct us. With them, I learned to attack while defending. Our forwards had plenty of quality, they could score and create, but football is much more than that.

After Željko left, Pepijn Lijnders returned to the club. Pep was already working in Liverpool's youth academy before Klopp and I arrived; he was responsible for player development. He's a real football enthusiast, forever studying the game; a true scholar. He's multilingual and, having worked in Portugal, speaks excellent Portuguese. We communicated well from the outset. And although Pep had left the club in 2018 to become the head coach of a club in the Netherlands, he then returned to Liverpool to be the new assistant.

Pep is an incredible guy, very intelligent tactically. Having him back proved a big help to me, both because we could converse in my language and because of his game-to-game advice on positioning. From 2019 we also had the presence of Vitor Matos, who is Portuguese, and who took on the player-development role that Pep held previously at the club.

They organized everything, ran training sessions alongside Klopp, and coached our pressing game before each match. I always listened to what they had to say, and we discussed the role of the false 9 over the years, but when it comes specifically to my position, it was something that happened naturally. There wasn't a grand plan, some blueprint or a brilliant idea – no Eureka moment. I had a few conversations with the Boss about the emergence of the false 9 and I credit him for it, but Klopp always told me that he didn't invent anything. He said it was about me adapting instinctively to this more expansive role on the field, driven by my playing style.

It had happened even with Coutinho, a natural number 10, on the team; after his departure, with Mané on the left and Salah on the right, my role made even more sense because the work I did was perfect for feeding them. When it came to the trio, once we had put the pieces together and found the right balance and chemistry between us, it was 'scary', to use Pep Lijnders's words. 'Bobby made the game flow and we always had an extra man in the middle – with his movements, his intelligence, and his incredible ability to hold the ball and make a simple pass. Players who create this balance are so vital for a team,' he told the club's TV channel.

My friend Alisson said: 'Take Bobby out of the team, and it's hard to replace him. On the field, he's magic. He was the one who could make those crazy movements.'

I am very grateful to God for having had the opportunity to work with brilliant people who helped me improve as a player and as a human being. We wouldn't have achieved so much success without everyone's work and commitment. The false 9 was crucial, but all the other 'real' numbers were giants as well. So too was the man who saw how it could all fit together, the Boss I gave the bear hug to on Boxing Day.

Chapter 8

The Three of Us

Why did I pull that face? I don't really know. But it was funny, that's for sure. To this day, memes still arrive on my phone or get sent to me on social media. We were in the tunnel, heading back to the dressing room after a convincing 3–0 victory against Burnley. The atmosphere was obviously tense. Despite the good result, the game had been marked by a burst of fury from Mané when he was substituted in the final minutes.

The cameras caught everything. Sadio wasn't only angry about being subbed off: a little earlier Salah had attempted a shot on goal when he had a clear pass on to Mané, who was free inside the box. Well, my English isn't wonderful, so I can't tell you *exactly* what Mané shouted when he came off. But it wasn't anything nice! James Milner tried to calm him down, but Sadio remained furious, sitting fuming on the bench, gesturing repeatedly.

I knew those guys very well, maybe better than anyone. It was me out there on the field, right in the middle of them. I saw first-hand the looks, the grimaces, the body language, the dissatisfaction when one was mad at the other. I could *feel* it. I was the link between them in our attacking play and the firefighter in those moments. For many, that disagreement between Sadio and Mo was the first; for some, the first and last. But I knew it had been brewing since the previous season, 2018–19. My instinct and my duty was to defuse the situation between them. Pour water on the fire – never petrol.

Tense moments usually passed quickly. In the next game, one would be passing the ball to the other – or passing it to me, who would then pass it to the other – and we'd be celebrating another goal for our team. Together. Salah and Mané had had their little problems before, but that time everything happened on the field, there for the world to see. That day, at Burnley, the lid came off. As we climbed the stairs coming off the field, the mood was heavy; there was none of the joy there should have been at another victory – our fourth in four Premier League games. And there I was again, in the middle of the two. Behind Salah and ahead of Mané in the tunnel, a camera looking right at us. When I saw it, I couldn't help smiling, making a face that said something like: 'Did you see that?! Things got heated between those guys today! Don't worry, though. It's nothing.'

Their argument wasn't funny. Potentially, it could have caused problems for us. But that ironic face I made was the face of someone who knew it wouldn't lead to anything serious. Maybe the Boss and some others were worried. I wasn't! I think the Liverpool fans, seeing my reaction, had a laugh, put their worries aside, and went to celebrate another victory with their friends.

I don't know if he was aware of it or not, but Salah used to frustrate everyone when he didn't pass the ball. I knew how to handle that situation better than most. Klopp addressed this issue in front of all of us: when a teammate was in a better position, the ball had to be passed. It was a clear hint aimed at Salah. Over the years, I must say, this aspect of his game improved significantly. He gradually learned to be less selfish and more cooperative – notwithstanding the fact that he is a striker, a goalscorer, and every goalscorer tends to be a bit 'greedy' in the pursuit of a goal. That's normal.

Mané was more intense in both good and bad moments. He was the most explosive of the three of us and he was also the person with whom I had the most freedom to discuss this issue. I was always talking to him, giving advice, trying to calm him down. I would tell him to find peace, play for the team, and stay relaxed.

They were never best friends; each kept himself to himself. It was rare to see the two of them talking and I'm not sure if that had to do with the Egypt–Senegal rivalry in African competitions. I truly don't know. But they also never stopped talking, never severed ties. They always acted with the utmost professionalism.

I never took sides. That's why they love me: I always passed the ball to both; my preference was for the team's victory. Many focus on what I brought to the attacking trio in tactical terms, but perhaps just as important was the human element: my role as peacemaker, unifier. If I didn't do that, it would be nothing but storms between the two of them on the field.

Maybe that's why I was the one most often substituted by Klopp. The three of us had very different personalities and the Boss knew I wouldn't throw a bottle to the ground or anything like that. If I was bothered, I'd talk to him privately afterwards. When a substitution was needed, it was easier to take Bobby off than to upset either of the other two. Everyone, including the other players, knew that's how it worked. It was the worst-kept secret in Liverpool – naturally, no one ever asked what I thought or how I felt. That's just my nature; the team comes first. The Boss knew it.

I arrived in Liverpool in the summer of 2015. Sadio Mané joined the following year and, in 2017, it was Mohamed Salah's turn. None of us knew what was going to unfold in the five years we played together. Klopp once said, 'Not in my wildest dreams could I imagine that it would work out like that.' In football, clubs are constantly searching for the same thing: victories and sometimes titles. They have huge teams of scouts, performance analysts and use advanced software, all in the pursuit of finding the formula for success. It's a sport that moves billions of fans, a lot of money and many hearts. Everyone seeks maximum return with minimal investment. But, still, you never know. Football is wonderful because it's impossible to anticipate or predict the magic that will unfold on the field when a boy from Egypt meets another from Senegal and one from Brazil. Only God knows; no one else. Not even Mr Klopp.

First, I should clarify something. Some people talked about how it was to my credit that I gave the number 11 shirt to Mo Salah when he arrived at the club and that helped the whole thing start off on the right foot. It looked like a selfless gesture that, in the context of the story of the trio I formed with those guys, fitted my style of play. I've always been seen as the most generous of the three, the attacker who did the dirty defensive work and played to make the duo shine in front of goal. It's the perfect story, so very like me: Roberto Firmino, the nice the guy who relinquished the number he wore at the club and gave it to his newly arrived colleague.

Sorry, folks, but it wasn't like that at all. Or rather, it wasn't *exactly* like that. I simply decided to wear the number 9. It had been available since the previous season, after Christian Benteke's departure, but it was only in that summer of 2017 that I thought I could transition from being a false 9 to becoming the actual number 9.

Being Liverpool's number 9 is no small thing. It's a historic shirt that has been worn by club idols like Robbie Fowler, Ian Rush and Fernando Torres. Perhaps it took me a little while to realize that.

I wore the number 10 in the youth categories and later, at Hoffenheim, I switched from 22 to 10 when I had the opportunity. For Brazilians, and almost everywhere else in the world, the number 10 is the shirt of the star player, the shirt Pelé immortalized. But the number 10 at Liverpool belonged to my friend Philippe Coutinho. The number 9, it's true, has always been a coveted shirt for Brazilians, worn by Ronaldo, and I did like it even though I had never worn it before.

Now the time had come.

In the documentary that Liverpool TV produced about my eight years at the club, Salah told the story as follows: 'When I came here, I knew that Firmino had the number 11. I think I asked him for it. He said, "Sure, sure. I'll have the number 9 and you can have the number 11." That was our first contact and I felt the click between us even before we started playing together. He is such a good guy, gave me his number . . .'

Couldn't be better, could it?

I had already asked for the number 9 from the club and now I even looked good by giving up the 11 for Mo Salah.

There was just one problem: the club had been selling the 2017–18 shirts since the end of the previous season and that included number 11s with 'Firmino' on the back. When I made the change from 11 to 9, they agreed that, to make up for it, fans who had bought shirts with what was now the wrong number could send them into the club and the club would send them back again – signed by me. That's when I found out the hard way how many of them had already bought my shirt. It was crazy. I spent hours after pre-season training sessions signing jerseys. At first, I signed my name. After about 50 or so, my friends, I must confess, I started using my initials: an R and an F. I signed over 300 shirts. My hand hurt more than my feet. Thinking about it, I should have asked Salah for help. He got the number 11, he could have also signed a few!

That was my first contact with Mo, who quickly integrated into our group because he's an easygoing, down-to-earth guy. He asks questions, enjoys conversation, chats away. And he can play: his impact was immediate.

Salah also had a childhood of struggle, just like mine. I heard that he had to take several buses daily and spent three hours getting to training sessions. His first stop in European football was in Switzerland, to play for Basel. We never knew it, but we were only 250 kilometres apart at that point – when he arrived there in mid-2012, I had been at Hoffenheim for just over a year. In 2014 Salah was pursued by Chelsea and Liverpool. How different things might have been, in his life and mine. Mohamed went to Chelsea, the adaptation was tough, and he ended up being loaned to Fiorentina and then sold to Roma, where he exploded in the 2016–17 season. That's when Liverpool came back for him, uniting our paths and purposes.

When he arrived, Sadio Mané had already been at the club for a year. We are all more or less the same age: I was born in October 1991, Mané in April 1992, and Salah in June 1992. Perhaps that's why our career movements were almost simultaneous. Mané was born in a small village in Senegal and must have faced similar or even greater difficulties to those Salah and I experienced. He had to leave the village where he lived and head towards the capital, Dakar, to fulfil his dream. Finally, he was discovered by scouts and, a year after I had those trials at Olympique Marseille, he was taken for trials at Metz, also in France.

Unlike me, at least he understood what people were saying there. Sadio quickly moved up to Metz's first team and made his debut in Ligue 1. In mid-2012 he was transferred to Red Bull Salzburg in Austria. So, at that time, he was about 500 kilometres away from me and about 500 and a few more from Salah, all of us in cities and leagues where the primary language was German. Coming from completely different places, we were already close to each other, but we had no idea.

After two seasons in Austria, Mané made his move to the Premier League. Again, the dates coincide. In the summer of 2014 Sadio was transferred to Southampton at the same time Salah went to London to play for Chelsea. I would have left Hoffenheim at that time too, after the season where I exploded in the Bundesliga. But my agents decided to hold off the move for a year and I would arrive in England a year later, in 2015. Unlike them, I went directly to Liverpool.

My first year in the Premier League was Mané's second, so I knew more about him than Salah. He had a great season with Southampton and caught the attention of many big clubs in England before God's will brought us together in Liverpool.

Klopp said I had 'absolutely everything' in my game except top speed. The team was looking for players who could accelerate our game on the wings and create space for the two Brazilians in the middle – me and Coutinho. First came Mané, then Salah. That part fit; what you never know is if everything else will, if the chemistry will be there. Take Messi, Mbappé and Neymar at PSG: three geniuses, world-class players, legends for their national teams ... yet somehow it didn't click. At Liverpool it did, and it brought immense joy to the fans and to us too.

The first time we were on the field together was on 1 August 2017, in a pre-season match: the Audi Cup, in Munich. We won 3–0 against Bayern Munich. It was a friendly game, but both teams wanted to field their strongest line-ups to get an idea of where they stood. Somewhere pretty good, as it turned out.

Carlo Ancelotti was Bayern's coach; Thomas Müller, Franck Ribéry and Robert Lewandowski were his front three. Let's face it, that trio was far more famous and established than ours but it turned out ours was even better. In the seventh minute, I stole the ball in midfield and provided the assist for Sadio Mané to score the first, a move that would be repeated a million times in the years to come. In the 34th minute, I started the play again from the middle, passed to Mané, who beautifully back-heeled the ball to Alberto Moreno, advancing from the left. He crossed it into the box and Salah scored the second. What a debut.

Just 11 days later we would play our first official game together. In the opening match of the Premier League, we drew 3–3 against Watford. Each one of us scored a goal. It was a frustrating result, of course, but, once again, we saw that the trio could work. It was a game that showcased what our season would be like: some defensive mistakes but a lot of attacking presence.

Mané scored the first goal in his characteristic style, breaking into the box from the left and shooting with his right. The second goal was mine, a penalty that Salah won. And on the third goal, I received a through pass and chipped it over the goalkeeper. Would the ball go in or not? I don't know. All I know is that Mo Salah appeared like a lightning bolt and that touch turned into an assist. The day wasn't perfect, of course, as we conceded the equalizer in stoppage time. Yet since pre-season we could already see that something good was happening. Because everything worked well in training, it was only natural for it to work in games too. I would drop back to get the ball, they would make runs behind the defensive lines. The coaches always told us that we would succeed together. After the debut in Munich and the first Premier League match against Watford, it felt like we had been playing together for eternity. And the rest is history: a beautiful story that lasted for five seasons. We were three hungry forwards eager to show the world what we were capable of.

That team also had Philippe Coutinho, but what the newspapers called the Fab Four (after the Beatles) didn't last long. Philippe had a strong desire to play for Barcelona and fulfilled his dream in the middle of the season, in January 2018. The Boss didn't want to lose him in any way. It became a battle between Philippe and the club. Our number 10 missed the start of the season due to a back injury. He wasn't in the Watford game, the first official match of the attacking trio. Even though we all knew how important he had been and, much as I wanted my friend to stay at my side, the debut gave us the confidence that we could generate a strong attacking presence and create chances without him.

While Coutinho was still on the team, I was, in practice, the number 9, positioned centrally between the two wingers: Salah on the right, Mané on the left, with Coutinho behind. The idea was for me to play closer to the goal. But, of course, I had never been the central striker, so it was natural for me to drop back to get involved in the build-up.

Philippe and I, perhaps due to our shared language and friendship, talked a lot during training sessions and even during games. We took turns dropping back to help in defence and press the opponents' build-up play.

By the time he departed, I had already become the false 9, even if it hadn't been entirely planned that way. Klopp must have liked what he saw in training and in games. Practice and reality are always stronger than drawings or elaborate plans on a tactics board. The Fab Four had become the Fab Three, topping the charts at Anfield instead of the Cavern Club. Even Klopp had never imagined it would be so good. This is how the Boss summed it up: 'It was about the boys, how they executed everything. The most important thing that the three up front did for a long, long time was the mix of offensive creativity, speed, finishing, plus the desire to defend.' Among the attributes mentioned by Klopp, two are very subjective: creativity and what he called 'desire to defend'.

Creativity is the essence of the game, especially in Brazil. And perhaps there is something of that in the football played on the streets of Senegal and Egypt too. Sadio, Mohamed and I all shared the struggle to make it, enduring lives spent far from our families, and frequent changes in countries, cultures and languages. We didn't know if we would make it: we failed trials, we experienced doors closing on us. It was a long, hard journey, but when the three of us came together at Liverpool it was like everything lightened. The pleasure was greater than the sacrifice; the sense of a collective cause makes the work worthwhile. With that chemistry, that mentality, playing becomes a joy. And we became a whole, building a beautiful story, day by day. On the field, we didn't need to speak. With just a look, we understood. It's incredible to think about the number of goals we scored together and the impact we had on the team's success; how natural it all came to feel, how *right*.

It worked so well for several reasons.

Salah possesses incredible speed, agility and a keen eye for goal. He can single-handedly turn a game with his mesmerizing dribbles and clinical finishing. His presence on the right side of the attack creates constant headaches for defenders. Mané has immense skill and flair, great ability to take on defenders and create scoring opportunities. Whether it's cutting inside from the left wing or timing runs into the box, his speed, technique and versatility make him a nightmare to face. And then there's me, the link between them, providing the creative passes and movements to unlock defences. It was also important that I wasn't obsessed with goals. I've always enjoyed providing assists, creating passages of play and serving my teammates as much as I can. What matters to me is winning.

If I had competed to be top scorer, I am absolutely certain we would have failed. For example, I could have kicked up a fuss or caused trouble in the dressing room when I was prevented from taking the penalties after missing two in the 2017–18 season and never had the chance to redeem myself. But it was never my goal, nor in my nature, to create internal conflicts or seek individual glory. The formation of a winning team has many nuances. God puts people in our path so that His will may be done, and it was He who brought Sadio Mané and Mohamed Salah alongside Roberto Firmino. I was the right person to help my friends shine and our team to win.

When my departure from Liverpool was finalized, many interviews and documentaries were made about my time there. It's very difficult to describe the feeling of gratitude upon hearing some of the comments from former team-mates, but I feel compelled to include some here. Because perhaps, for a while, they knew more about me than I knew about myself. Although we didn't become great friends in the sense of being like family or visiting each other's homes, our relationships developed off the field. To begin with, the language made it hard for me to establish smooth communication with my teammates. It wasn't for want of trying . . . by them, at least. Sadio Mané burst into the club with his joyful, positive personality and tried to talk to me in every way possible, even in German. But, in truth, I used to avoid him. I was very shy. I think he thought I didn't like him at first, but then he got to know me better and realized it was the opposite. In the first few years, I had more freedom both on and off the field with Mané. Let's say I was closer to him.

But, especially after Mané's departure to Munich in 2022, I also got quite close to Salah. He was my neighbour in the dressing room and a guy I learned to admire. He said this about me: 'Bobby has always been a humble and hard-working guy. He has the ability to do everything in a game and sacrifice himself for the team. Bobby always knew where we were.'

As I've said, on the field, a glance was enough. I already knew the movements they would make, where and when they wanted the ball, how they liked it to reach them.

Mané is the more explosive player. He can also play as a number 9 because he is a great striker and has the strength to withstand challenges inside the box. Salah is more of a dribbler and an opportunist. Sometimes I was amazed at how the ball would find him for him to just tap it into the net. He was always in the right place, alert and ready to score. He was very quick to anticipate the defenders' moves. If the defender blinked, Salah was already ahead of him. In his first season, Salah scored 32 goals in the Premier League, an absolutely unbelievable number. That was our best season together in terms of numbers: Salah scored 44 in all competitions; I ended up on 27, Mané on 20; in the Champions League each of us scored ten. I also finished with eight assists in European competition, which made me equally proud.

Everyone knows that, at some point in the following season, 2018–19, tensions began to emerge between my teammates. Both wanted to be top scorer, each was trying to get more than the other. That internal competition saw cracks appear. We started to have problems, of course, as some balls that should have become assists – from one to the other – turned into missed opportunities for the team.

But the only truly public moment of friction was that game at Burnley. Neither of them ever spoke badly of the other to me in private conversations. There was never an explosion inside the dressing room, as some believed. But there I was, right in the middle of them, and I could feel the atmosphere getting heavier and heavier. Their body language during games showed dissatisfaction. There were accusing glances when the ball wasn't passed properly, and the move didn't end well. I tried to calm things down.

The pair finished the 2018–19 season, our second together, tied as top scorers in the Premier League with 22 goals each, alongside Arsenal's Pierre-Emerick Aubameyang. That year we missed out on the title by just one point. We won the Champions League, so it's fair to say that the issues between them didn't hurt our results. There isn't too much wrong if you win the Champions League and finish the league with a single defeat.

Ego – vanity – is unavoidable in football. Players want to win and they also want individual recognition, the best contracts, awards, the Golden Boot, the Ballon d'Or. I understand that. After the Burnley game, though, Jürgen Klopp had to intervene. He called the two of them into his office and asked for that competition to simply end. We knew about the meeting through word that spread in the club's corridors. The team needed them, and they weren't even competing for the same position, each playing on a different side of the field. It made no sense. Things improved after that conversation with Klopp.

The following season, 2019–20, we finally won the Premier League. Neither of them was the league's top scorer: Salah finished with 19 goals, Mané with 18. By then they had understood that the most important thing was the team and their attitudes had changed for the better.

Yet there was still something there. At some point, it was going to come to the surface. I think Mané left Liverpool precisely because he didn't feel as valued as Salah within the club. He felt he was being treated as less important. I love this guy. I enjoyed playing alongside him so much, he was always smiling. Sadio is both fun and a man of strong character; a brilliant and determined guy. It was great to be around him and we formed a bond that remained strong even after his departure to Bayern Munich. This is what he said about me: 'Bobby changed something about my football. Because he makes things so much easier that you don't need to complicate. When we get the ball, Bobby always gives you options. I have seen many, many nice people in this business, but Bobby Firmino is far, far away my favourite one. I don't know a more beautiful stadium chant than Bobby's.'

Well, as I said, I love the song they made for Sadio Mané as well. But it was funny to hear him say that he preferred my song over his own. It reminded me of our goal celebrations: he also preferred mine. In the dressing room the lads would wind Sadio up, laughing and joking about the fact that he would always imitate other players' celebrations. I had so much fun on the field and my celebrations were always spontaneous, natural: it was just whatever came to mind at the moment of the goal. Sadio loved it and ended up doing the same. Whether it was a capoeira move, pistol fingers or even the pirate, he copied it. He just liked what he saw, but in the dressing room no one would let it go, ribbing him for it. He didn't always like that very much; sometimes he would even claim that he had come up with the celebration himself. But it wasn't true! Oh my God, how many cool moments we had together, how many laughs. I really miss Sadio.

Who, of the pair, do I think is better? There's no way to answer that. Who would I choose to play with? Both, of course.

They are two incredible players, two great footballers. They loved playing with me because I fought hard to serve them. And I loved playing with them because they were players who complemented my game and made the effort worthwhile. 'It was a lot of fun to see them working from where I was,' Virgil van Dijk said. He had a more privileged view than most, but I like to think it was just as enjoyable for those who watched in the stadium or on television around the world.

After five seasons together we reached an incredible 338 goals combined: 156 from Salah, 107 from Mané, 75 from Firmino. We provided 139 assists, two-thirds of them shared among ourselves. In these five years I provided 50 assists: 21 of them to Salah, 18 to Mané, 11 to other teammates. We won seven titles and received praise from all over, from Liverpool fans and teammates and even opponents.

This recognition from everyone, especially from the two of them, is very important to me. I feel deeply grateful, thankful to God for the opportunity to have played and experienced so much success alongside guys like Sadio and Mo; to have written unforgettable pages in Liverpool's history together.

Chapter 9

Shine On

Everyone talks so much about my teeth, don't they? And you know what? There's not actually much to say about them. I wanted to have nicer, whiter teeth. And that's the story.

When I arrived at Liverpool with those 'new' teeth, it caused a stir in the dressing room. A 'wow' here; a 'wow' there. 'What happened there, Bobby?' the Boss asked me. 'You're lighting up the place!' Little did they know that those dental veneers were temporary; I would show up with the permanent ones just a few days later. It was the talk of the club for weeks; everyone was amazed.

On the first day, I couldn't even talk because of the pain. I had a hard time breathing and, for a while, had to keep my mouth closed. The big smile soon returned, though. And now, it was even more captivating and shiny than ever. I endured a couple of days of pain, worried it would never go away. Then it did and right away I loved the decision to improve my appearance. Over the years, the Boss got dental veneers, Mané did too, then Coutinho . . . I set a trend and I think I helped that dentist in Liverpool quite a bit.

In my case, honestly, it was purely cosmetic. I never had trouble smiling, quite the opposite. A smile was my trademark throughout my childhood in Maceió, during my youth in Florianópolis and in adulthood in Germany. I always lived and communicated with a smile. I was never ashamed of my smile or my teeth.

One day, though, Larissa showed me an ad for these dental veneers. She already had veneers, had had them put on years before, and I didn't even know. It was Larissa who, let's say, encouraged me to do the same as her. We went to a clinic near our house. The price was quite high, which suggested to us that it was a good thing. That used to be our old measure of quality. If it's expensive, it's good. I know better now.

I wanted them right away, despite always being very afraid of dentists. I'd had an accident in childhood: I hit my teeth on another kid's head and one of my teeth went really dark. So I liked the idea of changing my appearance and chose to have white teeth. Whiter than white, in fact. I asked the dentist for a 'super white' shade.

That was in September 2016. It had been a little over a year since I'd arrived in Liverpool and our second daughter,

Bella, had been born a few months earlier. My life with Larissa was in one of those good moments. Aesthetics and appearances mattered a lot to both of us at the time – it was as if our value was in what we wore. Today, it's different: yes, we want to dress well, but what matters most is on the inside. Everything is in its proper place now.

In the first week with the super whites, it took me a little while to get used to the new look. It was impactful for me too, not just for the other players who saw me arrive with those bright teeth at Melwood. Suddenly, you have much larger teeth. They felt enormous, gigantic in my mouth.

They continued to hurt a lot at first, because the original teeth become sensitive due to the wear and tear, and the gums can become uncomfortable too. Gradually, I got used to it. I only had to replace the veneers seven years later and then I decided to go for the same white colour. They're even more shiny now, but more natural. That suits the new Bobby better.

I was never trying to impress others; that was never my motivation for buying a car, a watch, clothes or getting dental veneers. I always wanted to do these things to feel good, nothing more. Or at least that's what I thought. But on some level, I guess I did. I was a poor boy who became rich, who arrived in a new world and was looking for an identity, a way of fitting in and expressing myself. One of those ways was through possessions, which is what footballers do. I left Maceió wearing flip-flops and vests. I had nothing, just the gift that God gave me and a burning desire to become a football player. When things started going my way, it was like a child tasting chocolate for the first time. I wanted to indulge myself.

Football is a world full of vanity, one that's competitive in the dressing room as well as on the pitch. The best watch, the best clothes, the best car. As soon as a new luxury car is released, there will be a load of them already lined up in the parking lot at every big club. There are young players in the academy who are more concerned about the car they will buy than things that are genuinely important for their lives and the lives of their families. I advise everyone to have more control. Owning a luxury car shouldn't be a football player's top goal. I know: I went through it.

I wasn't trying to be better than others, but on some subconscious level, I was drawn into that. Today, I see it perfectly. I bought clothes or a watch to feel good, to fit in, to have a place, a status, in this new context of my life. In football, all the big players had fancy cars. Then I would buy a fancy car – or two or three – to be on that level too, to be one of them. And it wasn't enough to buy it, you had to show it. Take photos in the car, post them on social media. Deep down, you're trying to prove something, even if I couldn't identify it as such back then and didn't act with the arrogance that I know these words convey.

Above: Me at my birthday with Mom, Maria Cícera, as Grandma Lia carries cousin Zequinha.

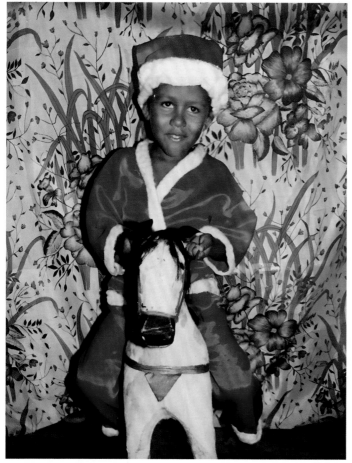

Left: Me as a kid in Brazil.

Celebrating one more goal at Anfield, but wearing the Brazil shirt. An international friendly against Croatia just before the 2018 World Cup.

Scoring my most important goal as a Red. FIFA Club World Cup against Flamengo, Qatar, 2019.

Liverpool vs PSG, UEFA Champions League, 2018. My trademark celebration after I almost lost my left eyesight.

A 'no-look' goal during Liverpool's 5–1 win over Arsenal in 2018. This was my first hat-trick for the club.

A big hug to the man who believed in me, Jürgen Klopp, after scoring against Brendan Rodgers' Leicester in 2019.

Seven is the perfect number. Never felt as loved as I did after scoring against Manchester United, just days after announcing my departure in 2023.

Above: Christian Rapp, Brunno Ramos, Eduardo Uram, me, Larissa, Marina Zini, Nenê Zini.

Left: My wedding in Maceió.

Below: Me and Larissa.

Revisiting the street where I grew up, Trapiche, Maceió. In the background is the blue façade of the Rei Pelé stadium.

Me with Dr Marcellus, the dentist, during my early days playing for CRB youth team in 2008.

A new life born in Christ. My baptism along with Larissa and brothers Alisson and Isaias Saad, in 2020.

Along with the Champions League and Premier League trophies, me with Julio Gomes who put my life into words. Maceió, June 2023.

Champions of Europe! One of those special moments, feeling the energy and passion of Liverpool fans in 2019.

Me in front of the giant mural on a wall close to Anfield. Just before my farewell party at Anfield.

Liverpool fans in front of the mural.

The complete family team. On the left, Cesinha with my father, sister, and mother. On the right, Larissa's parents, Marilete and Maurino. Crouching down, dear João and Lina.

Old days in Liverpool: me with Alberto Moreno, Juan, Philippe Coutinho, Cesinha Lucena and Lucas Leiva.

Me and Bilu, who arranged the trial at Figueirense.

Along with my dear friend Cesinha at home in Manchester, 2023.

My beautiful family: Liz, Valentina, Sophia, Larissa and Bella (2023).

Team ROGON – Dennis, Christian, me, Roger, Paul, Marten.

Manah Church – Juninho, Pastor Jairo, me, Larissa, Bella, Valentina, Pastora Keila, Camila, Gabriel.

Yes, of course, I know. I became a famous football player, a Liverpool star, a regular in the Brazilian national team, and people like me often influence the public to do or wear something similar. But, honestly, I never realized the extent of the influence I could have.

Even during my time with Figueirense, I started shopping and experimenting with my style. I was shy about speaking, but not about dressing. I also bought my first car, a white VW Fox.

I arrived in Germany with a great salary. It wasn't enough to make me a millionaire, but it was more than enough to live comfortably in Europe. It was more money than I had ever seen in my life and I wanted to do everything that had not been possible until then. The first thing I asked Meyer, who helped me with everything in Germany, including my finances, was how I could send money to my mother. That was my top priority. From there, the conversion from Euros to reais made me feel like I had a lot of money to spend. A lot!

When I arrived in Germany to sign the contract in the winter of 2010–11, Meyer had already set everything up so that I could focus on football when I returned for good in January. One of the first things I had to do was choose a car. I chose an Audi A3. I wanted a red car because I dreamed of having a Ferrari one day. I've always been a Formula 1 and Ferrari fan; I loved watching Michael

Schumacher, Rubens Barrichello and Felipe Massa driving the red car. But it couldn't just be any red car or even any Audi. I wanted the interior to be a shade like caramel or coffee. The Audi guy said he didn't know if a request that extravagant would be approved at the factory. But it was. And that was my first car in Hoffenheim. A red Audi A3 with a beige interior.

When I signed for Liverpool and became rich, my car collection grew a bit. I did get that Ferrari too: a 458 Italia. Thing is, I was a bit embarrassed to use it because when I arrived at Liverpool's training ground, everyone would stare at the car. That wasn't what made me happy and it wasn't what I wanted; I just liked having a Ferrari. I had it for two years and I think I only drove it a couple of times. I had wanted that status, but it didn't sit well. Showing off didn't either. Owning a Ferrari might have been the ultimate I could achieve, a sign that I had made it. Who doesn't want to have a Ferrari? But I didn't like everyone staring at me that way, those curious and admiring looks because of the car. Yes, I know. It might seem a contradiction. It is, in fact. Did I want to stand out or not? Well, yes. But no.

Today, I clearly realize that having a Ferrari or not doesn't make a person good or determine who you are. At that time, at 23 years old, I thought I knew; I was sure. Today I know that I lived in a sea of doubts.

The car I liked the most was the Lamborghini Urus. It was yellow with black seats and yellow stitching. It wasn't one of those low super sports Lamborghinis; it was a bigger but still a very powerful car. In England, at various times, I also had a beautiful white Rolls Royce, a Bentley, a Land Rover, five different Mercedes, a Porsche Panamera and a Cayenne, which was the car I was driving when I got pulled over by the police in Liverpool.

By the way, a funny story about that Cayenne: I gave it to Larissa as a birthday present. It came with a giant bow around it, balloons and everything; a lovely surprise. And then I went back inside to sign the lease. It was a gift, but only for a while, you know.

At one point I had five cars in the garage. I chose which car to use as if I were picking out a pair of shoes. 'Today, I want this one. Tomorrow, that one.' Cars and watches were my passions. I was a footballer. Nowadays, I'm detached from the material world and realize how excessive it all was.

The first car I drove in England was a white Mercedes. It was with that car that I learned to drive on the other side of the road. I went out with Meyer in the early morning in Liverpool, with no one on the road, to get used to it. Eventually I got the hang of it. Or at least, I think I did.

Driving was easier in Germany: the autobahns are magnificent roads with no speed limit. That's where I set my record, reaching 260 km/h in an Audi Q7. The steering wheel trembled a little, but I had the distinct impression that I could go even faster.

Cars are usually not bought outright. The vast majority of players lease them, meaning they pay while they use the car. Acquiring and swapping cars isn't complicated. It's not like watches or clothes.

In Germany, salaries are paid by the clubs at the end of each month. However, when I arrived at Hoffenheim I received an advance to start my life, open a bank account and send money to my parents. A few months later, I received a bonus, a larger amount. So, of course, I went shopping. I went to a store called Abseits in Stuttgart and made a massive purchase. I think I spent about 15,000 to 17,000 Euros, or something like that. Meyer helped me; we used three different credit cards, including Rogon's, which had a higher limit. I bought about five pairs of the same model of trainers, each in a different colour. I was crazy about style. I didn't even look at the prices of things. I had never had the opportunity to buy anything in my life, so I let loose. I wanted new clothes, wanted to wear different things, wanted to be fashionable. I liked to look for inspiration on social media. I followed fashion accounts on Instagram to see what was trendy, then mixed colours and accessories. Not that it always worked out: I remember one party in Hoffenheim where Larissa was horrified by my outfit: bright orange pants – what she called 'neon orange' – a red bow tie, a floral shirt, a velvet jacket and a cap . . . I thought it was extremely stylish!

I know I built an image of an extravagant guy, but I just wanted to express myself to be part of it all, something I couldn't do so well with words. I think the audacity with clothes and colours matched my audacity on the field. There, I wasn't so timid: I had the personality to wear different things, just as I had the personality to do different things on the pitch.

Another form of expression was tattoos. I got many over the years and, today, I regret all of them. Or rather, almost all of them: the ones that are related to my family really mean something special. But if I could go back in time, I wouldn't get any tattoos. I would prefer not to have had any. What attracted me in my youth is not what attracts me today. What I had to say through tattoos is not what I have to say today.

Another thing I always liked was perfume: all different types. Larissa says I'm 'the most fragrant person' she's ever met and that caught her attention on our first date, of course.

I still like going to shopping centres, I admit. I like shopping, I like having nice clothes. But today I shop moderately – before I was out of control. I still have more clothes and shoes than my wife, for sure. My style has changed and become more classic, less colourful and flashy.

I lost my passion for cars, perfume and watches. I matured, I found Jesus Christ, I changed. The Bible says, 'Do not store up for yourselves treasures on earth, where moths and vermin destroy, and where thieves break in and steal.' The luxury cars are a thing of the past. The teeth, I hope, are forever.

Chapter 10

On the Spot

W ho takes the penalty? Who picks up the ball, tucks it under their arm, walks up to the spot and takes the shot to become a hero (or a villain)? Things like that aren't decided in the heat of the moment, right there on the pitch. At Liverpool the penalty-taker order was displayed on the tactics board that the coaches used for the pre-match pep talk, the final conversation before each game. We all knew that James Milner, Mr Reliable, was number 1. At that point, I was number 2. Sometimes, the list didn't even appear on the board because this kind of thing rarely changes.

One day, I looked at the board and there was something new there. 'Penalty taker order: 1) Milner; 2) Salah; 3) Firmino.'

Eh?

I think I knew where that was coming from. I had missed a couple of penalties and, without anyone explaining anything to me, my name had moved down the list. I didn't like it – of course I didn't. And I didn't say anything, of course. I never spoke up. Mostly, I don't regret being that way throughout my career. But I do regret not fighting more for certain things internally. This is one of those cases. Yes, I would have liked to have been more involved in penalty kicks.

Out the 111 competitive goals I scored for Liverpool, only two were penalties. I have already mentioned one of them, which was the goal against Watford in the first Premier League match where Mané, Salah and I played together. If I had been the official penalty-taker during my eight years at the club, I could have scored more than the 111. When I arrived and, for a long time – almost all my time at the club – James Milner was designated official penalty-taker by Klopp. And he rarely missed. We all trusted Milner: he's truly a great and reliable striker of the ball. The next name on the list – mine – was ahead of both Mané and Salah. Mo had just arrived and Sadio had missed one the previous season, his first. That September we played Sevilla in the Champions League and we knew the importance of starting with a win. It was also our first European game together – we would end up as runners-up in that Champions League, with ten goals apiece from me, Salah and Mané – and although we were at home we trailed early. We turned the game around with a goal from me and another from

Salah before. Towards the end of the first half, the referee awarded us a penalty. And I hit the post. It was a huge disappointment, because 3–1 would have practically sealed the match, but we ended up conceding an equalizer that saw the points slip away.

Only those who have the courage to take a penalty and believe they are capable of scoring run the risk of missing it. The problem is wasting the opportunity. Worse still, to not even hit the target ... the Sevilla goalkeeper needn't have even been there. 'Hitting the post doesn't change the score,' say the lyrics of a song by the Brazilian band Skank. It was, in short, a complete disaster.

In late October that year we had a Premier League match against Huddersfield Town at Anfield, which we won 3–0. When the game was still level, I was fouled and awarded a penalty. Milner was on the field, I was on the field, but Salah took the penalty – and the goalkeeper saved it. I must confess I was surprised by the manager's decision. A few days after the match, Klopp explained and said it made sense for Salah to take the penalty after he had converted one in the final minutes of a vital Egypt game a few weeks earlier. He thought that Mo would be full of confidence, but it wasn't to be. The fans were surprised too; there was astonishment around Anfield.

The next time, it would be me again. It was January 2018, that same season, an FA Cup match against West

Bromwich Albion at Anfield. In a chaotic game I scored a goal early on, but we quickly fell behind. Then a penalty was awarded in our favour. Milner wasn't on the field, so I was given the responsibility. And I missed again, hitting the crossbar this time. We lost the match 3–2 and were eliminated at home. It's always very difficult to digest this kind of mistake; it was my second consecutive miss and, in both games, the team missed out on victory. That hurt. Even though I'd scored a goal and provided an assist in that match, the feeling of guilt for letting the team and the fans down was immense.

Three days later we faced Huddersfield Town again in the Premier League and once more won 3–0. The third goal was scored by Salah from a penalty. I was on the field, Milner was on the field, but the list had been modified. My two missed penalties had cost me. No one on the coaching staff talked to me or provided any explanations. At the time I was angry, but I respected the decision and remained silent. Today, I regret not speaking up. Mo Salah had just arrived at the club and had also missed a penalty, but he didn't allow himself to be removed from the list. I think there were moments when I was too accepting, too forgiving, and didn't fight my corner. I regret not discussing the matter with Klopp and his assistants. But, well, that's me. And there was never any resentment or disagreement between Salah and me.

Frustrations need to be left behind in the pursuit of something greater. And God is so good that, a few months later, He gave us the opportunity to completely turn this page. There was an important and unforgettable moment for me when it came to Salah, me and penalties – one that marked my first hat-trick playing in England in a 5–1 thrashing of Arsenal on 29 December 2018. Our London rivals took the lead, but by the 16th minute I had already scored twice and we had turned the game around. The first goal began at my feet in midfield. I passed the ball to Salah on the right, and he was dispossessed in the box, but the Arsenal defence got in each other's way, with one kicking the ball onto the other, and it ended up right in front of me, almost on the goalline, without a goalkeeper, or anything. It was the perfect occasion for a no-look finish. I tapped the ball in right-footed as I turned my head to the left, already anticipating the embrace from my teammates and the crowd celebrating in the stands.

The second goal came a couple of minutes later and is one of my most emblematic in a Liverpool shirt, a favourite of mine. Mané pressed for the ball in the midfield and passed it to me. I advanced with the ball at my feet, head up. I knew Mané was coming to my left, but he hadn't appeared in my field of vision yet. Salah advanced on the right, but there were two opponents blocking the passing lane. Shkodran Mustafi came to try to stop me. I think he didn't know whether to drop off or attack the ball and, in that split-second of hesitation, he became an easy target. I dribbled past him, cut inside and saw Sokratis Papastathopoulos already throwing himself to the ground in an attempt to tackle me. Everything happened so quickly. I cut to the left, evaded him and, in the blink of an eye, I was inside the box, facing the goalkeeper with no one to bother me. I struck the ball with my left foot into the corner and ran off to celebrate while Anfield exploded.

It was perhaps the most beautiful goad I scored in that stadium and it set me up for the hat-trick. Mané scored the third, assisted by Salah. Salah got the fourth from the spot – he was the man in charge – and then we got another penalty. This time, when the referee blew the whistle, Mo looked at me, I looked at him, and I flashed my smile. I didn't need to say anything; it was clear that he wanted me to take the penalty so that I could complete my hat-trick. I'm not sure if he knew that it was the opportunity for me to score three goals in a single game for the first time since joining Liverpool. Salah took the ball and handed it to me. It was a nice gesture on his part. He was ambitious when it came to scoring goals, but I was always very generous with him and I'm sure that influenced my friend's decision.

This time there was no way I could miss. I took a firm shot, to the left corner of the goalkeeper, the same spot where I had taken the two penalties I had missed. It was my first hat-trick and the last time I took a penalty during any game. Thank you, Mo!

After that I did get to take a few penalties in shootouts. In August 2019 we played against Chelsea in the UEFA Super Cup, in Istanbul. The match ended in a draw and went to penalties. Here was one list I was first on. I was going through a spell of real confidence and I volunteered, even though two months earlier I had missed one with Brazil in the Copa América quarter-finals against Paraguay, which thankfully we did still win, going on to be champions. Against Chelsea my penalty set us on the way to a 5–4 win and another trophy. That would be repeated when we beat Chelsea in the shootout at the end of the 2022 FA Cup final at Wembley, 6–5.

The coaching staff would always ask me if I wanted to take the first one, the last one . . . I would choose depending on how I felt. In shootouts for Liverpool I converted four penalties and only missed one – the last I ever took. It was the third round of the League Cup against Derby County in November 2022, a week after I had learned I wasn't in the Brazil squad for the World Cup. I was going through a really tough emotional time, shaken and sad about everything that had happened. The goalkeeper dived early and I went the other way, but I struck it carelessly and watched with disbelief as the ball went past the goal. It was a strange feeling, as if it wasn't me out there, like I couldn't grasp what had happened. I couldn't believe the mistake. Larissa said she cried seeing my desperation with the miss. Things weren't looking good. Thankfully, our keeper Caoimhin Kelleher was on fire, saving three shots to send us through.

Shootouts are extremely tense. So much goes through your mind during the walk from the centre circle to the spot. Originally, I used to think about what the goalkeeper had been doing in the previous shots, which corner to aim for. Later, once I was more mature, I tried to focus on prayer, on clearing my mind and asking the Lord to empower me so that I could take the penalty confidently and in peace. One thing was for sure: I wouldn't back down. Never in my entire career, from childhood to professional level, have I ever refused to take a penalty. I always volunteered for the shootout. I got most right. I missed a few. But when my team needed me, I was there every time.

Chapter 11

Hurt

Mason Holgate. There's a man who managed to do what few, very few, players – maybe no player – have done on a football pitch: wind me up enough to get a reaction out of me.

The extreme competitiveness never made me lose my head. I'm human, like anyone else, and on the field I've been nervous, frustrated, happy. Emotion and feelings are part of the job, part of what we do. But I don't confront anyone; I don't get into fights or brawls.

Except that one time. It was Liverpool versus Everton in the FA Cup. The Merseyside derby has always been and always will be a game marked by local rivalry; tougher and more tense than other fixtures. Too tense sometimes – and this was one of those times. With the play out near the touchline, Holgate pushed me from behind. Then, to make matters worse, he pushed me again when I was already off the pitch, sending me over the advertising boards. I tumbled into the arms of some friendly Liverpool fans in the stands on the other side, but I could have been injured, could have hurt someone; it was a nasty fall. And that's when I lost my cool.

I returned to the pitch, swearing at him in Portuguese and in Spanish, I was so angry. Back then, in January 2018, I still used a lot of foul language on the field. Later, after accepting Jesus, I became more respectful and mindful of my words, but that day I called the guy a 'son of a b****' not once or twice, but several times. I don't know what he understood or what he thought he heard. All I know is that he reacted and told the referee, and everyone else, that I had been racist towards him, calling him the 'n-word'. Maybe to English ears the sound of the 'n-word' is similar to 'son of a b****' in Spanish and Portuguese, and could cause some confusion? I don't know. In the tension of the game, maybe that was the case.

They started talking about the 'racist term' on the pitch and I didn't understand a thing. I didn't even know the word they were accusing me of saying. I didn't know the word, its meaning, nothing. I had never even heard of it. Holgate was mistaken. We were right in front of the referee and I hadn't said anything of the sort. There was an investigation. They put us in separate rooms, brought in lip-reading experts, watched the video from every angle, and I was exonerated.

Of course. It hadn't been pleasant, and I had been irritated by events that day and in the days that followed, but at no point did I fear that something might happen to me. I was at peace and had a clear conscience. I would never insult someone because of their race. Racism simply cannot exist. God made us in His image and likeness, and no one should ever be judged by their colour or race. We are all equal before the Lord.

I have difficulty understanding what goes through a racist's mind. I don't know if they are people who had a difficult childhood or were not educated by their parents. I think, for example, of what happened to Vinícius Júnior, who became a constant victim of racism in stadiums in Spain, and it makes me so sad. To see a friend go through that, to see anyone have to suffer it, is hard. In my country, racism is a crime. It should be considered so everywhere. It has to be taken seriously and dealt with properly.

The Holgate incident had hurt, but it didn't affect me too much on the pitch. The very next game, my first appearance since those unfounded accusations, I scored in our 4–3 win against Manchester City. When I received the ball on the left, John Stones had an advantage but I was faster and stronger, going shoulder-to-shoulder with him and getting past him and into the area. I looked up and almost all I could see was Ederson: he had come out to close me down and seemed huge. The decision came swiftly, spontaneously.

You train, you plan, but sometimes instinct and talent take over. I clipped the ball over him and into the net. People told me it was very similar to a goal that Robbie Fowler scored against Manchester United, which is an honour. That strike put us 2–1 up and, although the final score makes it sound close, we dominated, leading 4–1 until they got a couple of late goals.

I loved playing City. Some teams might have dreaded it, but not us. And definitely not me. From my arrival at Liverpool until that moment in 2018, I had faced them seven times, beaten them four times and lost just once – the league meeting earlier that season which we lost 5–0 and which had been conditioned by an early red card for Sadio Mané. Klopp had always been a thorn in Guardiola's side, going right back to their days in Germany, and he knew how to press his sides and make them uncomfortable. City are a fantastic team, of course. But their performance against other teams was one thing; it was another story against us. We showed on the field that we were better head-to-head and so, when we were drawn against them in the Champions League that season, we were quietly confident.

Things were falling into place. Although Philippe Coutinho and Lucas Leiva would depart that season – Lucas in the summer and Philippe in the winter – leaving me as the only Brazilian in the squad, I was happy and signed a new contract at the club; it still makes me smile to think of how we caught Mike Gordon having his lunch when we did a FaceTime call to say we were happy to sign. That trio, alongside Salah and Mané, was taking shape swiftly, even though it was our first season together, and we had also signed Alex Oxlade-Chamberlain and Andrew Robertson, who would fit perfectly on the left. In the middle of the season, the club also brought in a guy by the name of Virgil van Dijk. We had been scoring loads of goals; now the defence was tightening up too.

And while expectations hadn't been that high to start with, that attacking thrust meant we had been making good progress in Europe: we beat both Maribor and Spartak Moscow 7–0 and drew 2–2 and 3–3 with Sevilla. Then, with Virgil having arrived, we knocked out Porto. Which brought us back to City again. Everyone thought they were the favourites because they were leading the Premier League by a huge margin, but we felt good: we were calm, relaxed about it. We knew we could cause them problems. We were the better team and we won both games. In the first leg at Anfield we were already 3–0 up inside half an hour. We played with a lot of intensity, pressure and speed: the trademarks of our team. The focus was always on attacking, scoring as many goals as possible, never holding off. In the second leg, City started strongly, scored an early goal and put us under a lot of pressure, but gradually we managed to calm the game down and, in the second half, with the clock ticking in our favour, we exploited counterattacks. When Mo Salah equalized we breathed a sigh of relief. That settled the tie, but it wasn't over yet. I stole the ball from Nicolás Otamendi to score the winner, my fourth in nine games against City, along with six assists. I loved playing against them, *sí, señor.*

The path opened before us and we were flying, our goalscoring machine continuing to work perfectly in the semi-final. We opened up a 5–0 lead over Roma at Anfield before conceding two late goals. In Rome we led 2–1 and were in control. Although they scored two late goals again, our qualification was never really in doubt. That said, I must admit that I did get nervous when Roma were just a goal away from taking the tie to extra-time. Fortunately, that tension lasted only for a few seconds. We had reached Kyiv.

When I was young I didn't dream of the Champions League. My dream was to play football. Then, it was to play for a big team in Brazil. After that, it was to play for the national team. However, when you experience European football, you understand perfectly why the Champions League is the most coveted tournament of all. It's where the best players in the world come together. Maybe not even the World Cup has so many good players, because some play for countries that can't qualify. In the Champions League you have the best of the best, and you see it in the quality of every game.

For us, everything was new that year. That was the first final for our entire group. Liverpool hadn't reached the Champions League final since 2007 and we were just kids watching it on TV back then. Now, we were living the dream.

The story of the season was so magnificent that it couldn't end without the trophy. We'd lost Coutinho, but we'd signed Van Dijk; the chemistry between me, Salah and Mané worked better than anyone could have imagined, and we'd scored tonnes of goals. I had never won anything in my professional career. The thought of not winning that final never even crossed my mind.

Sure, it was Real Madrid. And Real Madrid had won it in the previous two years, with basically the same team. Everyone knew them by heart: Navas in goal; Ramos in defence; Marcelo on the left and as a creator; the historic midfield trio of Casemiro–Kroos–Modrić; and Cristiano Ronaldo and Benzema up front. We knew their greatness. We knew that Ronaldo had scored 15 goals in that Champions League, an incredible number. But he was just one player. We had Firmino, Mané *and* Salah. And we had scored ten *each*. Our team was better than theirs at that moment. We didn't have the same history or experience, but we had hunger and youth. It was the moment of transition. It was time for the best team in the world to pass the baton to the new best team in the world.

And then it all went wrong.

Everyone knows that our goalkeeper, Loris Karius, didn't have a great day, but these things happen in football and it wasn't just him who made mistakes. He had also made some important saves to get us there in the first place. That night, though, just wasn't our night.

A few days after the final, during the preparations for the World Cup in Russia, I talked to my friends from the Brazilian national team who played for Real Madrid. Casemiro thought that one of the keys was that we had not capitalized on the chances we created early on. That was our strength: to apply relentless pressure, score one or two goals early, and then exploit our speed on the break. This time, we didn't.

The most decisive moment of the first half, however, was the foul that Sergio Ramos committed on Salah, pulling him to the ground, landing on top of him and taking him out of the game, one of our key players gone. Mo was having a fantastic season and his absence made a big difference. It was an excessive foul, not in the spirit of the game, and it didn't seem like an accident. It was a judo move. I don't judge Sergio Ramos's intentions, but he could have been shown a red card. In the VAR era I'm sure he would have been sent off. The offender got away with it.

The goals came in the second half. There was Karius's first mishap, throwing the ball against Benzema's leg.

Mané's equalizer. That incredible bicycle kick from Gareth Bale. Mané hitting the post, which could have changed everything. And then Karius's second mistake, allowing Bale's shot to slip through his hands to make the score 3–1, removing any chance we had of a comeback.

Larissa told me that, high in the stands of the Kyiv stadium with the game still going on, Klopp's wife got up and went to hug and console Karius's girlfriend, who was shaken by what had happened. She probably knew Loris would be blamed, painted as the villain. Here was solidarity and support.

Karius suffered a lot after the game. He was crying in the dressing room; it was difficult to console him. Of course, errors like that are not normal, still less so in a Champions League final, but he didn't go out there to make mistakes and he didn't play alone. It happens. Nothing justifies what he had to go through – the threats on social media and the internet – and nothing could prevent the final having a profound impact on him. Loris had come from Germany, won the starting position over Simon Mignolet, and established himself as the first-choice goalkeeper. Sadly, after that game in Kyiv, it became impossible for him to wear the Liverpool shirt again.

Credit must be given to Bale's bicycle kick to make it 2–1. The momentum of the game had shifted in our favour before he came on and, within a couple of minutes, scored what was, in my opinion, one of the most beautiful goals in history. An overhead kick with his 'wrong' foot: a very, very difficult move to pull off. You have to recognize the incredible quality of that goal; it's not fair to only talk about our mistakes.

But that was no consolation. Kyiv was a very painful defeat for me; it was one of the greatest sorrows I've experienced in football. I don't like to lose. I hate losing. But this was even worse, a new situation for me and my family: the first time the smile had disappeared from my face. I didn't want to look at my phone, didn't want to see photos, messages, nothing. I had never been so close to a dream and let it slip away. There had been difficulties in my career, moments where it all seemed to be going wrong – moments when things did go wrong too – but somehow I had always found a way to overcome them. I always found a way to look ahead, a reason to smile. That time, I couldn't. That time was harder.

And yet ... it was also a lesson and things *were* going to get better. The final in Kyiv was the springboard for the 2018–19 season; we emerged from that defeat with a tremendous desire to fight even harder to achieve victories, which drove us towards another final and a chance for redemption. But in the days after Kyiv, I didn't have a sense of what lay ahead in my career. I couldn't have foreseen what we were about to do, or that we would be back for that very trophy the very next year, not least because I just couldn't foresee anything at all: a man who had always looked forward, I found myself capable only of looking back, picking over what had gone wrong, the pain. In those dark days after the final, it didn't occur to me that we would get another chance. I thought that was it, it had gone.

I couldn't control my bad mood. Sadness engulfed me – and that weighed on the atmosphere at home, which was no longer the place of joy and music it had always been. The pressure I put on myself was intense, the punishment. At night, I spent hours and hours thinking about what I could have done differently in the game, about the moves I had got wrong. I barely slept. Kyiv wouldn't leave my mind.

There was only one solution: to go and join the Brazilian national team. I wasn't due to meet up with them yet, but they were already gathered in London to prepare for the World Cup and I wanted to be there with them – forget the final, think about something else, leave the sadness behind. Time off would only make it worse, sitting there thinking about Kyiv. So I packed up early, boarded a train in Liverpool and headed south, leaving the nightmare behind in order to chase the only dream that could be even greater than the European Cup.

177

Chapter 12

Boys from Brazil

It might not have been the most beautiful or the most important, but it was the goal of my life. The match was Brazil versus Mexico, in the Round of 16 of the World Cup in Russia. It was 2 July 2018.

When I'm an old man, a very old man, and, God willing, I have grandchildren, I will be able to tell them: 'Your grandad scored at the World Cup wearing the Brazil shirt.' There are so many talented players who could only dream of experiencing that. I was lucky – I did – and the feeling was unique, unlike anything else. For those who look back upon my journey across continents, countries and clubs, upon the trophies I won and everything we did at Liverpool, it might not seem like the most important thing. But, for me, it was a gift from God and I will cherish that moment forever.

We were already leading Mexico 1–0 in a lively game

with chances for both sides. We should have sealed victory by then. I came on in the 41st minute of the second half, replacing my great friend Philippe Coutinho. A few minutes later, Fernandinho – another member of our 'Brazilian squad' from that Liverpool–Manchester home from home – surged forward with the ball from midfield and launched a counterattack. He passed it to Neymar on the left and I followed the play through the centre, waiting for the assist inside the box. The pass didn't come. Neymar shot directly for the goal, but the Mexican goalkeeper Guillermo Ochoa deflected the ball and it fell right in front of me. I just had to tap it in and celebrate.

The country comes to a standstill during a World Cup. Playing for the Seleção and scoring a goal gives you tremendous visibility. I made many people happy, moved my family, and also other families scattered across Brazil. It was a goal that made all the effort and sacrifice worthwhile; a moment that felt like, well, everything. I won't write that a movie played in my head, as many say. It's a worn-out phrase. No movie played in my head. The film of my life played in my heart.

I believe I didn't get the recognition I deserved from Tite during that World Cup, considering what I had achieved in the 2017–18 season with Liverpool – the first of the Firmino–Mané–Salah trio – when we reached the Champions League final and I scored 27 goals. I was surprised that he didn't take into account my connection with Philippe Coutinho, who I had played alongside for two and a half years.

The Brazilian national team is a unique and complicated affair. It's not just about the coach selecting the best players; it's about finding the chemistry, the movement, the space; creating the perfect bouquet by choosing the finest flowers from among endless varieties. In Liverpool there wasn't a Neymar in the space Coutinho and I occupied. In the national team, there was. I'm not saying it was bad news, far from it; it just required adjustments. Choices to be made.

In the coach's mind I was competing with Gabriel Jesus for the central striker's position. He had scored 17 goals in his second season with Manchester City and had been crucial for the national team since Tite took over in 2016. I wanted my chance, showed it in training, knew I could contribute more to the team. I should have had more minutes in the World Cup, but, of course, I respected my teammate and the coach's decision.

In the group stage I came on late in the matches against Switzerland and Costa Rica, and didn't play against Serbia. In the Round of 16, of course, I came on near the end and scored against Mexico. In the quarter-final the team was losing 2–0 in the first half against Belgium and Tite brought me on at half-time, replacing Willian.

The team and I had a great second half. We deserved to equalize in Kazan. Checking the statistics of that match, I saw we had 17 shots in the second half, while Belgium had only one. Thibaut Courtois made many saves; the referee could have awarded one or two penalties. That's football. I had a chance from a left-wing cross where I stretched out a leg, the ball touched the tip of my foot but didn't find its way to goal. In another move I received the ball in the box, pretended to pivot and pass to a player coming from behind, but spun and shot powerfully with my left foot – the ball narrowly missed the crossbar. And there was a header in injury time where I shot off-balance under pressure from the defender.

At the end of the game we went into the dressing room exhausted, completely frustrated at not having reached the semi-finals. I was unhappy at not being able to contribute with a goal or decisive play. The coaching staff and the players involved in those controversial moments were annoyed with the refereeing. Reviewing Vincent Kompany's challenge on Gabriel Jesus inside the box, it's incredible the penalty wasn't given. Jesus was right to be outraged. The margin is fine and your fate is not always in your own hands.

My relationship with the Brazilian national team had started in 1998 with the first World Cup I saw and remember – 20 years before my experience in Russia. We painted the streets green and yellow, adorned the neighbourhood with flags, paper and fabric in the colours of

Brazil. I cried when we lost to France in the final, but then came 2002, an unforgettable month for a ten-year-old boy, with the conquest of the fifth championship.

By 2006 I was already in CRB's youth team and my relationship with football had changed. In 2010 I had become a professional and was competing in Brazil's Série B with Figueirense. In 2014 I had some remote hopes of being called up, as I had had a remarkable season in the Bundesliga. But maybe I needed to have played before to be in Luiz Felipe Scolari's plans. Or maybe there was some lingering problem there, some hangover from the moment in 2011 that I had been forced to miss the Under-20 World Cup, a lack of understanding or empathy from the CBF (the Brazilian Football Confederation) for a young player put in an impossible position. Maybe I paid for my club's understandable desire for me to play for them.

It had happened not long after I joined Hoffenheim. I was called up by coach Ney Franco to play in the Under-20 World Cup in Colombia but, according to FIFA rules, Hoffenheim weren't obliged to release me – and they didn't. I was extremely angry and upset, left in tears. My dream of wearing the Brazil shirt had been ruined. My agents tried to convince Hoffenheim to let me go, but the management remained adamant. They sent a fax to the CBF saying that it wasn't an easy decision, but since I was young and an important player for the team, they couldn't afford to lose me for four rounds of the Bundesliga and some DFB–Pokal cup matches. I reported for pre-season training as agreed, in July, and trained hard for the upcoming year. Inside, though, I was hurt.

Several players who were part of the Under-20 South American Championship and World Cup that year were then called up for the London Olympics in 2012. Some, such as Oscar and Neymar, went on to the 2014 World Cup. I wasn't called up for any of those competitions after that, as if I were on a blacklist, even though it wasn't my choice, and even though I was desperate to play for Brazil. It was as if not going that summer had meant forfeiting opportunities in the future. If I had been in Colombia, who knows what would have happened? If I'd had a record of success in the youth ranks and added that explosive year at Hoffenheim in 2014, perhaps my first World Cup would have arrived earlier.

It didn't.

The first time I was called up to the senior team was under Dunga, on 23 October 2014, just three months after the World Cup and on my father's birthday.

I remember being emotional about that first call-up and feeling immense pride to be representing my country. There were two friendlies, one in Turkey and one in Austria. I travelled with some of the guys who were in English football, like Oscar, Willian and Philippe Coutinho. Couto and

I became friends right away, there was an instant connection – we didn't know yet that we would play together at club level, but there was already a plan for me to join the Premier League and I remember asking my national team colleagues a lot of questions about England. I was already curious.

I was also warmly welcomed by Luiz Gustavo, a midfielder who had played at Hoffenheim and had transferred to Bayern Munich just before my arrival at the German club. And by Filipe Luís, a former Figueirense player, like me. These guys made me feel at ease from the beginning; it was as if the Brazilian national team had always been my home.

I played about 20 minutes against Turkey, coming on for Luiz Adriano at the same time as Philippe Coutinho, who replaced Oscar. In the next match, against Austria, I came on again for Luiz Adriano, but this time a bit earlier, in the 17th minute of the second half. The game was level, tough. Twenty minutes after coming on I received a pass from Filipe Luís in the middle. I was facing the goal, had space and time, and didn't hesitate. I smashed a shot from outside the box that went into the top left corner. It was a superb goal, quite typical of the ones I had scored at Figueirense and continued to score at Hoffenheim. I wasn't afraid to enjoy myself. I dedicated it to my father, a big supporter during my childhood. It was a goal celebrated by my teammates, who might have been astonished by the audacity of that unknown kid. The Brazilian national team was going through a renewal phase after the 7–1 tragedy in the 2014 World Cup and it was the right time to seize the opportunity.

Dunga called me up again for the next set of friendlies where I scored my first no-look goal, against Chile – a sign that I was becoming a more confident young player.

In the middle of 2015 I participated in the first of three Copa América tournaments. I arrived in Chile knowing that I was close to becoming a Liverpool player, and the contract was secretly signed at the Brazilian national team's hotel, with a photo of me wearing the red jersey for the first time.

I was already close to Philippe Coutinho, who was also at the Copa América and, along with Lucas Leiva, was essential in my transition to England. Fernandinho, who had been playing for Manchester City for two years, was also part of the team – he lived in the neighbouring city and had quite a bit of experience. Lucas was instrumental. He had learned the hard way, struggling to adapt when he arrived in Liverpool, so he knew how difficult it could be for me and did all he could to help. Apart from Fábio Aurélio, there had been no other Brazilians at the club back then. Worse, Fábio was injured and had different schedules from the rest of the players, which left Lucas alone. Not knowing the language or culture, he had a tough, solitary start and wanted things to be different for the guys who followed him. Besides, the sooner we were settled, the better it would be for everyone. Lucas and his wife Ariana always welcomed me to their home.

That said, I didn't leave the best impression on Ari at first. When I arrived in Liverpool, Larissa wasn't with me, and I wasn't interested in getting married. I wanted to enjoy life and take advantage of the perks of fame. One of the first social events I attended alongside other players was a barbecue at Dejan Lovren's house. Dejan, the Croatian defender, seemed almost Brazilian, such was his positive energy, enthusiasm and love of life. This guy was fun! I was single and brought with me two girls I had met on social media from Brazil. It was a terrible idea. I can see that now, with greater maturity; I got a glimpse of it then, even if I didn't fully grasp it.

Ari and Ainê, Philippe Coutinho's wife, left the barbecue as they felt uncomfortable and had little in common with those girls. Yes, there were single guys at the gathering, but the environment surrounding the Brazilian players, who were my friends, felt like a family – some already had small children and had been with their wives for a long time. When they left, something in my mind clicked. There were two paths I could take on this new journey in England: family on one side, or the freedom to do whatever I wanted with whomever I wanted on the other. Although it took a while for that lesson to be learnt and properly understood, they had shown me a real example of the right path. If I was going to integrate into the social lives of my friends, mine would have to be a bit different.

That change happened gradually, not immediately; there were ups and downs. A few months after arriving in Liverpool, missing my daughter Valentina terribly, I asked Larissa to return. We got closer again and we had our second daughter, Bella. Slowly but surely I managed to change the negative image I had left with my friends' wives.

They helped us a lot in building our life in England. Every bit of advice matters. Where's a good place to live? Which are the best schools? Where to take guests for dinner? Where to eat Brazilian food? – those things we missed from home? Ari recommended to Larissa a Portuguese couple, Lina and João, who were fantastic cooks and helped with raising our daughters. They are wonderful people who came from Madeira, crossed our path in Liverpool, and have been a part of our lives ever since. Where we go, Lina and João come too – they're part of the family. In 2017 Lucas and Ari and Philippe and Ainê were our wedding witnesses, which shows how strong the bonds became.

In the middle of that year the paths of football led Lucas Leiva to Rome, away from Liverpool. Couto was determined to leave too; he had an offer to play for Barcelona. Philippe would go to Klopp every day to ask to leave. The club wouldn't let him, and he got more and more frustrated. Several players tried to convince him to stay, to show him that he'd be happier in Liverpool, where he was already established. Nobody wanted our magician to leave; we all loved playing with such a talented guy, but I respected his decision very much – after all, he was pursuing a childhood dream. I didn't want to interfere.

The transfer ultimately happened in January 2018, in the middle of the season. In the end Klopp was right: the Boss used to say that he would have less responsibility and status at Barcelona with Messi there; he wouldn't be as happy or feel as important to everyone. I think Philippe was deeply affected by the negative comments during his time at Barça. He was someone who listened to fans and social media critics, and it showed on the field.

Years later, there were rumours about Coutinho returning to Liverpool, but Klopp wasn't for turning back. He had his pride. Personally, I would have forgiven Coutinho and given him another chance. Coutinho was loved by all – Salah, for instance, was a big fan – and it would have been an honour to play with him again.

So Lucas and Coutinho left, but their legacy remained. Larissa and I made sure to do for newcomers what they had done for us. Our house in Liverpool – and, later, in Manchester – turned into a centre for parties, gatherings and, years later, worship and meetings with God, bringing together players from various clubs. For the start of the 2018–19 season, both Alisson and Natália and Fabinho and Rebeca arrived in Liverpool. Other Brazilian players had also started to come to the region, such as Danilo, Ederson and Gabriel Jesus, and were soon joined by Fred and Richarlison. Of course, my closest friends were my club teammates, whom I interacted with daily. But we always invited the entire 'Brazilian squad' and players and family members from other countries, especially those who spoke Portuguese or Spanish. Alisson soon became the champion of barbecues – he's from the South of Brazil, a region where *churrasco* is part of a big tradition. Ederson and Fernandinho became great friends with whom I talked a lot about football and life, although maybe they distanced themselves a little when the rivalry between Liverpool and City got heated. We kept inviting them, but they didn't show up anymore.

It's true that it wouldn't have been good for anyone if a photographer captured those gatherings of players from different clubs. You never knew how public opinion would react. But many of these guys were not just neighbours, they were also my Brazilian national team companions over the years.

In light of the crisis of results and the threat of missing out on the World Cup for the first time ever, the Seleção changed coach in 2016. Tite arrived. Highly respected, he had achieved significant titles with Corinthians. I'm very grateful to Dunga, who was the first to have faith in me and call me up for the national team, but with Tite's arrival, while I continued to be selected, I wasn't a starter any more.

Just before the Russia World Cup, we played a preparatory friendly at Anfield against Croatia. The crowd, mostly made up of Liverpool fans, chanted my name and didn't want me to stay on the bench throughout the match. They called for me to be introduced and their wish was granted. Not only did I come on, I scored – a special moment in my home and a great opportunity to momentarily forget the sadness of the defeat in Kyiv in the Champions League final just days earlier.

A regular place in the starting line-up would only come after the World Cup. The coaching staff called me in for a conversation before a friendly in Singapore and told me that I would be their number 9 from then on. And so it was, until my peak with the national team, the 2019 Copa América. I was an incredibly confident player at that moment, a Champions League winner, influential both at my club and in Brazil. Moreover, the tournament would be held on Brazilian soil for the first time in 30 years and we took on responsibility for winning the title.

Neymar was injured and didn't participate in the competition. Consequently, the team could be set up with Philippe Coutinho behind me, reviving our old Liverpool telepathy, and adopting a similar pressing and build-up style. We connected perfectly, on and off the field. The team's relationship with the demanding Brazilian fans was also positive – despite being booed off the field at half-time during our first game against Bolivia, which we eventually won 3–0. It's true that we drew 0–0 against Venezuela in our second group-stage game, but the crowd appreciated our effort and knew that but for several goals disallowed by VAR we would have won. I was involved in all of them – a hat-trick of disallowed goals.

In the third match, against Peru, in São Paulo, I scored the no-look goal that became famous throughout the country and became very special for me, proving to many people, even teammates, that I deserved to be there. In my home in Maceió I have a framed photo of that goal next to the shirt I wore in the final – which would be against Peru again. I'm not one to keep shirts, objects – I'm a bit detached when it comes to football memorabilia – but that moment deserved to be immortalized.

In the Copa América quarter-final we drew 0–0 with Paraguay and I missed a penalty when the score was level at 3–3 in the shootout. It was a dreadful moment, the first time I'd missed in a decisive shootout. Fortunately, the Paraguayan, Derlis Gonzàlez, up next also missed and Gabriel Jesus secured victory with the final kick. That was a huge relief for me; that miss was the kind of mistake that marks a player forever in Brazil. When you're wearing the Seleção shirt, it's like you have no right to make errors. Get it wrong and you'll forever carry a stigma. Some mistakes define losses or eliminations, and turn you into an eternal villain. Others eventually go unnoticed, as mine did that day in Porto Alegre. I was lucky.

In the semi-final we faced Argentina and Messi at Estádio Mineirão in Belo Horizonte. Our neighbours hadn't won a title with the senior national team in who knows how long – since forever, maybe. And they would continue without one. It was a hard-fought, intense game, where we rose to the occasion. Brazil versus Argentina is the most significant match in football, bringing together stars, extremely high-level football, history and a fierce rivalry. We won 2–0. For the first goal, Daniel Alves found me, his eyes looking left, the pass going right. I flicked the ball first time into the box, where Gabriel Jesus scored. In the second half, the roles reversed. Jesus initiated the counterattack from the left, escaped the Argentinians trying to foul him, and provided the assist for me. The ball bounced high and I nearly got it wrong, but I was never going to allow myself to miss a chance like that against Argentina. *Never.* I adjusted to hit the ball with the arch of my foot, sending it beyond the goalkeeper's reach. The Mineirão erupted.

There was still time to nutmeg Lautaro Martínez in midfield, what we call in Brazil *canetinha*. I enjoyed that; they didn't. Frustrated with the defeat, they started getting rough – and there's nothing better than responding to aggression with skill. I never dribble an opponent to humiliate them. Those who followed my career closely know that tricks – the back-heels, the dribbles, those flash moments – have always been about moving the team forward, creating scoring opportunities.

Well, almost always. That day, it wasn't *exactly* the same. But Lautaro opened his legs and what else could I do? He got angry, pushed me, wanted a fight and cursed a lot.

I just smiled.

For the final my whole family were in the Maracanã: Dad, Mom, sister, uncles, cousins, Cesinha and some of the other friends I brought for the game. We again defeated Peru and lifted the trophy in the great temple of world football. Tite was pleased with me at half-time as I'd stolen the ball in midfield, passed to Arthur who laid on an assist for Gabriel Jesus to put us back into the lead at 2–1 not long after they equalized. We went on to win 3–1. The only pity was that I had been substituted by Richarlison, who scored the winning penalty, denying me the chance to add to my goal tally. Everton's Cebolinha had scored the opener and became the tournament's joint top scorer with Paolo Guerrero of Peru, leaving me a solitary goal behind. Becoming a champion while wearing the yellow jersey is priceless and doing it there is just wonderful; a childhood dream fulfilled. God crowned us in front of our people.

*

The following year, the pandemic hit. The Brazilian national team didn't step onto the field from November 2019 to October 2020, and, although I played all four of our games in that brief period when football was back, we went a further seven months without a single game being played, between November 2020 and June 2021. In a year and a half, only four matches had been played and the world had changed, with thousands dying and the disruption huge. So much had changed; so many people had too. I was a different person, having embraced Jesus in my heart and been baptized. What football there was had to be played behind closed doors and that changed me too. It was a challenging time for a player like me – the fans are my greatest fuel, the whole point of the game – and the truth is that I struggled to find motivation and energy in 2021.

The season was terrible for Liverpool. I lost my place in the team and something changed in the mind of the Brazil coach. The promise made in Singapore that I would be the starting number 9 was broken when a second Copa América in Brazil came around in June 2021. There was no explanation, no conversation, no light shed on what had changed. I get the competition, I do. The Brazilian national team is colossal, blessed with a constellation of stars. But I believe that, in some instances, a bit more understanding from the coaches is needed. It's not that they have to justify themselves to the players, but a little empathy and a good conversation to discuss the paths taken wouldn't hurt.

It was a strange tournament. There was no one in the stadiums, public opinion was against the event and Tite made numerous changes. Everything was diametrically opposite to the 2019 experience – including the result. We lost the final against Argentina, who got their revenge and managed to give a title to Messi, before he would go on to win an even bigger one a year and a half later in Qatar.

I came on at half-time in the final against Argentina, but I couldn't change the course of the match. As time slipped away, little did I know that my international career was coming to an end too. Those would be my final moments wearing the Brazil shirt. I wouldn't step onto the field again for the remainder of the 2022 World Cup cycle.

Chapter 13

The Wall

If we make a mistake, don't panic: Alisson is there to save us.

That pretty much sums up the impact it had on us when the best goalkeeper in the world arrived at Anfield in July 2018. I called him 'the octopus'. He doesn't have two hands, he has tentacles everywhere. My life – all of our lives – changed when Alisson turned up. On a personal level, he held out his hand and guided me wisely, calmly, into the path of Jesus. On a sporting level, he guided us to a place where we felt secure. We had an extraordinary goalkeeper who could literally save us by making stops other guys just wouldn't make. Not once or twice, but dozens and dozens of times in the 2018–19 season – and in the years to come.

One particular save immediately comes to mind, a true miracle performed from point-blank range against Napoli in the final group-stage game of the UEFA Champions League in 2018. If we'd conceded that, we wouldn't even have made it to the knockout stage. Somehow, Alisson stopped it and we ended up becoming European champions.

That journey included the epic comeback against Barcelona in the semi-final. Many remember the goals we scored in the 4–0 win at Anfield; Trent Alexander-Arnold's corner kick; so many moments. None would have been possible without that save. The finger of God pointed constantly at Alisson, who kept us alive.

That was also the year we battled neck and neck with Manchester City in the Premier League until the very, very end. Without a doubt, the defensive wall that was built throughout 2018 is a factor that allowed us to dream big, fight for major trophies and contest a league title that the club hadn't won in three long decades. The arrival of Virgil van Dijk in January brought us crucial defensive consistency. In previous years everyone knew what we were like: we scored lots of goals, but we conceded lots as well. Somehow, we couldn't break that cycle. The saying is an old one, a cliche, but it's true: attacks win games, defences win trophies. As upset as I was about Philippe Coutinho's departure to Barcelona, the simultaneous arrival of Virgil in the winter transfer window changed the team's dynamic immediately.

I had played against him a few times when Van Dijk was still at Southampton and I had to go up against him in training too. I can tell you, he's the toughest defender I've ever played against. He also told me that I was one of the hardest forwards to mark, so there was mutual respect. It would have been well deserved if he had won the Ballon d'Or in 2019; he had a perfect season. It was clear that opponents were afraid of him. Apart from being tall, strong and naturally imposing physically, he's intelligent; he sees everything before the rest. He's a defender who doesn't dive in; he doesn't need to because he's already ahead of the move. For me, his main attribute is how well he reads the game. He was so engaged too: he studied the game, knew everything. I remember he used to ask me technical details about Brazilian forwards we would be facing. He was always seeking the knowledge needed to gain an advantage. He's an incredible guy: charismatic, humble; proud, too.

Over time I learned how to get past him when playing Southampton; how to take shortcuts. I didn't breeze past him – and I never scored against him in our games, I admit – but I wasn't intimidated either. Fortunately, we had only a few matches against him and he soon joined our team to play on our side. Virgil has had many centre-back partners over the years at Liverpool. I think Joe Gomez was the one who best fit his style.

After the 2018 UEFA Champions League final, which we lost to Real Madrid in Kyiv, it became clear to us that the team was capable of competing with anyone in Europe. It had only been the first season of the Firmino–Salah–Mané trio, and Van Dijk had arrived, of course, but there was still room for improvement. In the summer of 2018 Liverpool signed Alisson Becker from Roma and Fabinho from Monaco. I had been with Alisson during the World Cup in Russia and our wives had already met during that time in Sochi. Fabinho had been called up by coach Tite before, so we knew each other from the Brazilian national team, although he didn't make it to the World Cup and it also took him a little while to get minutes at Liverpool.

Alisson was one of those immediate solutions that transcended tactical considerations. He was the most expensive goalkeeper in football history at that time, but he proved to be worth every penny, seamlessly fitting into the team. Our squad needed a goalkeeper like him, reliable and confident, capable of keeping a significant number of clean sheets. Moreover, he is a consummate professional: principled, hardworking and responsible.

By the end of his first season with us Alisson had played 51 matches and kept a clean sheet in 27 of them, more than half. He was named the UEFA Goalkeeper of the Season and FIFA's Best Goalkeeper in the World, and appeared in countless best XIs. After bringing in the best defender in the world, Liverpool had now acquired the best goalkeeper on the planet. The difference, the step up we made, was huge.

As for Fabinho, he only started playing in October, but never lost his place in the team after that. Jürgen Klopp wanted him to adapt well to the country and the club before using him regularly, but once he overcame that hurdle, he became an undisputed starter throughout the latter stages of the season and the UEFA Champions League.

Fabinho is one of the most impressive players I've seen when it comes to stealing the ball from opponents. He was everywhere on the field, both in attack and defence, covering ground. Another crucial factor was Fabinho's attacking mindset – his incisive passing, getting the ball up the pitch quickly – which perfectly matched the style of play envisioned by our coaching staff. After winning the ball back, he could quickly find me, Salah or Mané, adding a great dynamic to our team.

In addition to Alisson and Fabinho, there were two other arrivals and an important return before the season began. The club signed Naby Keïta from RB Leipzig: a midfielder born in Guinea, who brought strength and presence. They also brought in Swiss idol Xherdan Shaqiri from Stoke City, who added experience and quality to our attack. On top of that, we also welcomed back Pepijn Lijnders after his spell at NEC. Pep had been at Liverpool when I joined the club in 2015, a prodigious coach: very young and multilingual, which was priceless for me. He already knew Klopp, our system, our characteristics and my position as a false 9. We had excellent, fluent communication and a highly promising start to the season. Up front we were ready to deliver once again. And, with the presence of Alisson, Van Dijk, Fabinho and the collective effort, we started conceding far fewer goals. We had at last found that balance we needed.

In my first three years at Liverpool, which were also Klopp's first three years, we conceded 50, 42 and 38 goals in the Premier League, respectively. In the fourth season, 2018–19, we only conceded 22. The numbers speak for themselves. This was the significant change that allowed us to compete for the domestic title. Football-wise, the signings of Alisson and Fabinho made a tremendous difference for the team, and on a personal level their arrivals transformed my life.

There's an interesting story about the negotiation between Liverpool and Monaco for my fellow countryman to come to England. Klopp called me in order to gather more information about Fabinho, as we had spent time together in the national team. Our coach knew Fabinho as a player, of course, but he wanted to know more about his off-field character, behaviour and so on. I responded honestly, saying that he was a great person, a family-oriented guy who was disciplined and wouldn't cause any problems. I had only good things to say. I spoke so highly of him that they wanted to sign him immediately – I used to joke that Fabinho should have paid me a percentage of his transfer fee.

As for Alisson, there was no need for me to say anything and no one called to ask. He was a fantastic goalkeeper. He's a great leader who speaks little, but when he does so everyone listens. He speaks with clarity and always chooses the right words.

On a personal and spiritual level, the two couples who arrived – Alisson and Natália, Fabinho and Rebeca – were the people we needed as a family. They were sent by the Lord. They came to show us the character of Christ through their lives to us. They preached the word, and my wife Larissa and I got to know Jesus through the word; the seed – faith – was being planted in our hearts. We've had many gifts in football, we've met many dear people who became close. But Nat, Alisson, Rebeca and Fabinho went far beyond that. Ours is a true, lasting friendship that will be forever.

The beginning was perfect, resulting in five consecutive victories in the Premier League – the club's best start since 1990, the year of Liverpool's last English title. Soon people started looking at us as genuine candidates. The fifth game on that list was the toughest and the one that best showed how things were changing: a clash against Tottenham Hotspur at Wembley. The previous season we had lost to Spurs 4–1 in a match that left our coach frustrated and epitomized our defensive inconsistency at the time. But we had evolved since then. I scored two goals in the first half, although the first was disallowed because of a marginal offside call. The second, which did count, started with Mané on the left. The ball fell to me almost on the goalline and I just had to nudge it with my left foot. Added to Gini Wijnaldum's opener, that put us 2–0 up and, although we conceded a goal late on and had to struggle to hold on, we did secure the victory. By then, though, I literally couldn't see what was happening on the pitch. Jan Vertonghen had accidentally poked me in the eye, leaving me in intense pain and with my vision almost gone.

As September turned into October we had a little moment of instability that would prove fatal in the Premier League. We played twice against Chelsea, once in the League Cup at home and three days later in the Premier League in London. Eden Hazard was the thorn in our side during both games, scoring the winning goal at Anfield and opening the scoring at Stamford Bridge, where we managed to salvage a draw in the dying moments. In the League Cup Klopp had left some starters on the bench. The manager knew it was difficult to keep many fronts open, especially with the physical intensity our style of play demanded, so that defeat, the first of the season, didn't raise doubts in our planning. After those encounters we had the second Champions League game against Napoli, in Italy, and then it was time to face Manchester City, the reigning champions in England, who were considered the favourites for the title, and going into that game shared the top spot in the Premier League with us, both sides having racked up six wins and one draw.

Despite going to Naples with a full-strength squad, it was as if our focus was elsewhere. We played poorly, didn't manage a shot on goal and Alisson was our standout player. Napoli scored in the last minute and won 1–0. Maybe the City game had been on our minds? Perhaps – but when we faced them a few days later, it was more of the same. We didn't play well and only avoided defeat because Riyad Mahrez missed a penalty in the final moments, to see it finish 0–0. It was our second consecutive game without scoring; our offensive machine had hit a problem. Fortunately, Alisson and the defence maintained their high level behind us. We were still level on points with City and Chelsea at the top of the league, and the result didn't seem so terrible. But, looking back at the season, that was a game in which we needed to perform better and win at home.

From the return from the international break until the end of 2018 we had an incredible run of 11 wins and one draw in 12 matches – and the draw came against Arsenal in London, a game in which we conceded a late goal. With Fabinho starting to get significant minutes and becoming an essential part of our midfield, we convincingly defeated our great rival Manchester United, won at Wolves and thrashed Newcastle.

As a team we were gathering momentum, playing really well; on an individual level, it was different. Three months had passed since the Champions League debut against PSG. In that period I had scored just three goals in 20 games. The team was winning and I was contributing, which was the most important thing. But, as a forward, when you're not scoring you always feel like you're letting people down and frustration is inevitable. It can eat at you. You need something to break that cycle.

I got it in the best possible way, with the 5–1 thrashing of Arsenal, in which I scored my first hat-trick for the club and perhaps the most beautiful goal of my career, leaving two defenders on the ground before finishing. I was up and running again.

The New Year began with a crucial clash against Manchester City. We were unbeaten in the league and had a seven-point advantage over them after they had stumbled a few times in December. A draw at City to go with the draw against them at home would have put us in a very strong position. A victory, meanwhile, would have left us almost with a hand on the trophy our fans wanted most. Liverpool hadn't been national champions since 1990, even before I, Salah or Mané were born. Our fans didn't deserve to go so many years without the title.

The match was fiercely contested and I believe we didn't deserve to lose. I was very confident after my hat-trick and put in a great performance, appearing all over the field. We might have scored right at the start. Salah initiated the play through the middle, we combined with a back-heel pass from me and he found Mané making a run into the box. Mo's assist was perfect and Sadio's finish was too. Or almost: it would have been a classic goal from our attack, but the ball hit the post.

If that was unlucky, what followed was even worse. In the aftermath of the move, defender John Stones kicked the ball onto Ederson, City's goalkeeper, and it was rebounding back into the net only for Stones to somehow recover and clear off the line. Goalline technology showed that the ball didn't fully cross the line by 11 millimetres. If I was a man who cursed, I'd curse those blasted 11 millimetres! Many of our fans still believe we didn't win that championship because of that. There are fine margins – and then there are those 11 millimetres.

I don't know what would have happened if we had scored the first. We were feeling good, confidence was high after eight wins from eight in December and, maybe if we had been in a position to play on the counter, we could have almost decided the title race there and then. Instead, Sergio Agüero scored the opener. In the second half we had more possession – which is far from easy against City – and fought for the equalizer. I scored with a diving header, after a play that went from one full-back to the other: Alexander-Arnold to Robertson to me. But City got the second on a quick attack and a cross-shot from Leroy Sané, which felt unfair to me: a draw would have better reflected the balance of the game.

Our lead was reduced to four points after that defeat, which was our only loss in 38 games. That said, it wasn't there that we lost the Premier League and we were handed another opportunity to go seven points clear when City were defeated by Newcastle, only to draw 1–1 with Leicester. Instead, it was the month of February (and the first weekend of March) that hurt us, when we drew three games and dropped six huge points.

I'm not fond of blaming referees. But it's impossible to look back on that game against Leicester, and those two vital points dropped, without mentioning Martin Atkinson. There were two crucial controversial moments. In one, Harry Maguire fouled Mané when he was about to run clean through on goal. It was a clear red card, which would have put us with an extra man to go with our lead. But Atkinson only showed yellow and Maguire was the one who scored for Leicester minutes later. The other incident, in the second half, was a clear penalty on Keïta. This time Atkinson didn't signal anything at all. Jürgen Klopp publicly criticized that refereeing and we were very upset in the dressing room after the match. In the end, the 1–1 draw allowed us to open up a five-point lead, instead of seven.

I will say it again: I have never been one to complain about referees. I am a player who rarely goes down, who always tries to stay on his feet, who doesn't try to deceive referees. I don't like the attitude of players who dive and spend so much time rolling on the ground. I also think the refereeing in the Premier League is good, contributing to the speed and quality of the game. But that day? There were big mistakes made that changed the course of the championship.

Which is not to overlook our share of the blame. Three away draws cost us the lead in the league and allowed City to pass us in the table. We drew 1–1 against West Ham and 0–0 against both Manchester United and Everton. In the space of a month, we squandered everything we had built throughout the season.

In the game against United at Old Trafford I took a knock on my ankle and had to leave the field before half-time. Jürgen Klopp said after that match that my injury was a 'catastrophe' for the team and that we had 'lost rhythm' without me. I spent hours in physiotherapy in an attempt to return as quickly as possible. I couldn't play against Watford (we won 5–0) and couldn't start in the Merseyside Derby either. I only came on in the second half to try to help. That game was one we should have won comfortably – the ball just didn't want to go in.

Fabinho also mentioned to me that the team had really felt my absence. Maybe, as some said, I really was the most crucial piece of our offensive machinery at that time and my injury had truly been catastrophic. I couldn't assist my teammates and two crucial matches against our greatest rivals finished in draws. Right then, Manchester City over-took us. I can assure you, few things are more frustrating for a footballer than not being able to be on the pitch when it matters most.

We won the last nine games of the Premier League but Manchester City got into that routine where they just never let up, never gave you a glimpse of a chance, winning all 14 matches they played after that defeat to Newcastle. Some of our players avoided watching their matches. There was no use in suffering and hoping for them to stumble, because the reality was that we knew they wouldn't falter. The moment we became dependent on them, we lost the championship.

Fair or unfair? Honestly, it doesn't matter much. We finished the Premier League with 97 points and only one loss: an incredible campaign that would have secured the title in almost every 20-team league ever played in football history.

But God had something even greater in store for us.

Chapter 14

David and Goliath

I'd love to describe the scene, look back on my goal and tell you everything I could see that night at Anfield. But what I could see was . . . well, nothing. Not clearly at least. Almost blind, I had to play on instinct. I think if the Boss had known my true condition, he wouldn't have put me on the pitch at all. I could hardly see anything with one eye. With the other, everything was blurry. I saw only shadows. I made the moves I made because I'd been doing that my whole life and knew the paths. In the end, the Boss had no reason to regret that craziness even a bit – or his excessive confidence in me. When the ball came to my feet at the edge of the penalty area, I knew what to do. I would've done the same blindfolded. I went at Marquinhos, pretended to shoot with my left foot and then quickly cut back, creating enough space to shoot low and hard with my right foot. It was 3–2 against Paris Saint-Germain. It was the winning goal and, in a huge match against massive opponents, one of the best I scored for Liverpool.

In the celebration I covered my left eye with my left hand. It was the gesture that came to my mind, because when I covered the bad eye, I could just about see something with the good one. And that became one of the standout images of me in a Liverpool jersey.

It had all started when I almost lost my sight days before, after the Tottenham defender Jan Vertonghen poked me in the eye, his finger going in deep. It was an accident and he was not to blame, but it was excruciatingly painful and, for a moment, I thought I was going to lose all sight on my left side. When I opened my eye, everything was blurred and I couldn't see a thing. The doctors told me that with a little more bad luck, depending on the angle of impact, I could have indeed lost my vision permanently. In the following days, I couldn't even get up on my own to go to the bathroom. My wife had to hold my arm to help me move around my own house. Those were terrible days, full of pain and apprehension. Bad thoughts crossed my mind; I even feared for my future in football. My eye was hypersensitive to light, so when I opened my other eye, the right one, it hurt a lot. I relied on medication on Sunday and Monday. But on Tuesday I decided I needed to leave the house and go to training. That was a risk and I wasn't in a fit state to train, even though I wore a pair of protective glasses like Edgar Davids used to wear. But I wanted to be at the opening game of the Champions League against Paris Saint-Germain at any cost. That was our first game in another Champions League campaign. We had lost the previous final and were desperate to make amends from the very beginning, but we had been handed a tough group, alongside PSG, Napoli and Red Star Belgrade. Had the opener been a smaller game against lesser opponents the club might have sent me home; instead, I was included, albeit on the bench. They did ask me to wear the glasses in the match, but I refused. I just took more medication to numb the area.

The atmosphere at Anfield was incredible. It was always special playing in front of our fans, but that night the noise was different, the stadium even louder. I was quite angry to be a sub and sitting there on the bench I was still struggling to see what was happening just metres from me. The team started the game well and by the 30th minute Daniel Sturridge, my replacement in the starting XI, scored a header. Five minutes later we were 2–0 up: Gini Wijnaldum was fouled and James Milner converted the penalty with his usual calm. But, still in the first half, PSG managed to pull one back with a goal from the Belgian Thomas Meunier.

At half-time Thomas Tuchel, the PSG coach, surprised me. There in the tunnel leading to the dressing rooms, I think without knowing the seriousness of my eye issue, he spoke in a friendly tone in German. 'Hey, Roberto, the game is great like this! Just relax on the bench, no need to come on.' I started laughing and replied, 'What am I going to do? If the coach decides to put me on the field, am I going to say no?' I didn't know Tuchel personally. It was a curious episode. It was just a joke, but it seemed like he had some sort of premonition about what would happen.

Klopp decided to send me on with 18 minutes to go. It didn't start well: Salah played me a ball in a difficult situation in midfield. PSG won back possession, Neymar accelerated the move through the middle and Mbappé equalized with a right-footed shot inside the box. A draw would be a terrible result for us and it felt very unjust as we had clearly been the better team. We also knew that we needed to start the competition with a win, so went in search of it in the final minutes. We were attacking with the entire team forward. The ball was lost and Mbappé had the chance to break. But James Milner made a great tackle and quickly the ball reached me at the edge of the penalty area. What happened next, you all saw better than me.

I am convinced that my impaired vision heightened my hearing. And what I heard was Anfield erupting. In life, I've witnessed few sounds like the ones that night, no roar quite like the one that greeted that goal: an explosion that felt like it came from within. Those fans, there in good and bad times, carried me. A competition that started that way could only end well! But the journey to glory was long.

After the victory against PSG we lost to Napoli. And we had two matches against Red Star Belgrade, one in Liverpool and another in Serbia. It was crucial that we win both, or else the group and our qualification could be beyond us. At Anfield we won 4–0 quite comfortably. I scored the first goal, after a left-wing cross from Andy Robertson, and I celebrated with my hand over my left eye again.

The ease of that first encounter was no indication of what the return game would be like; in fact, it might even have worked against us. We were already without Jordan Henderson and Naby Keïta when we went to Belgrade a few weeks later, and the coach decided to rest me as well. I hated being rested, hated sitting on the bench. Players always want to play. I was very upset. I didn't understand what Klopp was doing. In his mind, it was always about resting. But I always wanted to play. There was no reason to be stuck on the bench unable to get out there. I was on fire.

Maybe it was due to a lack of focus; maybe the quality of the opponent; maybe it was the absentees or the noise from the stands; maybe it was all of those things combined – whatever the reason, we conceded two goals in the first half and the game was out of our reach. I entered at half-time, but the result remained unchanged. Now we were in trouble. With the two draws between Paris Saint-Germain and Napoli, the group became a mess. Napoli and Liverpool had 6 points, PSG had 5 and Red Star Belgrade 4. Everyone had a chance and everyone was on edge. We still had to play in Paris and face Napoli at Anfield.

The game in Belgrade wasn't a complete write off because there, in the capital of Serbia, the coolest tribute I've ever received from Liverpool's fans was born. I learned about this years later, of course; about how a group of fans at a bar in the city came up with '*Sí, Señor*', drawing inspiration from a song sung by the River Plate fans, which they found on YouTube:

> Our nuuuuuuumber nine
> Give him the ball and he'll score every time
> *Síííííííí, señor*
> Pass the ball to Bobby and he'll score

Now it's back in my head in full force. I'll bet it's back in yours, too.

We were left even more on edge by a 2–1 defeat in Paris, beaten by an inspired performance from Neymar. Going into the final game Napoli led the group with 9 points, PSG had 8 and we had 6. Nothing less than a victory would do, or it would be over almost before it had started. The good news was that our destiny, if not top spot, remained in our own hands: win and goal difference would take us through.

Before games like this, the coaching staff always inten-sified training, constantly reminding us of the upcoming match's importance, piling on the pressure. And, in contrast to the match in Italy, we produced a great performance at home. Salah scored a stunning goal in the first half and we had several opportunities to seal the match on the counter in the second. Sadio had an unlucky night, missing two clear chances. As had become a habit, I was substituted for Keïta as we tried to hold onto the lead.

We almost didn't. In the very last minute of the game Napoli had an incredible chance. Arkadiusz Milik controlled a cross and prepared to shoot from inside the six-yard box. For a split second everyone's heart stopped, mine included. You could almost feel Anfield hold its breath. But Alisson leaped on him like an octopus to make an extraordinary save.

Alisson had rescued us. Without that monstrous save, we wouldn't even have been in the Champions League knockout stage, and we'd have had to settle for the Europa League; instead, we ended up as champions of Europe. See how thin the line is that separates success from failure? Many goalkeepers would've conceded that goal – and it wouldn't have been their fault. But only we had Alisson.

First place went to PSG and the punishment for finishing in second was handed down during the draw, which placed us against Bayern Munich in the Round of 16. We were going to have to do this the hard way. Worse, that meeting came at a delicate moment. In the 32 days between late January and early March, we drew five out of seven games, hurting our chances in the league and threatening to derail us in Europe too. One of those draws was the first leg at home against Bayern, denying us the chance to take a lead to Munich.

As it turned out, it didn't matter – thanks to the Sadio Mané Show. He scored a fantastic goal, deceiving Manuel Neuer and giving us the away goal that put us in a perfect position. A great match was unfolding: Bayern equalized and had chances to turn the game around, but we had our opportunities too: Van Dijk, following a corner, and Mané, after a beautiful cross from Salah, scored headers to take us into the quarter-finals.

In the next round, our opponent was Porto, who we beat 2-0 at home and 4-1 away, with me scoring in both games. We had regained our form from December and were practically flawless in March and April, securing ten consecutive victories. It was a shame that we were one point behind Manchester City in the Premier League. We were doing our bit by winning matches, but they were not letting up. Fortunately, we still had the Champions League to pursue.

Alas, against Cardiff my personal drama returned. I suffered an injury to my adductor muscle. The strain forced me to miss out in the Premier League against Huddersfield and work around the clock in an attempt to be fit for the first leg of the semi-final against Barcelona. It would be my first time facing Barcelona, my first at the Camp Nou. I was obsessed; I didn't want to miss that for anything. My priorities were clear: we had only two matches left in the Premier League and it already seemed clear that Manchester City would snatch the title from us. We had to win the Champions League!

Jürgen Klopp asked me: 'So, what do you think? Do you want to be on the bench?' I kept saying, 'I'm in, I'm in, I'm in.' I am a professional, I am stubborn: I want to train, I want to play, I want to travel with the team. I wanted to go to Barcelona. And I went.

Camp Nou is a massive stadium, nearly 100,000 people packed in. Barcelona has always captivated me. For Brazilians there is a mystique about the place, a sense that it was ours too, in that we had seen so many great moments there, seen so many of our idols play in their colours – from Romário to Ronaldo and Rivaldo, and, of course, my great hero, Ronaldinho Gaúcho. By then, though, it wasn't the Brazilians who dominated, even if my friend Philippe Coutinho was on the field; it was Lionel Messi, a genius. It gave me butter-flies just to think about playing there, but my injury ruined everything.

Not fully fit, I watched from the bench as everything went wrong for us. Barcelona dominated the early part of the game and Luis Suárez scored the first. We reacted well, gradually getting into the match, becoming the better team and creating chances to equalize – but it was one of those nights where the ball just didn't want to go in. With 15 minutes left Barcelona scored their second. Messi built up the play, Suárez hit the crossbar, and the ball, which could have gone anywhere, rebounded off Messi's chest. It was easy for him. Trailing 2–0 Klopp sent me on with just over ten minutes left. There wasn't much I could do. Shortly after my entrance, Messi scored *that* free-kick. From my place in the wall, I saw the ball fly past Joe Gomez. It's Messi, so you're already afraid; if the ball goes past the wall, you can only pray the goalkeeper reaches it. This time Alisson couldn't get to it. It was impossible, even for him.

We immediately created a goal-scoring opportunity that might have given us a little hope. Mané fought for the ball in the penalty area and it fell to me. I shot with my right foot, perhaps the only ball that got past Ter Stegen in the entire game. But several Barcelona players were rushing towards the goalline and one of them miraculously cleared. Later, I found out it was Ivan Rakitić; at the time I had no idea and no idea just how miraculous it was for him to have reached it. It was unbelievable that the ball didn't go in then, or when the rebound came to Salah and he shot and hit the post.

The bad news didn't stop there. At the very moment when

I almost scored, I felt my adductor again: the exact same spot we had been treating all the week. I thought, 'This can't be happening again.' I was devastated: I knew immediately that I would play no part in our remaining league matches or the second leg against Barcelona. I stayed on the field until the end because there were no more substitutions left. We lost 3–0 and I had suffered a relapse of the injury. It could hardly have been more of a nightmare.

Only one good thing happened and it turned out that was just enough of a lifeline for us to hang on. Already five minutes past the added time, we had a corner, one last desperate attempt to leave there with a goal. Instead, Gerard Piqué cleared and suddenly Ousmane Dembélé was leading a counter, three on one. Messi received the ball on the left, our players sprinting after him. Messi slipped it to Dembélé, alone in front of Alisson, for an easy fourth. Luckily for us, he took a weak shot that went into the hands of our goalkeeper. If they had scored that fourth, it would have been all over.

Actually, it already was. Or so everyone thought.

Everyone except us.

You know what fantastic thing happened that night? When we returned to the dressing room, there was an atmosphere of total confidence among all the players and the coaching staff. Genuinely, there was a conviction that it wasn't done yet. Jürgen Klopp was the first to speak, as he usually does after matches. He gathered the team and said, 'Nothing is lost. I believe. As long as there are chances, I believe. We will turn this around.'

Believe, believe, believe. This was the verb of the night, the verb of the week. The word Klopp kept saying all the time: '*Believe*. And that's an order.'

You might think: 'Well, yeah, sure, but a coach has to say that. He has no choice. He's obliged to tell his players there's still a chance because he's trying to lift them after a tough defeat. It doesn't mean he truly believes.'

This time, it did. A player can tell when there's no real conviction. And a player can tell when what he is listening to are not just empty words. Klopp said that because he actually did think it was possible. And we believed it too, because we had played a great game, despite the final score. Our leader showed a lot of faith: he was strong, convincing. He led us to a better place, right there in the Camp Nou dressing room.

The pre-match talk before the second leg was also powerful. Klopp communicates so well; he motivates players like no one else. He emphasized intensity and the need to close down Messi. It wasn't about marking him individually, but rather we had to mark him collectively. If the ball reached him, no one could give him space, even if it meant leaving other players free.

I already knew I wouldn't be physically fit to play in the second game. What we didn't know was that Mo Salah would also be out of the match, after a collision with the Newcastle goalkeeper in the weekend game. There was no room for resting players or taking our foot off the gas as we were simultaneously in a Premier League title race and now Mo couldn't face Barcelona either. Of course, we had confidence in our teammates, but the news wasn't exactly uplifting.

At that point in my life I had already started embracing Jesus. Many things happened in the week between the two matches against Barcelona that left a profound impact on me and somehow came together that night of the second leg at Anfield. Larissa had decided to be baptized. Rebeca, Fabinho's wife, brought Isaias Saad, a successful gospel singer from Brazil who later became a great friend of mine and the family's, to visit. On the way from the airport to our house, Isaias told Larissa and Rebeca that God had put the story of David and Goliath in his heart. A few days later, on the Sunday, we gathered at Fabinho's house and his mother, who is a pastor, brought exactly the same message: the story of David against Goliath. She spoke about how sometimes we feel small facing a giant, when confronted by life's difficulties, but nothing is impossible for God.

Anfield staged David's battle against Goliath. There David was stripped of his armour – Salah and I – but still defeated Goliath because he believed in the Lord and the Lord fought alongside him. Today, I see that what happened that night was God's will.

Those who stepped onto the field gave their all and defeated Barcelona 4–0. I love revisiting that match.

It was a game where Alisson saved everything, as we had to open up and Barcelona had several chances on counterattacks. Divock Origi played in my place and was inspired, as if guided by a light. He scored the first goal early in the match, which was absolutely crucial.

At half-time Gini Wijnaldum came on and within ten minutes he'd scored two goals. Gini was flying that season; I think he was unhappy about being on the bench and there was vindication in the way he played, a man who was laying claim to his place, proving he was worthy of being there on the field. We had the entire second half to get the fourth goal, while Alisson held Barcelona at bay. A momentum and a feeling of destiny began to take over.

It's very difficult to sit out of a game like that, but just being in the stadium was so emotional. I was sitting in the stands, watching with Alberto Moreno. We looked at each other and he said to me, 'What is this? What's happening? This must be the hand of God!' Alongside us, Salah was wearing a shirt that read 'Never Give Up'. Somehow it all made sense when the fourth goal came with Trent Alexander-Arnold's brilliant decision, a moment of inspiration from a 20-year-old kid that was simply unbelievable. He was about to leave the ball for Milner to cross, but he had the presence of mind to look at the area first. He saw Origi all alone, saw that no one from Barcelona was paying attention, span back and took the corner himself. Origi, very attentive, scored the goal. It was one of the loudest explosions I've ever witnessed. People were crying tears of joy and tension. I felt more and more of God's presence in my life.

And I knew in my heart that we would be champions now.

The day after our comeback, Tottenham achieved an equally epic feat playing in the Netherlands. They had lost the first leg of their semi-final to Ajax and were trailing 2–0 at half-time in the second, but turned it around in the second half with three goals from Lucas Moura. A game that also entered history ensured that they would be the team awaiting us in the final. Like us, they must have felt invincible after that.

That season we had beaten Tottenham twice, 2–1 each time, and we were very confident. Of course, we needed to respect the opponent, who had knocked out Manchester City and shown so much heart in the semi-final. They were the team of Kane and Son, but we felt it was beneficial for us to face a team we knew and had an advantage over. My goal now was getting there. In the lead-up to the final I did physiotherapy all day every day. Training without the ball, training with the ball, I was desperate to be in perfect shape when the final came.

The Premier League title race was still running but, of course, we ended up losing by that solitary point to City.

After that the club organized a training camp in Marbella, southern Spain, and allowed our families to join us. We had intense training days followed by two days off. It was important to make the team even more united, as well as relaxed and happy. This was about body *and* mind.

As I said, I knew we would be champions. I knew it wouldn't be like the previous year against Real Madrid. This time we had Alisson, Van Dijk and Fabinho; we had the experience; nothing could bring us down. With all due respect, we were better than Tottenham.

It wasn't my best game. I didn't play much and was substituted for Origi, who scored the second goal in the final minutes, sealing the victory initiated by Salah's early penalty – a clear handball in my opinion. When the referee blew the final whistle I went back onto the field to celebrate with an epic somersault!

The title was the crowning achievement of a very special group of players who liked each other and enjoyed playing football together. We had truly been the best football team in the world since 2018, and this victory did justice to what we had built. I was so happy that I even made sure to buy a full-sized replica of the trophy. Most my teammates bought the miniature replica, but I wanted the big one. I keep the trophy with care in my apartment in Maceió. From time to time, I lift it.

Larissa managed to come down to the field at the

Metropolitano Stadium in Madrid and hand me a shirt that said 'To God, all honour and all glory'. I put it on right away. She had already gotten very close to Jesus and, of course, been baptized that week, while my transformation had been unfolding throughout the year. I started changing my behaviour off the field, getting closer to the truth and my family. I prayed a lot for the trophies to finally come. In my hotel room in Madrid, before the final against Tottenham, I got on my knees. 'Why have I never won a title, Lord? If it's your will, Lord, give me a title. May everything be done for your honour and your glory.'

He delivered the thing I wanted the most: the UEFA Champions League. And He kept on giving. I asked for a trophy and, in two years, the Lord gave me seven.

The European Cup made up for all the work, all the pain; it compensated for all the frustration and revealed the path I had travelled along to be the right one. That night in Madrid will forever be in our hearts: Liverpool, champions of Europe.

Chapter 15

Top of the World

Those two years, 2018 and 2019, were relentless. The football kept coming, every game was huge, seemingly even bigger than the last; there was barely time to breathe. Within a couple of days of Liverpool losing the Champions League final to Real Madrid in Kyiv, I reported to London to join up with the Brazil squad at Tottenham's training centre. I was very, very upset. Losing the Champions League final had hurt, possibly more so than any other moment in my career. I believe we had chances to win the game and we basically handed them the victory. I kept thinking about it, couldn't get it out of my mind. I was desperate to get away from it, to go somewhere else and think of something else.

In that sense, having a World Cup to prepare for was good; going there for the Seleção is a dream for every child born in my country. But it is also true that it meant there was no rest, no chance to switch off. And, it seemed, no end in sight. Less than a month after Brazil had been knocked out in Russia, I was back on the pitch for a pre-season friendly against Napoli in Dublin and another exhausting season. For the second consecutive year we reached the final of the Champions League, this time against Tottenham in Madrid, of course, while also being immersed in the insane battle, game after game, with Manchester City for the Premier League title. The day after the final in Madrid I was back with the Brazil squad, this time for the Copa América at home. And by July I was playing for Liverpool again, against Lyon in Geneva. Then came the Community Shield against Manchester City and then the Super Cup final against Chelsea in Istanbul. And then . . .

Well, in short, I hadn't stopped since 2017 and everything was taking its toll. I hadn't had a decent break, time to phys-ically and mentally recover. Long seasons with Liverpool rolled straight into competitions with Brazil, which rolled into Liverpool and back again. And in the middle of it all there were Jürgen Klopp's intense training sessions. His demands and those of the ultra elite – a competition where you could not give an inch, where almost 100 points still weren't enough – were huge. Maybe my body was starting to give in? I don't know. But I know I went through a terrible spell for a forward. Between 22 September 2019, when I scored a header at Stamford Bridge in the victory against Chelsea, and 23 November, when I scored against

Crystal Palace, I went two months and nine matches without scoring. And then after that Palace game I went on another six-match goal drought. The press and social media were saying that I was tired; some said I needed time on the bench.

Until the trip to Qatar for the FIFA Club World Cup. Although I had only scored one goal in 16 matches, the team was flying high and had won 14 of those games, with two draws. I never lost my starting position or the coach's trust; I was contributing to our collective play. And that pleased me. But, you know, even forwards like me who are not defined by the goals they score struggle when they go through a spell like that and it's inevitable that the doubts accumulate. Yours, and everyone else's. I finally rid my mind of them at the best possible place.

We Brazilians value the FIFA Club World Cup trophy a lot, unlike the English, who usually see this tournament as an inconvenient friendly in the middle of a busy schedule. Sure, we were tired too, but there is a cultural question there: we grew up watching the old Intercontinental Cup, which served as a forerunner to the Club World Cup – and the chance to compete against the big European clubs was never viewed as a friendly. My friends Alisson and Fabinho and I desperately wanted this trophy; we wanted it to be part of our story. And we knew that our opponents, Flamengo, would feel the same way. So, although Fabinho got injured and couldn't travel with the team, Alisson and I decided that we needed to have a word with our coach. Lots of people had told us that English teams thought this competition didn't matter; we wanted to make sure he knew that it did. At the end of a training session in Qatar, when the opportunity presented itself, we went to Jürgen Klopp: 'Coach, we want to tell you that this trophy is very important to us. And it is highly valued by Brazilians. Expect a fiercely competitive game against Flamengo. They defeated Liverpool in the final of the Intercontinental Cup in 1981 and they still sing songs about it. It's the game of their lives. We can't go into it as if it were just any match.'

I could see the surprise in Klopp. Maybe he wasn't aware of the Brazilians' obsession with this trophy, but he got the message. He definitely became more engaged after that. He started asking questions and showing more interest, probably out of curiosity because it was something new for him. Before that, let's be honest, nobody really cared. After we had that chat with the Boss, he and the coaching staff started treating the fixture the way they treated other important matches. He couldn't help but see the significance in the streets, too. Flamengo fans had come to Doha in huge numbers; they were everywhere. They were determined to do their bit in the stadium as well. This wasn't a friendly to them. Or to me. It was the World Cup.

I also made sure to talk to all my Liverpool teammates.

'Hey, guys, I really want to win this game!' Alisson did the same. We were already thinking about the game against Flamengo, but before that, we had to win the semi-final. Our opponents were Monterrey from Mexico. The Boss decided to give some starters a rest and it turned out to be a tough game. Sadio Mané came on in the second half and I joined him with five minutes to go. Fortunately, the little time I had was enough to score that winner, ensuring our place in the final without needing to play a long period of extra-time that no one wanted.

The final was a battle. Flamengo fought for their lives, despite having had a long season with the Copa Libertadores and the Brazilian Championship. In our first attack I had a clear chance to score the opening goal. I received a wonderful left-footed pass from Alexander-Arnold, who is naturally right-footed, controlled it on my chest and shot, only for the ball to go over. It was a missed opportunity that could have eased everything and confirmed that my drought was over. Instead, it was going to be a long night. We had two more great chances, one for Keïta inside the box and another from Alexander-Arnold from long range, before the match became increasingly complicated. Bruno Henrique, a strong, tall attacker, was causing problems on their left. Still, I was confident that we would keep creating chances and that, at some point, one would go in. I was right, for a while, at least.

When the next chance fell, it fell to me. I flicked the ball over the defender's head and shot left-footed past the keeper. But it hit the post, ran all the way along the line and out again. I couldn't believe it. In that moment, you wondered if maybe it just wasn't going to be our day; if we were going to regret that opportunity slipping away. Chances kept coming for both sides. With the best of them, Gabriel Barbosa, my teammate in the national team, forced a great save from Alisson with a shot. And so we headed towards extra-time.

The good news was that, for all our fatigue, we were in better physical condition than Flamengo. We were in the middle of the season, gathering momentum on our way towards the long-awaited Premier League title, while Flamengo had heavy legs from having played 74 matches that year. And in the ninth minute of extra-time, in a classic Liverpool counterattack, Henderson's long, precise pass sought out Mané's speed. Rodrigo Caio from Flamengo tried to intercept the ball and failed, leaving us two on one. Mané found me in the area and I cut inside to score the winner, the goal that justified everything: the tension, the tiredness, the time I had gone without scoring. It was a trophy Liverpool hadn't won before, so we could add another award to the wall at the training ground. Off came the shirt in an explosion of joy. The Brazilian club wouldn't win the trophy, but it would at least be lifted by

Brazilian hands, hands that knew what it meant to hold the Club World Cup.

'No player deserved to score the title-winning goal more than Bobby,' Klopp said. He understood perfectly, as he always did. A coach with less empathy could have pretty much ignored what Alisson and I had said to him on the eve of the FIFA Club World Cup, but the Boss embraced our feelings.

The only thing I didn't like about that World Cup was leaving without the award for the tournament's best player. They gave it to Salah, maybe because it was in Qatar, or maybe because he was the team's biggest star, I don't know. But I think I deserved it after scoring the two decisive goals in the semi-final and final.

It had been an amazing game. Teammates talked about how well Flamengo had played, how well Jorge Jesus's team had competed against us. Many were surprised; they didn't expect it to be so difficult. They talked too about Flamengo's fans, who made an incredible noise. I hadn't really experienced that before, not having played in Brazil's top division, and while not many Liverpool supporters had travelled to Doha, the Brazilians had turned up in huge numbers. When we returned to England, I was happy to see that the FIFA Club World Cup had been embraced more this time. As for Klopp and the other players, they all had big smiles on their faces.

Back home in Brazil they didn't need telling how big it was. I get reminded about my goal against Flamengo whenever I'm there. Maceió has its two big teams that have always competed for the state titles, CRB and CSA, of course – but like in every city in the north-east the majority are Flamengo fans. Sure, they're from Rio de Janeiro, but they're the most popular team in the country, definitely so in Maceió. When I was a little kid in my neighbourhood, I even played for Flamenguinho – little Flamengo.

Whenever I return home, get stopped and asked for photos or autographs, I remember I've been on the other side; I know how important it is to give something back, to give fans time. When I get stopped in Maceió now, almost everyone, especially the kids, says to me, 'Roberto, you didn't need to score against us!' Others say, 'You killed us! But can I have a picture anyway?' What can I say? I just smile. Sometimes, I even apologize, but I was just doing my job. Except that for me it meant much more than that.

At the beginning of this book I talked about what the most remarkable goal and moment of my eight years at Liverpool was. It's hard to look beyond that day: 21 December 2019. I don't know if it was the happiest day or the most important title, but for me it will always be the most significant goal I scored in the red shirt of Liverpool. And there was something else too, something that made that final more important even than the goal or the trophy. That day, guided by the joy I felt, I took the most important decision of my life. The Lord spoke to me: the time is now. I called my wife Larissa immediately after the game and told her that I wanted to be baptized; that I wanted to become a new man in Jesus.

Chapter 16

The Right Path

When I stepped into that temple in London, my life changed forever. It was a blessed day, a Sunday – 10 February 2019, the day the Lord touched me.

Perhaps, for a moment, you might have thought that this book would be only about football. But this chapter is one of the most important parts of my life. Regardless of what you believe, or even if you don't believe in anything, I would like to ask your permission to invite you to continue reading with an open heart. This is my story, my experience. And it started that morning.

Larissa was going to leave at 7 a.m., very early, for a service at the Cathedral International, located in Norwood, south London. Isaias Saad and Luma Elpidio, two successful Brazilian gospel singers, would be there. They weren't over in the UK that often; Larissa had accepted Jesus with one of Isaias's songs, called '*Ousado Amor*'

(Reckless love), and wanted to meet him in person. She was going, no matter what. I wasn't sure.

We had just been through one of those difficult moments in our marriage. We were in different places. She was already in the spiritual realm; I was still immersed in the physical world.

It only takes a look or a moment of desire. 'But I tell you that anyone who looks at a woman lustfully has already committed adultery with her in his heart' (Matthew 5:28-29). And I had done more than just look and desire on one of those Liverpool trips, organized to build bonds and team spirit among players. Larissa knew what could have happened and our relationship was strained. Even after getting married, there were moments of temptation, moments that seemed made for sin, where I fell.

This whole religious thing was starting to go too far; it had become serious. I noticed how Larissa had changed: her behaviour, her attitudes. It wasn't temporary, just a phase, as I had initially thought.

After the 2018 World Cup and the arrivals of Alisson and Fabinho at Liverpool, my teammates and their wives and Larissa began holding frequent prayer meetings. I didn't usually attend. But all of that was starting to pique my curiosity. So that February weekend I was torn about whether to attend the service in London. Should I stay or should I go? I wanted to go, but I'd have to wake up at 6 a.m. to catch the train and arrive on time. I hated waking up that early, especially on a Sunday. Should I go or not?

I went.

I woke up determined, as if God was calling me. And He was. When I entered that building, I felt out of place, somewhat uncomfortable. The cathedral is like an auditorium with a stage, a large screen behind it and chairs in front. The stage is where the pastors and musicians are. There were about 300 people there for the service that Sunday. When Isaias began preaching the word through music, I felt a shiver throughout my body. I felt the presence of God. I cried a lot, non-stop. 'What have you done to me?' I asked Larissa. 'Why am I crying like this?'

'It's Jesus touching you,' she said.

How could Jesus still love me after so many mistakes? I wasn't a religious person. I grew up in a Catholic family, but we weren't very involved in the church. My mother attended mass on Sundays, but not much else. I prayed very little and had a spiritual barrier. I believed in God, yes, but I didn't exactly know what that meant. I had no idea who the real Jesus was. When I played for Figueirense I even attended an evangelical church for a while. A player named Luan was friends with a pastor in Florianópolis and I went with him to some meetings. But I couldn't open my mind, my heart, and didn't fully commit.

Larissa also had a Catholic upbringing in her childhood

and even dabbled in spiritualism. Like me, she never fully committed. We had a life that had nothing to do with Christ – quite the opposite.

The song '*Liberta-me de Mim*' (Free me from myself) by Luma Elpidio, which had the most impact on me that Sunday at the cathedral, has a passage that goes like this: *'The good that I want to do, I do not do. And the evil that I do not want, that's what I end up doing.'* Not that we were bad people; it wasn't about that. But the mistakes were numerous. Ours was a life of sins and excess. Our values were connected to possessions, image, external values – never internal ones. We were young, rebellious and empty in our relationship with God. We were poor in terms of respect between husband and wife, poor as parents, unstable. We didn't have the right priorities. We were lacking in true friends. We were poor in the things that money can't buy.

Transformation came for Larissa in 2018. While I was completely focused on the World Cup, the families of the Brazilian national team players were staying at a hotel nearby in Sochi. There, some gatherings were organized for preaching the word of the Lord. It began in Fernandinho's wife's apartment. The meetings were led by Douglas Costa's mother, who is a pastor. Among the wives and other family members who attended was Natália, Alisson's wife. Larissa started going to the meetings and identifying with what was said, with Jesus's word. She cried a lot during the testimonies and felt good in that environment.

After the World Cup, though, we returned to normal life, until an unexpected moment that didn't seem important at first brought Larissa back to Jesus.

A housekeeper who worked in our Liverpool home, named Viviane Montesso, needed a space to organize a lunch for women who attended the same church as her. Viviane helped us with cleaning, she was also from southern Brazil, like Larissa, and she was a missionary. She had been sent to Liverpool to help expand the MSBN Church (Sowers of Good News Ministry) to the north-west of England. MSBN is a church focused on missions and preaching the Gospel around the world. Larissa offered our house, on a day when I wasn't there. At that gathering, she was touched by Christ. It was a very powerful experience for her, one that changed her perceptions and led her to question her own life and behaviour. She says she couldn't stop crying. When she then looked at our daughters, she felt unworthy of having two such beautiful, pure girls; perfect gifts that God had given us. She began to question things like going out for dinners and parties and leaving the girls with Lina at home. She started to question the need to drink to have a good time.

At the same time, Alisson, Natália, Fabinho and Rebeca arrived in Liverpool: two Christian couples who began to spend time with us and became great friends and – why not? – guides to lead us along straighter, more righteous paths, away from rough, crooked ways and sin.

Larissa used to pray alone. Then she started doing the same with our girls. She would hide it around the house so I didn't see, because she was afraid it would be met with rejection.

She also began to organize gatherings at our house with my Liverpool friends. It was intentional, because she wanted me, in some way, to feel compelled to join. I have always been a very respectful person. Yes, I enjoyed parties, chaos, loud music and drinking, but I wasn't rude. If there were visitors at home, of course, I would be there, not holed up in a room. And my wife knew that better than anyone. That's how I participated once, then again. I felt absolutely awkward, sometimes uncomfortable. There was one particular meeting in December 2018 that was the turning point for Larissa's conversion. At that meeting a minister from the MSBN Church whom we didn't know, named Ramon, said things that I can't reveal to respect the privacy of others. It was a tense moment, somewhat embarrassing, as he discussed sad and, until then, unknown details of a marriage that had been restored. The couple was present at the meeting. Larissa was disappointed at that moment, upset by the embarrassment her friend had experienced in front of the group, and disillusioned to the point of giving up on the path she had been following.

The next day, though, the same friend told her that everything the minister had said was true and that he had revealed things she hadn't even told her mother. There was God's voice and He knew. If God had been able to put that girl's marital life in order, then He could do the same for Larissa. From disillusionment came confidence that Christ was indeed manifesting Himself in her life.

In that same meeting, the church minister had taken Alisson aside and delivered a powerful message to my friend. He told him that God had brought him to that place for a great reason: Alisson was responsible for bringing Roberto Firmino onto the path of a new life in Christ. Alisson and I never talked about this. I only found out about it much later because Larissa told me. And I am very grateful to Alisson, who did indeed assume and fulfil his mission. We would talk about healthy things: family, books, the Bible. This great brother in faith became a true friend for life. He showed me the ways of a responsible man, the paths of regeneration; leadership through example, not material possessions or empty words.

A little while after that impactful meeting, after the turn of the year, came the meeting at the Cathedral International in London; the moment when I clearly, powerfully, felt the presence of Jesus Christ.

But these things don't happen in the blink of an eye. It took me a whole year to fully accept Jesus into my heart.

It was step by step. Through Larissa and other people, or even events, I began to feel Christ's presence in me more and more.

In this transformation process I went through, two fundamental people were Pastors Jairo and Keila Fernandes. They were the pastors of the MSBN Church in Manchester and appeared in our lives for the first time when Larissa offered our house to Viviane to organize that lunch for church members.

Even though they lived over an hour away, Jairo and Keila attended many of the gatherings held at our home. Their sons, Juninho and Gabriel, were always with them. Juninho played the keyboard, Gabriel the guitar. The boys led the worship, while their parents, the pastors, delivered the word of God.

Jairo and Keila were essential for my encounter with Christ because they knew how to respect my time. Maybe everything would have gone wrong if, in this moment of doubt when Larissa and I were out of sync regarding faith, I had encountered pushy, determined people demanding something from me that wasn't yet deeply rooted in me.

Just because my wife started attending church services and organizing gatherings didn't mean our lifestyle had changed. We still went to parties and drinking remained a part of our lives. At the same time, though, I wanted God to be present. More and more. In such moments, Jairo and

Keila always appeared to bring me the word of God. In other moments, when maybe I didn't even want to receive them into my home, they gave me hugs and smiles without asking for anything in return.

Our pastors are zealous, diligent in their evangelical mission to convert. But they guided my transformation differently, understanding that it wouldn't happen overnight and respecting my space. At no point did they force Christ into my life. Despite the ups and downs I went through, they never gave up on me and, with immense, genuine affection, patience and wisdom, showed me the path to salvation.

Over the years, we've welcomed many people into our home: singers, influencers, famous individuals. And I always felt like there was something these people expected in return from me. There was always a price. Jairo and Keila lived far away, had a financially uncomfortable situation, and never asked for a single penny to help pay for the petrol they bought to get to us. They never asked for a photo or a post. Nothing. They were people with very little. And the little they had, they offered to us.

In 2019 Larissa completely changed her stance; I could see the transformation in her after she had said yes to Jesus. For example, she began to drink less when we went out at night. She stopped posting provocative messages on social media that emphasized the body. She became a more present mother in our daughters' lives. The Holy Spirit began to reach me, convince me, because she started praying for me. She started praying that I would be impacted too, like she had been.

In May 2019 Larissa was baptized. I asked her if she was sure she wanted to do it and she replied without hesitation: yes. I was the one who wasn't sure. Yes, I was afraid of losing my wife to the church. Things were different; this was a playing field I didn't know. I had many questions, and the change I felt happening in me both excited and frightened me. Little angels and devils were in full battle.

'This is between me and God, don't worry about it,' she told me. She wanted to show the world that the old Larissa had died, that there was a new person there, whose commitment was to God.

Her baptism was a very emotional event and, on top of that, it happened a couple of days before the Champions League semi-final in 2019 when Liverpool beat Barcelona 4–0. We were surrounded by friends, including Isaias Saad, who became a great brother and stayed at our house.

Isaias is a young, talented guy who also had nice white teeth like mine and showed me that it was pure prejudice on my part to think that believers and religious people were dull. It was possible to have faith and be fun at the same time. I used to ask Larissa, 'When are these believers leaving so I can turn on the music and listen to my *forró*?' *Forró* is a lively Brazilian dance and music style known for its infectious rhythms. In my mind, highly religious people were boring.

But maybe I was the one who was boring. Childishly, I insisted that Isaias have a glass of wine with me. He didn't drink, but I had always had this habit. I liked it when guests had a drink with me. I was determined to make this guy break his promise not to drink alcohol because of God.

Until Isaias disarmed me, made me see that I was wrong: 'If this is so important to you, Roberto: no problem. Pour a little wine into the glass.' He sipped a tiny bit and then left the glass full. This kind of attitude from a mature and confident person began to show me that it was possible to be nice, well-mannered and sociable without needing to drink. There were other ways to have fun besides going to clubs. I'll never forget when we spent hours and hours laughing and playing charades. We had a blast.

The seeds were being planted in my heart. Increasingly, my life was surrounded by people who believed in the power of Christ, who lived for Him. As Pastor Keila says, if you stand near a campfire, you will inevitably feel the warmth. It was impossible not to feel the fire when everyone around me had a heart burning for Jesus. God used people like Isaias, Alisson, Jairo, Keila and Larissa, among others, as instruments to bring me to Him.

In the week of Larissa's baptism, I felt that something was changing in me. And I was shocked by God's hand in that victory over Barcelona. He moves. David against Goliath, the biblical passage delivered days before by Isaias and by Fabinho's mother, was being played out right before my eyes. Those were intense days and something was already burning inside me.

I began attending meetings more regularly. Deep down, I knew I had already accepted Jesus, but still I resisted. Stubbornness was stronger than faith. I was afraid. I had doubts. What would become of the old Bobby? Would I have to give up everything I liked? Would I have to stop listening to my *forró* and the music I loved?

In the midst of the transformation my family was going through there was my career. Liverpool had reached another Champions League final, this time against Tottenham in Madrid, and we couldn't lose. I was confident we would win the title, especially because of how we had reached that final. In almost ten years as a professional, I had never won anything, which left me frustrated and bitter. In the hotel room in Madrid, I knelt down, prayed and became emotional. 'If it is your will, Lord, give me a trophy. Let everything be done for your honour and glory.'

I asked for only one and He gave me four in 2019 alone. With Christ in my heart, I became the champion of Europe.

Despite all the messages, despite Jesus's love for me and all the demonstrations of His will, I still resisted complete transformation. I had highs and lows. During the holidays in

Maceió, I organized an *'arraial'*, a huge June party, with the presence of famous local and national singers, lots of drinks and fun. *'Festa Junina'* is a lively Brazilian celebration featuring music, dancing and typical food, especially grand in the north-east of the country. At the same time as I was organizing the *arraial*, I invited Isaias to come to Maceió. We held a family service, a very emotional celebration that marked Larissa's reconciliation with my mother – they hadn't been getting along well in the previous years.

But the same Bobby who did this still had monumental slips. At the farewell party for that holiday, as we were preparing to return to Liverpool, I was ready to misbehave. In fact, I was determined to. I wanted to drink, I wanted to go wild, I wanted to activate the mechanism that 'freed' me for pleasures of the flesh. The problem was that Larissa was there at the same club, in the same VIP area. I was already drunk and my strategy to get her to go home, leaving me free, was pretty basic: irritate her. I went up to Larissa and 'invited' her to dance. When, as expected, she refused, I threw a glass on the floor and caused a bit of a scene. The problem was that the man who came to restrain me was Sven Kampmann, my friend and physiotherapist. I clenched my fists and pushed him away. Security at the venue thought Sven wanted to fight me and they came after him. A bit of trouble became a lot of trouble. There was press in the place and people were taking photos. Larissa 'rescued' Sven, to whom I of course apologized, and even had a beer with the next day. The plan to 'stray' at that party had failed. It was a time of transition for me: the old Bobby and the new one both appearing in actions and feelings.

If in Maceió I had been determined to do something that I would have regretted, at a private birthday party for a Liverpool player in London I behaved differently. Larissa prayed for me at home and I felt out of place for having even gone. Regretting not having declined the invitation, I sent a bouquet of flowers to my wife – with a Bible verse on the card. I knew that detail would please her. That was a pivotal moment in our lives. Formerly, in a situation like that, I would have gone to the party, engaged in my antics, and Larissa would have been upset and annoyed. She would have taunted me with social media posts. We would have argued. And we would have been estranged for a while. None of that happened. Something had changed in me.

When I called her that night and asked if she was angry, she replied: 'No, I'm disappointed. Now, more important than the commitment I made to you is the commitment I made to God and I will follow the path He shows me. God is trying to call you, Roberto. Don't let the storm arrive first.'

Amidst errors, relapses, meetings, worship sessions, repentance and tears, my transformation was taking place. In the second half of 2019 I went two months without scoring a single goal. Still, I felt loved and supported by Christ. 'Trust in the Lord; with all your heart, and lean not on your own understanding. Wait for the Lord; be strong and let your heart take courage; yes, wait for the Lord' (Psalms 27:14).

Jesus did not give up on me. Jesus died for us and is the only path to forgiveness. 'You will cast all our sins into the depths of the sea of forgetfulness' (Micah 7:19).

He empowered me to score the goals that gave Liverpool its first-ever world club title. He saved it all for the most important moment. The love of Christ burned in my heart. The old Roberto Firmino was no longer present. The Bobby who scored those goals in Qatar was a new man; a new life in Christ had been born and it was time to consummate that love with my own baptism. I had no more doubts, only certainties.

'And Jesus replied, "Very truly I tell you, no one can see the kingdom of God unless they are born again. No one can enter the kingdom of God unless they are born of water and the Spirit. Flesh gives birth to flesh, but the Spirit gives birth to the Spirit"' (John 3:5–6).

On 14 January 2020 I was baptized in the swimming pool at my home in Formby. It was one of the most wonderful, blessed days of my life. I cried while embracing my brothers Alisson and Isaias and my wife Larissa, who had been so important in my journey towards Jesus. Among many beloved people, brothers and sisters in faith, Gabriela Rocha was also present – a very successful gospel singer in Brazil. On the day of my baptism, eight others also decided to fully accept Jesus into their hearts. It was a special and emotional moment for all who experienced that demonstration of faith. God made His presence felt in the hearts of all.

The following month Larissa and I travelled alone to the Maldives. We confessed our sins and started a new, pure relationship, without resentment or doubts. 'If you declare with your mouth, "Jesus is Lord," and believe in your heart that God raised Him from the dead, you will be saved. For it is with your heart that you believe and are justified, and it is with your mouth that you profess your faith and are saved' (Romans 10:9–10).

The trip to the Maldives was just before the coronavirus pandemic. With the greatest respect for all the sadness that the pandemic caused in the world, I open my heart here to say that those events too were fundamental for the new life we wanted to establish. We were locked at home, which provided months of healing for our lives. We looked inside and realized that our family was more than enough to be happy without the need to seek anything outside. We had all we needed to sustain us: love.

Until then I had not paid proper attention to the two wonderful daughters that God gave. When the pandemic came, I began to value Larissa, Valentina and Bella more. With the children, we did activities that were unimaginable a year or two before. I gave myself completely because the truth was that I had participated very little in their lives until then. We engaged in activities to ensure they didn't forget the English they were learning, held picnics, let creativity flow with new recipes, played games and blew bubbles. And, of course, we played a lot of football in the garden. My girls didn't have it easy. When I have a ball at my feet, I can't just play; they started their football lessons at the 'hard' level.

I became a father at last. Years had gone by without me understanding what it meant to be a real father. My encounter with Jesus and the pandemic allowed this to finally happen in a complete and conscientious way. There was real intent now. We found true, deep joy – not the supposed joy of parties and nightlife. We found a joy that didn't depend on drink and carnal pleasure, but on love.

Larissa and I set ourselves the goal of reading the entire Bible in three months. We studied the word of the Lord, took a course to educate our children based on Christian values, and I started participating in online meetings to speak about and hear from God. Fernandinho, Ederson, Fred . . . Brazilian Premier League players gathered through screens for worship services with the word of God and hymns. On Instagram I started recording videos to talk about the Lord's word. I would spend hours trying to make a 30-second clip. That was new to me; it was unimaginable that I would do something like that before.

We also participated in live sessions with gospel musicians, singing and praying. It was during one of these powerful moments, in a live session led by Isaias Saad during the pandemic, that God spoke to me clearly and told me to give up drinking.

Throughout my transformation process, I hadn't thought about quitting drinking. Yes, I had become aware of a desire to control it, reducing what I drank, but I still had a beer or a glass of wine here and there. But God spoke to me: He knew I was ready. There would be moments later when I felt the desire to drink with friends, situations in which I could have done so, but God had drawn a line and I would not cross it. He told me clearly to stop. And I stopped. God does everything for a Purpose and we are here to glorify His name, not to challenge it. From now on, there would be no alcohol at all. Nothing, not a drop. Towards the end of the pandemic, when the players started meeting again and football was about to resume, my Liverpool teammates couldn't believe how much I had changed. The Bobby who went to every party, who was always among the first to enjoy going out, had just stopped completely. Mo Salah, who didn't drink because of his Muslim faith, was one of those most struck by my transformation, truly shocked at the new Bobby. Sadio Mané, another non-drinker due to his religion, was curious about my Christian transformation, and we started having many conversations about spiritual matters. Even on the field and during training, my attitude changed. I became more affectionate with my teammates, more open; I was warmer, I paid them more compliments, I took time to talk to them more, to get deep into conversation with them. Meeting Jesus liberated me: at last I started breaking down the barriers that shyness had imposed on me.

I was a new me.

So much had happened in our lives, and something even more special was yet to come.

The Lord had given me the trophies I asked for, set my marriage on the right path, led me to my daughters and showed me the happiness I had right beside me at home but couldn't see. In 2020 we were experiencing an overflow of God's blessings. How could we repay all of that? What could we truly give in return?

The answer came on a night when we watched a Christian movie. It was the story of a pastor's son who had experienced a tragedy in his family, but needed to fulfil the mission of building a church. Larissa was deeply moved. She looked at me and said she'd had a vision of a church in Maceió. She was seeking answers about how to use all the material wealth life had given us in order to help others, to have an impact on their lives. God had helped us prosper, took care of my football career and opened doors for us, and we'd spent so much money on filth, hell and sin. How could we give back to God what was God's? The answer was to bring God's power – salvation – to as many people as possible. He gave us the answer through that vision. And He was telling me the same thing, although I didn't have the wisdom to understand. When Larissa told me about the image of a church in Maceió, I instantly knew what His plan for us was.

There was fear, of course. There was uncertainty; an awareness of what we were taking on; a respect for the task ahead of us. If we were going to do this, we had to do it right. You don't play around with this kind of thing. We didn't know anything about how to build and run a church – what to do, where to start – and so we humbly sought the guidance the Lord could provide.

We called Jairo and Keila to tell them about our vision. They were cautious at first, hesitant. They were already responsible for a church in Manchester and they had been in England for years. Besides, we were in the midst of a pandemic. However, a family illness brought them back to Brazil. God acted so they could fulfil His will. Jairo and Keila went to Maceió, found a good property in a humble but well-located neighborhood. They organized everything with our support and Manah Church was born in January 2021 – an extraordinary work that only the Holy Spirit could raise so quickly, although it was six months before we managed to return to Brazil to visit the church. It's important to say that the church is not 'ours'. It belongs to Christ. Larissa and I are only backers, offering ourselves to the Lord so that a transformation can be brought to the lives of many people.

Before Manah, or even my encounter with Christ, I was already someone who tried to help the less fortunate in my city with donations. Today, I understand that more than giving money or toys or food, it's important to bring God's word to people. To embrace them, listen to them, go beyond their physical needs and care for the spiritual side of each individual. That's what I do every time I return to Maceió. Our missionary work brings more than just food – which is essential and necessary, of course. It brings hope to many poor children in the interior of my state of Alagoas. I participate whenever I can. I talk to the girl who saw her father kill her mother in front of her. The boy whose arm was burned by his stepfather. The 14-year-old who takes care of four younger siblings in a house abandoned by their parents. I show them that I came from a similar place and that Jesus is the only path to salvation.

In addition to Manah in Maceió – and the missionary work – in September 2022, Manah Church in Manchester was also established, and our pastors, Keila and Jairo, returned to preach the word in England.

Neither of the two churches is, nor should be, maintained by us. They belong to Christ and are administered through tithes, the offerings of the faithful. Of course, our financial support is greater than that of most, as God enlightened us and empowered me to accumulate so much material wealth with my gift.

When I entered Manah for the first time in Maceió, I felt the presence of Christ the King powerfully. I love that place. The atmosphere created is perfect for encountering and hearing the word. The church is known for being quite dark, so that people don't get distracted. The hymns are sung at a very, very high volume. But none of that matters like the presence of God. If people don't feel His presence, if they don't feel something different in every service, they leave. At Manah, God always makes Himself present.

The first service had 80 people in attendance – that was during the pandemic, at a point when church services were allowed but there were still some restrictions. Over the few years since, the 80 have multiplied and turned into thousands. New people arrive every Sunday.

Manah is my home. It's the place where God's presence allows families to be restored and addictions to be left behind. I fell in love with Manah as soon as I set foot in it. The hymns largely filled the void I felt from not being connected to music. I have a passion for music, love to play, listen and feel the Lord through music. The songs I used to listen to are in the past. They remind me of things I'm ashamed of and a place I won't return to. I wandered the world, but I didn't find what I have now. My new place is spiritually powerful. I love the church's energy and I participate in services with my brothers and sisters, singing at the top of my lungs in praise of the Lord.

My encounter with Christ gave me the courage to overcome my fear of public speaking. Love casts out all fear, and God has given us strength and sound judgement. To speak of Christ is boldness, bravery and power. We need not be scared when we talk about His love.

The shy Bobby Firmino apparent in interviews continues to live within me. I slay a giant every time I step on stage to preach. So, I seek the Spirit of God to guide me. To empty myself, and let the Holy Spirit fill me with His word and message. He gives me the peace to let go. I feel the fire burn inside me when I preach the word and share my life's testimony. People need to know everything Larissa and I felt and went through. And that Christ saved us.

Believe me, all that you've read here is just a brief summary. I could write an entire book about this part of my life, telling you all the coincidences or 'Jesuscidences', as I like to call them, that happened along this journey, confirming every step. Jesus's touch didn't just transform my marriage or make me quit drinking. His touch brought me an identity that goes beyond football; it brought me responsibilities, values. And all of that was, I have no doubt, reflected in my football too. His touch revealed to me the greatest proof of love ever known to humanity: that He died so that I could live. Even more than the desire to tell you my story, my genuine desire is that one day, you who are reading this page, also feel the touch of Jesus. This is my prayer.

Chapter 17

The Wait is Over

It's no secret to anyone. We'd conquered Europe, we conquered the world, but something was missing: we still hadn't conquered England and that Premier League trophy was the one the fans wanted most of all.

I have no doubts that we were the best in the world during the period that spanned from the end of the 2017–18 season until March 2020, when the planet came to a halt due to the coronavirus pandemic. We had demonstrated our strength with two Champions League finals, an entire Premier League season in which there was just one, painful defeat, and in our performances against Barcelona, Manchester City and even Real Madrid, against whom, despite losing, we were the better side.

But the Premier League was still missing and we needed it. Liverpool hadn't been English champions since 1990. We'd come close a few times, but we had never been able to clinch the domestic title in this new era when the Premier League became the most powerful league in the world. We had a score to settle. Our team was just too good not to have a Premier League title.

As everyone knows, in 2019 we were Champions League winners and had an epic Premier League campaign, amassing 97 points. Yet, still, it eluded us. In the 2019–20 season, the same couldn't happen again. It just couldn't.

I arrived for pre-season having just won the Copa América with the Brazilian national team and I felt in the prime of my career. I couldn't have been more confident, even though we knew we needed a near-perfect campaign if we were to win the league. Determined, we had made a sort of pact during pre-season: this was it, we couldn't let a single game slip through our fingers, couldn't ever ease off. We went into the season incredibly focused, committed to starting strongly, knowing that every point was decisive, that there was no margin for even the smallest error. And so it was. We won one match. Then another. Then another and another . . . and another after that. No one could stop us. In our first 27 games we won 26 and drew just one, against United at Old Trafford. We were an unstoppable force, everything fitting together like clockwork. Relentless: don't pause until it's over.

With a substantial lead in the league, we secured the Club World Cup in Qatar – I'd scored the goals in our victories over Monterrey and Flamengo, of course – and when we faced second-placed Leicester, managed by Brendan Rodgers, on Boxing Day we thrashed them 4–0. For many fans that was the night we won the league; for others, it was the 2–0 win over United in January when we opened up a 16-point lead. As for us, honestly, we hardly glanced at the league table; we just kept on, committed to that original promise. Not one point gifted, not one game wasted. Match after match. It was like a race where the runner sprints down the track, way ahead of the rest, and never looks back until it's done. When you finally pause for breath and glance behind you, there's no one even close. After 26 wins in 27 games, it was clear that the title was just a matter of time and the objective had already shifted: now we wanted to win the league undefeated. We discussed this among ourselves – and why not? After all, it was win after win every week, and that finishing line got closer with no sign, still less any intention, of slowing down.

But then we had a dip in the season; a small one but enough to cost us dearly. And one that perhaps, in the long run, contributed to us losing our European and global dominance.

In February 2020 we travelled to Madrid to face Atlético Madrid in the Champions League last 16. It was a tough game, just as we expected. They scored an early goal and then defended for the rest of the match. That wasn't the kind of game we liked: we preferred to play with speed, exploiting open spaces. Diego Simeone, Atlético's coach, perfectly identified our style, finding a way to nullify us.

It was our first defeat in five months, only the second of the season – the other had been against Napoli in the group stage – and the truth is, it shocked us. By that point in the season we had felt invincible, with a united and powerful squad.

But, of course, we weren't truly invincible. Rocked by the Atlético result, we found that out the hard way. After Madrid there were three more defeats, which ended up being even more significant than we could have imagined. We lost 3–0 to Watford, a scoreline that ended our run of 18 consecutive Premier League wins and a 44-match unbeaten streak. Our last Premier League loss had been to Manchester City more than a year earlier. Now our hopes of an undefeated Premier League title had been destroyed. It was a dreadful game. Everyone played poorly, the team seemed all over the place. I was very frustrated and irritated that day; I felt as if our wonderful campaign had counted for nothing. And after all that time, I no longer knew how to lose. Larissa told me to look at everything we had achieved, but I didn't want to know. I didn't take the defeat to Watford or the performance there at all well.

We also lost to Chelsea in the FA Cup. We usually didn't pay much attention to the Cup competitions. But since it was the fifth round, against big opponents, with the latter rounds approaching and the Premier League title secured, the Boss fielded a mixed team of starters and substitutes. We lost 2–0.

Then came the second leg against Atlético Madrid, where we were without Alisson. Unlike the other two games, where we felt we had not been right, there was not much to regret about this match except the result. We completely dominated, played with the same quality we had displayed throughout the season, and had 34 attempts on goal but only one of those went in, forcing the tie into extra–time. I then scored a header early on and it seemed like we were on track for the quarter-finals. Honestly, when the ball hit the net, I thought it was done; we'd won it.

I'm still not quite sure what happened from there. Atlético Madrid scored three and knocked us out at Anfield. Marcos Llorente was their hero, with the goals that turned the tide against our substitute goalkeeper Adrián San Miguel.

Suddenly, in the blink of an eye, we had lost our unbeaten record in the Premier League, and got knocked out of the Champions League and the FA Cup. It was heartbreaking. Honestly, that was the team to win it all (something we almost achieved two seasons later). We had the best goalkeeper in the world, the best defenders, attacking full-backs, a solid midfield, a lethal trio of forwards, positive leadership, a winning mentality and an experienced, intelligent manager surrounded by an excellent staff. And, of course, the best fans. To me that was a perfect team, a perfect combination. It should have delivered the perfect season.

But it had gone. The slip-ups cost us the chance to once again prove our superiority in Europe and make history at home.

And then, almost overnight, all that was made to feel trivial. We'll never forget March 2020, when everything changed; everyone's lives became affected by the coronavirus pandemic. Many lost family members or loved ones, and we all had to adapt to a different and ever-changing reality.

Professionally, it was challenging too. Defeat at Watford wasn't just the end of our unbeaten run. Looking at what happened afterwards, it also took away our chance to be champions before the pandemic forced a halt, denying us the opportunity to share that moment with our fans. When the authorities decided that football had to stop, we had a 25-point lead over Manchester City with just 27 points left to play for. In other words, we were champions, but we weren't champions yet. Three more points – those three Watford had taken – and we would have been. That was incredibly frustrating. There were even discussions about cancelling the league altogether, which made me nervous. Can you imagine? We'd had an extraordinary, epic campaign and they were going to deny us the title? We didn't deserve that. Nobody knew what would happen; it was a massive question mark.

The doubts caused by a terrifying and unknown disease came first, dealing with the fear that provoked in everyone. Then came the concerns about the championship and how we could maintain our physical fitness on our own. The club organized daily routines to keep everyone fit: morning yoga, afternoon training. All the players stayed connected via Skype, with the fitness coach overseeing and leading the training sessions. It was also a way to keep us connected and bonded. Liverpool arranged our supermarket shopping; we didn't have to do anything. I didn't pass my front gate in two months.

Gradually, those terrifying numbers slowed and some countries resumed playing. Germany was the first; watching a football match go ahead was a great and liberating feeling, even if it hadn't come to us yet.

The Premier League finally resumed in June, three months after the suspension, but without the fans. We had to walk out alone.

There's no place like home. And Anfield will always be home to me. There are football grounds and then there's Anfield. There are many fanatical, loyal, noisy sets of fans. In England, Brazil, Germany and Saudi Arabia: where there's football, there's passion. But I can tell you, at Anfield, things are different. Listen to my Brazilian friends, rivals from other clubs. They always told me, 'How tough it is to play at Anfield!' Tough for them; a blessing for us.

Liverpool's fans play. They understand the game, know when to push the team, when it's needed. I've never heard them boo or criticize their players, regardless of how the season is going. Never. Not here. I've been through that elsewhere. When I played in Brazil, I was booed by the fans of my own team, Figueirense. I was young and bold, always trying things, always attacking. I would lose a ball, lose two, and become the target of their fury. Some players would be intimidated, but not me. I'd do it again and again and again. I wasn't going to change, even if they did boo. That was Roberto Firmino on Brazilian and German fields. That was Bobby Firmino in England, where there was never any doubt: one or two former players might criticize errors or moments where you played badly, the mistakes you made, but the fans always stood by me. In success and failure, in victory and defeat, on the Anfield pitch I *always* felt loved. I always had my special place and they never wanted me to leave it.

But at that moment, they were the ones who had to leave. The pandemic took away the Liverpool fans' chance to support us, share with us the moment they had waited for even longer than us; to release a cheer that had been trapped in their throats for 30 years. How sad that felt! How sorely they were missed!

When football returned, there was still no vaccine, and we all had doubts about Covid-19 and how the virus could infect us. The league and the club subjected us to strict protocols to protect players and staff, as well as our families. It was weird, totally different. Every day, I went to the club already in my training gear. Upon arrival, I would take a PCR test and have to wait to find out if the result was negative before I could be cleared to go to training. There was no shared space, no dressing room together. Greetings were different, just a little fist bump, avoiding much contact. It was the right thing to do. Some might think all those protocols were excessive, but I respected the rules and people's health; this was bigger than we were. Which isn't to say the football didn't matter: it played an important role in bringing joy and distraction to people amidst all the agony, and put a smile back on their faces. It provided solace to some, a reason to think positively. In England the beginning of summer marked the start of a gradual return to normality: the rules we had all been rightly subjected to were gradually relaxed, allowing families to reunite.

On the field, the title didn't take long to arrive. In the first game back we drew 0–0 with Everton in a derby that didn't feel like a derby, in front of an empty stadium. Then we won 4–0 against Crystal Palace, with an incredible performance from my friend Fabinho. All that was left was for Manchester City not to defeat Chelsea the next day for our title to become mathematically certain.

The club gathered the entire team of players at a hotel in Formby. Families couldn't be there because the team bubble had to be maintained. Together, we watched Chelsea's 2–1 victory, with a penalty goal from my friend Willian. Less than a week after the restart of the Premier League, we were champions. It was a special moment. And different, of course. The joy was there, we jumped and embraced each other, but it wasn't a celebration like the others. There was no escaping the feeling that something was not right, that something had been denied to us. And, above all, to our supporters. It was such a pity not to have secured the title before all of that happened. Liverpool fans had waited 30 years to celebrate the title and, when it came, they could only shout, 'We are the champions!' from within their own homes. It wasn't bitter, of course not. It was a moment of great joy that I shared with my teammates, but it could have been better.

A month later we played our last game at Anfield. I scored, as we defeated Chelsea 5–3, and we finally lifted that trophy we had dreamed of for so long. A huge stage was set up in the Kop, where our loudest fans should have been standing. It was the ideal place for the celebration, a gesture of solidarity with our absent supporters. There, one legend, Kenny Dalglish, presented the trophy to another: Jordan Henderson.

Families were allowed to attend the stadium on that day. Although they had to stay in the VIP boxes, isolated, they could at least witness the victory and celebration up close. That was priceless. Outside the ground, big crowds were expected, even though gatherings were prohibited. I don't know how many, but several thousand fans were there with us, through the walls on the other side of the stands. Fireworks painted the sky red. I wanted to be out there with them, or have them in the ground with us, but couldn't.

One season ended – a mini-season played out in silence – but there was almost no time before the next, 2020–21. Larissa and I enjoyed a few sunny days in Sardinia, but it felt like I hadn't really had a holiday. The adrenaline from that mini-end of the Premier League season had worn off and I didn't feel physically refreshed. In other words, I started the next season tired. And it was clear that I wasn't the only one. Others felt the same way.

The start wasn't bad – although we suffered an incredible 7–2 defeat to Aston Villa. That was the only loss until the end of the year, and we even took the lead in the league, but consistency was lacking, then disaster struck with several poor results between January and early March. We lost to Burnley, ending a 68-game unbeaten streak at Anfield in the Premier League, a run that had been going since 2017. Worse, that was the first of six consecutive defeats at home, a series of games in which we scored only one goal – in a 4–1 defeat to Manchester City, who would go on to reclaim the title.

The reality was that our ground had become just a patch of grass and concrete. Some teams suffered more from playing without fans during the pandemic, some less. We suffered much more than anyone without our supporters. It just never felt right. Playing football without a crowd is horrible. The fans are our fuel: we play for them, perform for them; we want to bring them joy. Without them, there's no spectacle, no sentiment. They even tried to pipe crowd noise in through the sound system to simulate some kind of atmosphere, but you can't replace real people or emulate the emotion.

We could also hear perfectly everything that was said on the field. Henderson especially: he is one of those captains who likes to 'commentate' the game. During the pandemic you could hear him accompanying every move, every play: it was like someone had left the radio on. Then there's the manager. Sometimes, a coach shouts at you, but with all the stadium noise you can pretend not to hear. Let's just say we could 'select' what we listened to. During the pandemic there was no more pretending, no place to hide, and definitely no excuse. You could hear everything that the Boss shouted perfectly clearly – and he knew that.

Without the fans, it was a very tough season for me. It took me a while to get used to their absence, the lack of pressure and atmosphere. In fact, I'm not sure I ever did. This was a show with no audience, which made it hardly a show at all. I think our whole team felt it – the other guys, like Thiago Alcântara, told me they were also struggling – but I might have been the one who felt it most keenly. It's no coincidence that we went 68 games without losing at Anfield and then suddenly lost six times in a row. We were missing 40,000 players.

That wasn't the only thing that made the new season a more difficult one for me. In addition to Thiago, who came from Bayern Munich for the 2020–21 season with the European title in his luggage, Diogo Jota joined from Wolves. He started in many matches during the season, especially in the Champions League. I didn't feel threatened by his arrival. He was a guy to give our attack some breathing space, another quality option. He played more on the wings, sometimes taking the number 9 role, and he made the most of the opportunities. But it did mean I spent more time than I wanted to sitting on the bench, and in some big games too. That was new for me. It wasn't nice to watch from the sidelines as we were defeated by Real Madrid – them again – in the quarter-finals of the Champions League. We lost 3–1 and couldn't reverse it at home, inflicting another European disappointment on ourselves.

Looking back, I believe I can divide my eight years at Liverpool into three parts. In the first two seasons, I earned my place, gained the respect of the fans and the club itself, and Klopp began to build a winning team. The next three seasons were about transforming and establishing Liverpool as the best team in the world. I was at my peak, and shone at the club and for the Brazilian national team. The last three seasons, starting with the empty grounds, were tough for me. Sitting on the bench at a stadium is worse than being in detention at school. The Boss made me go through that a few times that first season after the Premier League title.

Another moment around then that bothered me was what I thought was an exaggerated telling-off over a haircut.

Well, actually, it wasn't that simple. It *was* my fault – and I should make that clear from the beginning. We were still in the pandemic, during another reopening phase, in 2021, and players were allowed to receive visitors. In this case, the hairdresser. Lots of us footballers like to change our looks and go for different hairstyles. Our next game was against Arsenal in London and Klopp asked us on the Thursday not to have anyone come round the day before the match. Most of the guys had already had their haircuts, but my appointment was scheduled for the next day. Honestly, I didn't think it would be a problem. When I arrived at the club, of course, everyone noticed that I had had a cut and someone must have mentioned it to Klopp. The Boss came to the gym, where I was working out, and gave me a real going over. Then after training, when we had a team meeting about the game, he did it again – in front of everyone. He said that nobody should disrespect his orders and that I would be fined.

I was in the wrong and I knew it. I didn't say a word. But was all of that necessary? Did I get a telling-off that was, well, a little over the top, *because* he knew I would stay quiet? Alisson and Fabinho, for example, told me later that they would have reacted differently if the Boss had spoken to them that way.

That Friday night, I sent a message to the coach: 'Boss, sending this message to apologize again. I didn't intend to disrespect you! It was done without thinking. I had already organized it with the barber and we took all the safety precautions, as always. Nothing justifies my mistake. I'm upset that I disappointed you. It won't happen again, see you tomorrow.'

Klopp replied: 'Don't worry anymore. I said what I had to say. You got a fine and now it's forgotten! Sleep well, Bobby.'

The next day, we defeated Arsenal at the Emirates. And the fine I was going to receive was forgiven.

That was just an isolated incident, but it shows how strange everything was during the season. With all the competitions overlapping, no break from one tournament to the next, and with the exhaustion, the lost minutes and lack of a crowd, I couldn't find a way to reach the level I had been at in previous years. Everything felt strange from the reduced pre-season. I never got into the rhythm, I scored only nine goals; it was my least productive year at Liverpool.

Not that it was a season to forget entirely. In the end, we secured direct qualification for the Champions League. And that happened because of a historic game, a truly epic moment that will be remembered forever.

On 16 May 2021 I stepped onto the field for the first time wearing the captain's armband of Liverpool Football Club: a very special, emotional moment for me, one of great responsibility. The game was played at West Brom and we were fifth, chasing Chelsea and Leicester for a spot in the Champions League. After all those losses and being knocked out by Real Madrid, the team had improved again and found its attacking form. But to keep our objective alive, we needed to beat West Brom and it was fast becoming one of those days when things just didn't seem to be going our way. There were many missed chances, including me hitting the crossbar when I should have scored. We reached injury time with the score at 1–1, a result that virtually took us out of the race for a top-four finish.

Then an angel appeared, flying high. It was Alisson. My brother of faith had received the saddest news of his life three months earlier: the death of his father, José Agostinho Becker, who drowned in a lake on the family's property in southern Brazil.

Alisson's father had been baptized at my home in England, along with my sister, Marcella. He was a great man and very close to his sons. He was an amateur goalkeeper and an inspiration to Muriel, his oldest son, and Alisson – both of whom became professional goalkeepers. José Agostinho always asked his son to go up for a header when the team needed it most, in the final minutes of any match. On that rainy day Alisson did just that. He rose higher than everyone else, as he usually does, and gave us victory. The stadium was empty and the cheers that came from our throats echoed everywhere. A goalkeeper's goal! It was simply unbelievable, one of the most emotional moments I've ever experienced wearing the Liverpool shirt – especially as captain. Alisson dedicated the goal to his father, the goal that would eventually secure our place in the Champions League. There wouldn't be another European final, no attempt at the quadruple, nothing of what was to come ahead, without that epic afternoon.

We won the last two games, ending the season with the five consecutive victories we needed. On the final day we had help from Aston Villa, who defeated Chelsea, and Tottenham, who came from behind to beat Leicester. We did our part with a 2–0 victory over Crystal Palace. That day, for the first time at Anfield since March 2020, the authorities allowed a limited number of fans to attend. The

UK had vaccinated almost the entire population quickly and the pandemic finally began to recede. Ten thousand people were present as life returned to Anfield at last.

And if the crowd was back, we would be back too.

Chapter 18

Red Party

A few days before the 2022 Champions League final, Jordan Henderson went around asking us whether we wanted to do an open-topped bus parade around Liverpool – even if we lost in Paris. The captain listened to the players and then reported back to the club. Although we had just missed out on the Premier League title by a single point on the final day *again*, destroying our dream of winning the quadruple, and despite the fact that we could still be denied another European Cup by Real Madrid, and much as some harboured doubts over what to do, the answer was: yes.

Whatever happened now, we felt we owed the fans that. We owed ourselves too. The quadruple had already escaped us and, of course, we knew there was the possibility of being left standing on the top deck with only the two domestic cups, but the fact we even had a chance to win all four right up to the very last week of the season was something to be proud of; 2021–22 had been extraordinary. Up until that point, we had played 63 games – every single match it was possible for us to play – and lost just three all season. We hadn't had the chance to celebrate winning the League Cup or the FA Cup because the campaign had been so relentless. In fact, the pandemic meant that we hadn't had the chance to celebrate the previous year's Premier League title either, not properly with our supporters: this, at last, was the first opportunity to share those achievements with them. And, of course, we still believed that this time we could defeat Madrid and return as European champions.

We didn't.

Instead, we came back having suffered another devastating, even more incomprehensible defeat. It was painful and, truth be told, the parade now felt like something we could do without. All those reasons to board the bus without the Champions League trophy didn't feel like very good reasons any more. The two trophies we had won were, we knew, the two least important – and, in that moment, felt like none at all. As we flew back from France it was hard not to feel like the whole season had been worth nothing; like everything we had worked for was gone. There had been a gathering for all the players and their families in Paris after the game – a party that went on a long time even if it lacked the jubilation we had hoped for – and we were all exhausted and sad. The atmosphere was completely flat, no consolation possible. We also didn't know how the fans would react, what the reception would be like. They had been defeated and, for many, the experience of that final had been horrendous, with all sorts of problems around the stadium. They were hardly going to be in the mood to line the streets now. Their dreams had been destroyed too. We weren't sure how we could look them in the eye.

While it had been an extraordinary season collectively, for me, on an individual level, it was the worst of my life: a difficult year in which I had struggled with injuries and at times had felt disconected, separate, like I was not part of it. We didn't even get the ending that would have made all that suffering feel worthwhile. Instead, I felt empty. I was upset, angry: we had been beaten by Madrid again and maybe our last chance to win another European Cup had gone. I had played just 13 minutes in the final. I was hurt; I didn't have the enthusiasm to do anything. How were we, or the fans, supposed to enjoy the parade? It was going to feel like a punishment – or so we thought.

And then we landed in Liverpool.

And there, over a half a million people were waiting for us. The best fans in the world. We had fallen short on our mission, but it had meant something, after all.

'Mission' was the word. This was not one of those situations where, as the season went on and something extraordinary started to look plausible, no one dared mention the word '*quadruple*'. This was something we had set as a target from the start. Usually, the cups were not a priority for the Boss. But that year, perhaps due to what had happened the previous season when we had finished empty-handed, and perhaps because the cup competitions were the only thing we had not won under him, Klopp started by saying he wanted to compete for every trophy. In practice, he still rotated the team in the League Cup, but there was something about the discourse that was different.

Above all, what was different were the grounds – and that also gave us the hope that this could be a better season, provided the motivation to make it so and make up for lost time. After winning the Premier League title in the pandemic year, 2020–21 had been a sad season. We were deeply affected by the empty stadiums: the team's intensity dropped and we couldn't compete in the same way. Personally, as I noted, I just couldn't get used to playing without anyone watching. Now, though, the crowds were back: even pre-season against Spanish sides Osasuna and Athletic Club Bilbao, there were 40,000 people at Anfield. We hadn't seen a crowd like that since we had faced Atlético Madrid in the Champions League a year and a half before and it was wonderful. I felt good and I could tell that my teammates did too. Maybe that's why the Boss decided to go after everything we could win – and, sure enough, we went unbeaten in our first ten league games and won all six of the group matches in the Champions League.

Winning the title would mean beating Manchester City, we knew. And I can tell you something, for sure: we weren't afraid to face them. We respected them, of course. But fear? Never. And most of the time we were better than them when we faced off. I believe some of the City players didn't enjoy playing against us at all because we took them out of their comfort zone – something other teams rarely did.

Klopp or Guardiola? Who's better? Many years have passed with fans, journalists and former players debating this question. Naturally, there's no correct answer. It's a matter of taste and opinions. It can also be about results or titles, depending on how you want to analyse this show-down of super-coaches that I had the privilege to experience from the best possible place: the pitch.

Guardiola is a brilliant coach, a true genius. It was incredible how often during a game it seemed like we had one less man on the field, as they were always seeking overloads. If you give them space, they destroy you. And the one with the solution to that was Jürgen Klopp – who had been involved in a similar battle in Germany where, as a Hoffenheim player, I had seen his Borussia Dortmund side take on Guardiola's Bayern Munich. Klopp is really great at playing with a high press, which is exactly the way you need to play against Guardiola's City: take risks, run relentlessly, close every space, never let them play.

Of course, it's easy to say and a lot harder to actually do. Many coaches have tried and few have succeeded. None quite like Klopp, though; no team challenged them like us. I always felt like we were the better side overall. And, before anyone comes up with a list of titles or something, let me tell you how the numbers turned out during the period I played for Liverpool while Klopp and Pep were in charge: in Premier League games, we won four, lost five and drew five. In knockout matches, with me on the pitch Liverpool won four times, drew once and never lost. In total, we won eight, drew six and lost five times to them in 19 matches. We had the psychological advantage. That season we drew both games 2–2 and were determined to push them all the way to the finish again.

The problem was that it was all well and good *us* competing against them – we needed other teams to do the same.

As for me, I had problems of my own. On a personal level it felt like 2021–22 was all bad news. Every time things looked like they were falling into place, something else went wrong. It's strange to look back on a season that was building towards being Liverpool's best ever and reflect on how awful it was for me, disconnected from that mission. I suffered four injuries, each of which kept me out for a month or more, denying me the opportunity to make a contribution that might have carried us over the line as we chased the quarduple, and also ruining my chances of making it to the 2022 World Cup.

To understand how I began to lose my place in the national team, we need to go back to the previous summer and that transition from one season to the next. The pandemic had affected Liverpool badly and me especially; it had also meant that Brazil went a long time without playing, breaking the momentum and bringing uncertainty. Brazil coach Tite seemed to have lost some of his previous convictions about certain players. He shuffled the team a lot, even rotating the goalkeepers, and the promise that I would be the starting number 9 in the cycle between World Cups was fading. Richarlison gained favour with the coaching staff and I found myself back on the substitutes' bench. The feeling within the group wasn't the same either and, although the Copa América was again played in Brazil because of the pandemic, it was in empty stadiums and we lost the final to Argentina at the Maracanã.

Again, the summer break was short, but unlike at the Copa América, when the football restarted in England the fans were back and that gave me a huge boost, a feeling of optimism. I felt like I was starting anew, like life was returning to normal. Alas, the optimism didn't last long. In just the third game, a draw against Chelsea, I left the field with a hamstring injury. It was the start of a run of physical setbacks that scuppered everything.

There's nothing harder for a professional than being in treatment and recovery. Kept away from what you love, the loneliness feels endless. The training schedules differ from those of the other players; you don't even see them. Isolated, you lose the camaraderie, the contact, the fun. In this challenging year, I learned a lot on a personal level. I deepened my relationship with Christ. God tended to my heart while I was off the field. I spent more time with my daughters, began to appreciate other things that were close to me. But, still, how I missed football.

I always tried to bring a positive attitude to my teammates whenever I saw them. I would go to every game at Anfield, even if I couldn't play. I'd arrive two hours before and hang out with the guys in the cafeteria, trying to create a good atmosphere, always offering words of encouragement, helping them in any way I could. It helped me too; it made them see me as part of the team and made me feel part of it. This is something every player should do when they're injured.

Although I started playing again in September, that injury delayed my return to the national team and to Liverpool's starting line-up. When we drew 2–2 with Manchester City at the start of October, I was on the bench, and when the Brazil squad was named for the three South American qualifiers later that month, I wasn't in it.

I hadn't sat out an international break for a long time; with so many tournaments the routine had been brutal, so at least there was an opportunity to clear my mind and recharge, to get back to my best. Those were difficult days at home. Larissa, who was 37 weeks pregnant, had contracted Covid, which left us very worried. Lina and João, who supported us, also got Covid and had to go into quarantine at home. I stayed isolated from the family, spending much of my day working at the club and praying for everyone's health. When they improved and the Premier League returned, I was in good shape. A starter again, the next couple of weeks were wonderful, like an entire season distilled, hope returning.

I scored my second hat-trick in a Liverpool shirt in a 5–0 victory at Watford, celebrating the third by placing the ball under my shirt in honour of our daughter Liz, who was due to be born any moment. Next we had the chance for a little revenge over Atlético Madrid, beating them 3–2 in the stadium where we had won the Champions League three years earlier, but not before Antoine Griezmann was sent off for kicking me in the face – which really, really hurt. After that, we smashed Manchester United 5–0 at Old Trafford in another massive show of strength from our team. And then, at the end of October, Tite called me back to the Brazil squad.

The next day, I was in the team hotel preparing for a home

game with Brighton when I got the wonderful news that our third daughter had finally been born. God had given me another beautiful and healthy child; I was playing well and feeling good, up and running properly, and was back in the Brazilian national team. Everything was fine, right?

Not for long.

On as a substitute, I lasted just 33 minutes of our next match, against Atlético Madrid at Anfield. Another hamstring injury forced me to pull out of the Brazil squad and sent me back into that spiral, that terrible routine of pain, recovery and isolation. Two long months passed before I could play again, in an epic League Cup game with Leicester that we drew 3–3 and won in a shootout, during which I scored my penalty. I had needed that – the adrenaline, the excitement of playing again – and although the team stumbled a bit, allowing Manchester City to open a lead at the top, by January I had reclaimed my starting position from Diogo Jota.

I felt I was playing well again, but Tite didn't include me in the Brazil squad for the February international break. For the first time, I began to worry about my future in the national team. It was already 2022, a World Cup year, and this was the first time I wasn't included for footballing rather than medical reasons. Worse, I then got injured yet again. I had scored a header against Inter in the San Siro as we continued our superb form in the Champions

League, where we had won every game, but as I sat there in the dressing room afterwards I could feel a pain in my thigh. It was unbelievable, just so frustrating, and it was becoming the story of the season. I'd get an injury, work hard to come back, regain my place, and just when I was getting back into the groove, finding my form and helping the team again, bang, another injury would strike. This latest setback kept me out for another month, forcing me to miss the League Cup final against Chelsea, where we won our first trophy in an extraordinary shootout which ended with our goalkeeper, Caoimhin Kelleher, scoring the winner with the 11th penalty. It wasn't until mid-March that I was fit again, by which time I had been left out of another Brazil squad and lost my place with my club. It was frustrating, hard to take. In the mind of a competitive guy like me, you think: 'I fought back. I worked for this. I should be back on the pitch.' It's difficult when that doesn't happen. And that was increasingly the case.

Collectively, the momentum was building. In Europe we were on the verge of the semi-final, having beaten Benfica 3–1 in the quarter-final first leg. We were in the semi-final of the FA Cup, against Manchester City. And in the Premier League, ten consecutive wins had seen us catch up with Manchester City. Always them. Between us we had dominated English football over four years and now, yet again, it was going to become a straight battle for the title.

The date marked in red was 10 April, billed as a 'final' for the league. A direct showdown in Manchester, it was the start of six days that would define our season, in which we played City twice with Benfica in-between. Win at the Etihad and we would go top.

Did I mention that I hate being on the bench? Well, I hate being on the bench. It was 2–2 in Manchester and there were only six minutes left when I finally came on, denied the opportunity to help my teammates. That midweek I started against Benfica in the Champions League, scored twice in a 3–3 draw and thought I had done enough to be back in the line-up when we faced City again. But guess what? None of that happened. I was benched again and, when I came on with only five minutes left, I managed to get injured once more. This felt never-ending now, a vicious circle that I just couldn't get out of. Still, 3–0 up on 45 minutes, although City pulled two back and we were made to hold on towards the end, we had reached another final. The issue was, I wasn't sure I would get there. I felt a pain I had never felt before when I kicked the ball or twisted my foot. It felt like a sprain, but wasn't. My foot didn't swell on top and neither did my ankle. Only the sole swelled. It was unbearable, as if there was a knife under my foot cutting into me constantly. I underwent countless tests, but nothing serious showed up. I tried physiotherapy, tried everything. All that was left was to kneel down and pray. The doctors called it *plantar fasciitis* (inflammation of tissue along the bottom of the foot); for me, it felt like the end of the world. It was the fourth time that season that I had been kept away from training and the teammates I loved spending time with; away from the big moments I lived for; away from the dream of the World Cup; away from the pitch, the place I was happiest. It crushed my heart and my mood.

Already League Cup winners, in the FA Cup final, in the Champions League semi-final, and just a point behind City in the Premier League ... everyone was talking about a historic quadruple and I wasn't part of it. Not playing, not participating, not involved. I was not happy.

I watched us beat Villarreal in the Champions League and slip three points behind City after a draw against Tottenham, but with the season reaching its climax and a shot at history appearing before us, I did manage to make another comeback in time for the FA Cup final against Chelsea at Wembley on 14 May. There was another target in my mind too: I was absolutely determined to make it to the Champions League final two weeks after that. Kyiv had hurt so badly; it was time for revenge against Real Madrid and I was preparing for a shot at redemption. The FA Cup final against Chelsea ended in a goalless draw and we won on penalties again. The tension was astonishing. When it came to my spot-kick – the third – Édouard Mendy read my intentions, dived the right way and reached the ball. There's a moment, a tiny fraction of a second, when everything stops: you can see the goalkeeper's glove on the ball and, in that instant, you think he's going to save it. Thankfully, this time he couldn't and, a couple of penalties later, with the score at 5–5, my great friend Alisson saved Mason Mount's penalty, leaving Konstantinos Tsimikas to score the winner. Kostas couldn't have been more delighted: it was the biggest day of his career so far and his happiness was infectious. Football is a team sport where everyone has a role to play, but sometimes it's down to a single man to become a hero or villain, to live a unique moment. That time, Tsimikas was our hero.

Not that there was time to celebrate, which was a pity. Looking back, we never really had a chance to enjoy it: the pursuit of everything was too relentless, the margins too fine. There were three games left and two more trophies; our entire season depended on them.

Except that we knew our fate was not in our own hands; with City three points ahead, it was likely that the league was beyond us, but we had to do everything we could just in case something unexpected happened.

Something like this: three days later we came from behind to beat Southampton and Manchester City, who had been thrashing everyone and didn't give us the slightest hope of winning the title, stumbled to an unforeseen draw with

West Ham. Once again, just like in 2019, we entered the final Sunday separated by a solitary point.

I've already told you what I think. We were a better team than City in our direct clashes. Between 2019 and 2022 they won the Premier League three times while we only won it once. In my view, that statistic distorts reality. Add up those four seasons and you'll see they only got one point more than us (358 to 357). It would have been more just – a more faithful portrait of our battle – for both sides to have won two leagues each.

For one brief moment it looked like it might actually work out that way, that justice would be done. In 2019 somehow we knew that City were going to win every game, that they just weren't going to give us the chance, but 2022 was different. There was hope, however small; a belief that maybe, just maybe, City could drop points. It had happened against West Ham; now we needed it to happen once more. In the days before that final weekend in the Premier league, I sent Philippe Coutinho a message telling him he and his Aston Villa team, managed by Liverpool legend Steven Gerrard, had to help us out. They tried. On the final day, Aston Villa went 2–0 up against City. With only 20 minutes left in the whole season, City needed to score three times. As for us, we needed to score as well. We were drawing 1–1 with Wolves, but there was real hope, a genuine chance. The roar from Anfield had told us that. It was actually in our hands, or so it seemed. We could do this. We could win the league. The whole lot. That impossible mission was close now, real. We went for it, with everything we had. Anfield was urging us forward. *This was it.*

And then, suddenly, there was silence. From the away end the Wolves fans started celebrating. And kept celebrating. It didn't matter to them, but they enjoyed watching us fall, the banter. We knew from their reaction, from the silence, that something was going wrong. Somehow City scored three times and, although we kept going, although we got the goals we would have needed through Mo Salah and Andy Robertson, it had gone. We had lost the Premier League by a single point on the final day.

Again.

Same story, same frustration.

And yet also the same wonderful shot at redemption, the same chance to end it all in triumph.

In that crazy 2021–22 season there was no time to celebrate, no time to lament your fate. Did you lose? Did you win? It doesn't matter. There's a game tomorrow, go again. My word, we had to be mentally strong that year. Just like in 2019, there was a Champions League final to come days after the Premier League disappointment. And there were familiar opponents too; the team that, like City, had denied us what we felt we deserved. Real Madrid again, this time in Paris.

I had never been able to swallow that defeat by them in 2018 in Kyiv. That had been a very peculiar game, with Salah's injury and Karius's mistakes. Now maybe we had a chance to overcome that. We had proven we could be champions, both in Europe and in England; we were more experienced, stronger, a better team than before. Although Madrid had reached that final again, it had taken the most incredible, almost surreal run of miracles against PSG, Chelsea and City. You could talk about luck, but maybe there was something else, and maybe that run was a warning. I don't know why things never went right for us against Madrid. We always came into our meetings with them flying, playing better than them; we always approached the match thinking we were better, believing we would win. Often we played a way that meant we should win too. And then, one way or the other, it didn't happen. Perhaps some players felt the pressure of facing Real Madrid. There's something about them, about that shirt, their history, their ability to win.

Despite my admiration for Barcelona as a child, despite my passion for Ronaldinho Gaúcho, I have to admit it would have been really cool to wear that white shirt – the winning mentality they have suits me. In fact, there were inquiries after my departure from Liverpool, and I would have given up a lot to play for Madrid, but it didn't work out because the timings didn't quite fit; my family and I preferred not to wait for the end of the transfer window in 2023. But I would have liked to have seen from the inside what I suffered from the outside. It's not that shirt alone that wins games, but when those players pull it on they feel capable of anything and maybe some opponents feel intimidated by that.

And yet, we still thought we could win in Paris.

I have to tell you that in all my years at Liverpool, that was the moment when I felt most disappointed with Jürgen Klopp. After so many injuries and setbacks, I was fine, ready to play. I had worked so hard to be fit. Our trio – Firmino, Salah and Mané – had unfinished business with Madrid. I should have started. But Klopp picked Luis Díaz, who had arrived a few months earlier. I have nothing against Luis, of course: he's a talented player and a really nice guy. But that was a game to draw on the experience of those who had lived through it all before, who had that extra motivation. I felt like it would be my last Champions League final, like this opportunity wasn't going to come around for me again. We already knew that Sadio Mané wanted to go and, although I had tried to convince him to stay, that this could be the trio's last game together.

It wasn't just me who was surprised by the Boss's decisions. At the end of the match Vinícius Júnior, who scored the winner, came to me and asked why the manager hadn't put me on from the beginning. I think Klopp's decisions made things easier for Madrid in that final. Vinícius wanted me to play with him at Real Madrid, and I was told he did pull some strings to try to make it work, but it didn't just depend on the two of us. He's a great lad, a star.

I can't deny it. I was left with a bitter taste. The season ended with two cups, true – two I hadn't won yet at Liverpool. But it also ended with two titles lost in a painful, frustrating way; the two biggest titles as well, the two that really mattered. To lose just four games *all year* and for that to end with 'only' the FA Cup and League Cup was hard to take. To watch us dominate Madrid and not find a way through, to watch them score with the only chance they had, hurt. To have to do it from the bench hurt even more. Thibaut Courtois had the game of his life, saving everything. I was furious at not playing. I only got on for 13 minutes, and such a short spell rarely works: you don't get into the game. I didn't get a single chance; if I had, that was one shot Courtois wouldn't have stopped.

We had played every single game that season and had little to show for it. By the end some of my teammates were exhausted. Klopp's work is intense – all the time, every training session – and it was starting to affect some of the older guys. I have the same mentality as Klopp, though: I like to run, to work. But the truth is: the guys were getting a bit tired of it all. It works and the team is always in good shape; the problem is that the repetition, over and over, wears you down mentally. There's also the fear of injuries. I'm not saying my injuries were related to that, but the fact is, my body suffered, it paid for those years of intensity with no respite. And while things improved subsequently, with more rest days granted, the pursuit of that quadruple took a toll, which perhaps was most felt in the following season, when the adrenaline subsided.

That night in Paris there was a meal and a party. Klopp was the one who celebrated most; it was as if he felt the responsibility to cheer us up, to encourage us, to convince us that despite the way we felt, we had done something special, we were not to let defeat sink us. That wasn't easy, and facing our fans wouldn't be either. It was a long night, we hadn't slept much, we were tired. Some were hungover too. All of us felt flat. I was upset: another Champions League final lost, another defeat to Real Madrid, and I hadn't even played. The last thing I wanted to do was go around the city on a bus.

But, of course, when we arrived in Liverpool and saw our fans, everything changed. They brought me back; they brought all of us back. The sadness and the anger began to fade and was replaced by something better. The parade was epic. All along the nine-mile route, the fans were packed in, waving, singing, welcoming us home. And it *was* home; there was no place like it. There were people *everywhere*. They had climbed onto roofs, clambered up traffic lights and hung from road signs. Everything was engulfed in red smoke. Above all, we were engulfed in love.

The season had started with the fans as the protagonists, with the grounds finally full again – and it ended in the same way. These Liverpool supporters are truly unique, there's nothing like them in the world. I was so moved by what they did for us, the way they showed their appreciation for our efforts, for everything that the team had done for Liverpool. It all felt worthwhile again. I had started the day stepping off the plane from Paris looking like a man eating rotten food and ended it having one of the happiest, most fulfilling, most emotional experiences of my life. No, there was no quadruple, but there was a big and well deserved party, *sí, señor.*

Chapter 19

A Fond Farewell

On 3 March 2023 I began typing the farewell message on my cell phone that I was going to read to my coach Jürgen Klopp, a friend I'd made in football and with whom I'd achieved so many things over eight years. As you already know, English isn't a language I have completely mastered. It was a significant moment in my life, so I preferred to write the message beforehand; it was better than standing in front of the Boss and choosing my words poorly. 'Meeting' was the title of the note on my iPhone. It consisted of just four paragraphs to tell him that I was leaving:

MEETING . . .

First of all . . . I want to say thank you to God, for bringing us together for a great purpose at this amazing club.

Yesterday I spoke with my family and I made a decision that I no longer want to stay here at the club.

I believe that my cycle here is ending . . .

Thank you so much . . .

But, I'm here to tell you that I'm still very motivated and I want to keep up the hard work, and am looking forward to these last three or four months, to reach our goals.

Those words hurt deep inside. Because the truth is, I didn't want to leave Liverpool. If someone had told me in July 2022 that, a year later, I'd be writing a book about my eight seasons at Liverpool, looking back on a period that had come to an end, I probably would have laughed. I'd have thought it was a joke. I couldn't see myself outside Liverpool; there was no chance of me leaving. But not everything in life goes as planned, for it is God who is in control. Why did things change so drastically in just a short eight-month period?

After the new disappointment against Real Madrid in the 2021–22 UEFA Champions League final, it was vacation time. The season had been dreadful for me in terms of injuries and not starting many important games, like the final in Paris. It was time to clear my mind and rest my body, as a World Cup was on the horizon. I've said it before, but it's worth repeating: there's nothing greater for a footballer than representing their country in a World Cup – at least for us Brazilians. A year had passed since

I was last called up and I needed to be ready to make up for lost time. We returned to Maceió with our three daughters – Valentina, Bella and seven-month-old Liz. The final year of my contract with Liverpool was about to begin, but, honestly, that was irrelevant to me. I was not entertaining the idea of moving.

Then during those days on holiday, Roger Wittmann – a partner at Rogon, the agency that has always managed my career – spoke to me and Larissa. 'Start imagining, perhaps, living in other countries. Tell me your dreams. Where do you want to live? The United States? Somewhere else? Give me a club, a dream, and we'll go after it. Tell me what you want me to do for you.' It was as if he already knew that my time at Liverpool was coming to an end.

'I want to stay,' I replied.

And I did want to stay: the thought of leaving Liverpool never even crossed my mind. I didn't want to hear offers or consider other options, didn't want to even contemplate living anywhere else. During those same holidays in Maceió, the Lord alerted me of His plans through Pastor Daniel. This event occurred when I was at church, and God spoke to me clearly, but I was stubborn and didn't want to listen. The pastor said, 'Yes, son, you're leaving, I know. But it's okay. God is in control and He will guide you; the Lord will give you a better place.' I didn't think much of it at the time; I would only remember this conversation, this warning, many months later, and then it felt like it made sense.

In August 2022, while still on pre-season, Liverpool told my representatives that they wanted me to stay as well. A contract renewal wasn't something I lost sleep over back then; it seemed like a formality, a matter of time.

True, Liverpool had signed Darwin Núñez in the summer transfer market and, before him, in the middle of the previous season, Luis Díaz had arrived. Both came from the Portuguese league: Darwin played for Benfica, Luis for Porto. Some people had already speculated that I might lose playing time, but I never saw their transfers as threats and we welcomed them with open arms. Our family was known at Liverpool for warmly receiving new players and their families. We wanted to give what we had received, to do for them what Lucas, Philippe Coutinho and others had done for us.

Luis integrated seamlessly and joined our dinners. Darwin attended a few times. They became friends. Internal competition is healthy, but it mustn't turn into rivalry, or the whole group suffers. They were always invited to birthday parties, barbecues and lunches. We would meet to play pool, listen to music, chat – all of which was aimed at helping them integrate. Everyone went crazy for our Brazilian version of hot dogs: with sausage, bacon, vinagrette dressing, peas, shoestring potatoes, grated cheese, mustard and our spectacular homemade garlic mayonnaise.

Díaz started in the final against Real Madrid in Paris and also in other crucial games towards the end of the 2021–22 season. As I've said, it had been a terrible year for me in terms of injuries. I missed the final of the League Cup and the Champions League semi-finals. I wasn't called up for the Brazilian national team. But I believed the space I'd lost was due to injuries and physical matters, not the manager's preference.

The transfer window was also marked by Salah's three-year extension and Sadio Mané's departure to Bayern Munich. I was deeply saddened by my close friend's departure, someone I had shared six years with, experienced great moments with, and learned to love. It marked the end of our historic trio. My repeated injuries meant the trio had already been playing less anyway, but now the separation was definitive. Díaz was showing that he could be a natural replacement for Mané on the left. Diogo Jota had been with us for some time. Looking back now, Darwin Núñez's signing indicated the club was looking for another number 9 for the years ahead. But I still felt ready to continue. My mindset was to stay with the club as a key player and regain my place in the Brazilian national team.

On 12 July we kicked off the pre-season with a friendly against Manchester United in Thailand. We lost 4–0. We would get our revenge in style in the Premier League, but perhaps that was an early sign of the tumultuous season ahead. And yet, besides the initial thrashing, everything went normally during pre-season until the first competitive match of the year: Manchester City, again, for the Community Shield. We began the game with the new attacking trio: Salah, Firmino and Díaz. We won 3–1, starting the season by lifting a trophy against our long-time rivals.

Díaz has a slightly different style from Mané, who had a greater presence in the box and scoring instinct. The young Colombian still had some way to go to adapt to the rhythm of the Premier League and the intensity of the game, but he was progressing.

We knew, from the experience of previous years, that starting the Premier League strongly was crucial. You could not afford to drop points, even early on. The totals would be too high for that. But that's not exactly what happened. The truth is, the first two months of the season were terrible. In the Premier League we won only two out of the first eight games, and suffered a 4–1 thrashing by Napoli in our Champions League debut. By the time we lost 3–2 to Arsenal in October, we found ourselves 14 points behind the leaders. Nobody wanted this, of course; nobody had expected it either. It was, by far, our worst start to a year since Klopp's arrival.

Some of our players started the season fatigued, following the strain from attempting to secure the quadruple the previous season. We had played every possible match in 2021–22 and I could see that some players were bothered by the extremely high intensity of Klopp's work and repetitive training. It's true that those demands produce results – we always performed at a high level – and that intensity had been a trademark of our team in recent years. But I believe fatigue slipped in. I love running, working, helping my teammates, but not everyone is accustomed to that German mentality and those seasons had been extremely hard. Players don't mind playing all the time; it doesn't matter if the game is big or small, if it's a more or less important competition. But training is a different story and maybe it was inevitable that it would have an impact.

And yet that wasn't the case for me. I was far from tired: I had missed four months of games due to injury, recovered during the holidays, and felt ready to start again, determined to make up for lost time. I could see though that others were tired, especially mentally, after many years of relentless, intense grind, repetitive training and so many games. We had lost Mané, Thiago Alcântara had injuries, young lads were joining the team. There was a shift and the squad was not yet on the same page. It was yet to become a united group with a single purpose and identity; a transitional period was already underway.

On a personal level, I was starting to find my best form again. I scored in the only games we won at the beginning of the Premier League: the incredible 9–0 against Bournemouth and the 2–1 against a strong Newcastle side – I had an exceptional performance that day. A few days later, the final call-up for the Brazilian national team for friendlies before the World Cup was announced and I was back on the list. I felt like things were starting to fall back into place.

I had been part of the entire cycle since the 2018 World Cup, starting in the Copa América we won and then in the South American qualifiers. I believed that injuries and Covid had kept me out of the recent call-ups, and I had now overcome that. The return to form and that September call-up showed that I was back, the dream was alive. It was wonderful to reunite with my teammates for so many blessed moments wearing the yellow shirt. I love the players, the atmosphere, the conversations – everything that comes with representing my country. I sent several messages to my wife during those days, sharing my happiness for being there and the love I felt for the Brazilian national team. The friendlies would take place in France. I couldn't have been looking forward to it more.

But I didn't play a single minute. Against Ghana and Tunisia in September, I watched everything from the bench. Coach Tite didn't say a thing and questions swirled in my head. It was all or nothing. Why had he called me up? If he didn't put me in to play, was it because I didn't need to prove anything anymore and was already in the World Cup squad? Or ... well, I didn't want to dwell on the second possibility. It didn't make sense. All I could do was keep working and hope.

Back home, Darwin Núñez had also started the season playing well and Klopp began alternating our presence in the line-up. Of course, this bothered me quite a bit. Unlike what had happened years ago, now the Boss wasn't offering many explanations about my selection – or lack thereof – as a starter. Previously, Klopp used to say that he was sparing me, keeping me fresh for important moments of the season. He usually offered a comforting word, some kind of explanation, knowing that I hated being on the bench. But now he didn't say anything. Perhaps he didn't feel he owed explanations for the decisions he made. I felt that we didn't have the same freedom as before to chat.

Meanwhile, my representatives were talking with the club about the contract renewal and disagreements were starting to arise. The club saw things one way, we saw them another. But I didn't want to know anything about that. I just wanted to play, work hard, score goals, help the team and head to the World Cup with Brazil. I didn't want to get distracted by those discussions, especially since leaving Liverpool simply wasn't an option for me and my family.

I wasn't a starter in the first two Champions League matches or the game against Arsenal, but I did come on at the Emirates and soon returned to the side. We thrashed Glasgow Rangers 7–1 in Scotland. We conceded the first but I scored a brace to turn it around and assisted Núñez for the third. The two of us started that game together, a tactical option the Boss hadn't tried yet.

At that point I had eight goals in nine matches. There were less than two months left until the World Cup and Klopp called me for a conversation in his hotel room before a match. 'We really want to keep you', he said. He insisted that if we just sorted out the salary, we could speed up the renewal process. I agreed with him. It shouldn't be a problem. I told him I would discuss the matter with my agents and ask them to finalize the deal. He reached out, showed interest, and I was happy. There was no way this could go wrong.

Not least because on the pitch things were improving. We beat Manchester City again, 1–0, which was a sign that we had the quality to become competitive once more. In the Champions League we managed to recover, winning five consecutive games after the heavy loss in Naples. The last match of the group stage was against Napoli again, and we won 2–0 with goals from Salah and Núñez. Tite, the Brazilian manager, attended the match to watch us. After the game Alisson, Fabinho and I were directed to Klopp's room at the stadium. The space had been lent to Tite for a conversation with us. The dialogue was quite interesting.

He blamed a planning mistake, a misuse of players, and apologized for not playing me in those September friendlies against the African teams. I was surprised. I said, 'That's fine.' I reiterated that I respected his work greatly, that we had been together for a long time and I trusted the decisions of the coaching staff. Fabinho later mentioned that, at the beginning of the conversation, he thought Tite was going to tell me I wouldn't be at the World Cup. But later, with the apology and how the conversation unfolded, he left the room with the opposite impression – that I would be in the squad.

Everyone knew that Alisson and Fabinho would be on the 26-player list for the Qatar World Cup, so it was easy to imagine that the coach had come to Liverpool specifically to watch me play and assess my physical condition. I didn't dwell on such thoughts while on the field; I played my usual game, getting involved all over the pitch. What I had done my whole life had brought me to the national team so there was no need for theatrics, no need to change. I just had to be myself. The Napoli game wasn't my best or worst; it was an ordinary game. A week later, the squad for the Qatar World Cup was announced.

I wasn't on the list.

As I write, the words come from my fingers with pain. It was deeply, unexpectedly hurtful. I was so disappointed. I had been part of the previous World Cup cycle, part of the

2022 World Cup cycle, the starting number 9 for almost three years. It was hard to understand and accept.

Today, looking back, I might be able to understand the coach's doubts about my physical condition. In the previous season, 2021–22, I had been sidelined by injury four times. During one of those spells, I was called up to play in the World Cup qualifiers for Brazil only to have to pull out with injury. In two other instances I had just returned from a month-long period without playing and it's natural that Tite didn't include me. But in the World Cup season, during those three months leading up to the call-up – August, September and October – I was playing and playing well. No injuries. I was flying!

My club coach, Klopp, was quite surprised, publicly saying the decision was 'crazy'. To this day, as I write my book and tell my story, I have never received a single message or a phone call from Tite, and that's something that hurts me deeply. We spent many years together, sharing many moments of joy and sadness, of camaraderie.

A week later, the squad was announced, I received an audio message from César Sampaio, the former Brazilian national team player who was part of Tite's coaching staff and who is a fellow Christian. César thanked me for all those years and said, 'It's never easy, but decisions had to be made by the coaching staff.' He also asked me to stay prepared and alert; I was the first reserve if anyone had to pull out. Hoping that someone gets injured is impossible. That thread of hope was much smaller than the sorrow I was feeling. Friends from Liverpool, Alisson and Fabinho, also sent me messages, saying they would miss me in Qatar. And Claudio Taffarel, the goalkeeper who won the World Cup in 1994 and trains with Alisson at Liverpool, did the same. No other players called me or messaged me.

I believed that everything I had done in all the previous years, and the form I was in during the season, should have been enough to earn me Tite's trust. With the news, it felt like the world was collapsing around me. I thought about many things, tried to find answers. So many thoughts go round your mind, so many reasons why it might have happened. You search for something to make sense of it all. And the more you think, the more it hurts, the more it eats away at you.

I had never played for a big Brazilian club so I was never really favoured by the media back home, which is more focused on domestic football during moments like these, more likely to favour the footballers they see daily. There was never any support, any media or public pressure on my behalf. Perhaps I'm partly to blame for this, for not being the type of guy who courted attention, or tried to build relationships with journalists so that they would lobby for me. I didn't give interviews, rarely appeared in public, didn't talk much. It just wasn't me. I was too shy for that and never believed I needed it either; it didn't even occur to me. Surely, those who followed football closely knew I was good, knew what I was capable of? Were there other interests that went against me? I don't know.

This is how the Lord wanted it to be; this was His plan.

I wouldn't be going to Qatar.

It was time to lean on Jesus Christ and my family, which would grow again. Larissa was pregnant with another girl: Sophia was on her way.

On Instagram I posted a message wishing my friends luck in their quest for the sixth World Cup title – and then I forgot I had social media. I wanted to isolate myself from the world. Such sorrows make me unbearable: I get irritated with everything and become moody. We thought about several destinations, places to get away from it all, but, in almost all of them, it was clear that escaping football was impossible. In the end we went to clear our minds and enjoy a break in the Maldives with the children. The deep sadness and the desire to be in Qatar made it impossible for me to watch the World Cup. The two biggest sorrows I've had in football were losing the first Champions League final against Real Madrid in 2018 and not being called up in 2022. I saw the results on my cell phone, but didn't want to see anything. I felt rejected by everyone.

In the Maldives I felt loved again; a place of great hospitality, people there treated me with real kindness. It was also a period of deeper connection with Jesus, when I found an inner peace. I learned to trust in the plan the Lord had prepared for me. Reading the Bible became my routine.

Refreshed after the short holiday, it was time to start thinking about Liverpool again. The club organized a training camp in Dubai. There, of course, it was impossible not to see football or the World Cup. Having avoided the opening matches, I did watch the Brazil versus Croatia quarter-final with some of my club mates. A very strange feeling came over me. Honestly, I didn't know whether I wanted Brazil to win that game and the cup or not. That haunted me; it bothered me deep inside. Representing the national team is every boy's dream. I had cheered so much for Brazil in so many World Cups, played in one, and I am proud to be able to tell everyone that I scored a goal in a World Cup wearing that yellow shirt, to have served my country. And I felt bad in that moment: I felt that selfishness and resentment were trying to take over my heart. I stopped watching the game and went up to my room to pray. I asked God to enlighten me, remove that bad feeling from me and help me overcome it.

When I left the room and was going down the stairs back to the area where the game was being broadcast, one of the staff at Liverpool told me Brazil were winning in extra-time, that Neymar had scored. And I was very happy. I thought about my close friends, about what the national team meant, and the feeling that came over me was one of joy – and also of relief for being happy.

But what followed was only sadness. Even before I reached the TV, Croatia had equalized. I watched the entire penalty shootout, in which Brazil were knocked out. After that, I didn't watch any more World Cup games. Would the story have been different if I were in Qatar? Who knows? I'm someone who likes to look forward, not backward. And in my mind that meant just one thing: Liverpool.

We returned from Dubai, and then it was time to definitively sort out my contract, which had always been my desire. I made my intentions clear to my agents. I wanted to stay. I didn't want to hear about offers from other European clubs or other parts of the world. My life was in Liverpool, my family was well adapted to the city, my older daughters were in school, the third was still a baby, and the fourth was in my wife's belly. We had friends there, the church that had been born in Manchester under our care, the affection of those people. Sure, people say Liverpool and Manchester are grey, rainy cities, but that never bothered us. Liverpool was home. Klopp had already called me into his hotel room to tell me he wanted me to stay at the club and, in an interview in January, he said he didn't see any problems with the extension going through: 'Bobby is very important to us, he knows his importance, and negotiations like this are completely normal.'

But the two sides were drifting apart instead of aligning. A difference in opinion about my role was emerging. In the view of my representatives, I was a top-tier player in world football and should be given a renewal that reflected that. From the club's business perspective, Roberto Firmino's peak had passed. My salary was quite high, significant investments had been made in new players and some contract extensions. There was also an expectation that the club's revenue would be reduced since securing a spot in the Champions League was looking less likely.

What complicated matters further was that I couldn't play. After the short vacation in the Maldives, back in December, I injured my calf in a training session and the recovery time was estimated at two weeks. I was anxious to play and, after ten days, I felt fine. I went to do some stretching before training and tore my calf again, which meant another five or six weeks of recovery. My wife was trying to open my eyes and she kept saying to me, 'Roberto, you're not able to show your football. It's as if something is always put in the way, hindering you. God isn't allowing us to stay. He's not allowing us that option. He will close doors so that His will is fulfilled.'

In January Cody Gakpo, the young Dutch player who had shone at the World Cup and had similar playing characteristics to mine, was signed. In the club's view, the future was secured with Gakpo, Darwin, Luis and Diogo Jota. And, of course, Salah had renewed his contract.

I still thought there was a place for me in this attack. I had experience and a deep connection to the club; the team improved when I was on the field. I could help the younger guys and, of course, play – the schedule demands a lot from the squad. Klopp had told the management he wanted me to stay, but the club's view was that I would no longer be a protagonist. And, honestly, I don't know if the Boss wanted to go into battle with management, backing me no matter what it cost. The season wasn't going well, he had other concerns, and he was also under pressure for better results.

I accepted a shorter contract – one year instead of two. I told the club I would accept a significant salary reduction. That wasn't an issue. Money didn't matter. But communication was muddled and responses were slow. One week ... three weeks ... a month. We kept compromising, but it didn't seem like there was a real willingness on the other side to finalize negotiations. Things dragged on through January and February. By that point, my agents told me that they were only continuing negotiations with the club out of respect for my desire to stay and the love we had for Liverpool.

On the field, I wasn't the figure I had been, my grip on a place ever more precarious. I returned to play in

February after the calf injury and remained on the bench in every match. My wife can tell you what it was like having to endure my bad moods during the last two seasons in Liverpool, how irritable I was as I spent more time sitting on the sidelines than anywhere else.

I was ready. I was back, but I wasn't playing. The Boss was avoiding me now. I wanted to demand an explanation for what was happening, but I couldn't get his attention. Those weeks were filled with anguish for me and my family due to the uncertainty. If the World Cup had been my top priority before, now it was my future at Liverpool. A concern that didn't exist before, a possibility I had never truly imagined, was becoming real. Maybe they really didn't want me. Maybe it really was over.

The straw that broke the camel's back was a match against Wolves, in which I came on as a substitute in the last minute. That was it. Right there, I understood. As we say in Brazil, the penny dropped.

I knew now.

I called my agents. Roger Wittmann and Christian Rapp met with me for a face-to-face talk. We left the living room and went to my room: just me, Christian, Roger and Larissa, no distractions. Christian and Roger were perfectly transparent about everything that was happening and the club's view of my future. It wasn't a war. It was just a difference in understanding about what I could offer to Liverpool.

I reflected a lot and realized that God's plan was to take me somewhere else. The signs were all there since that conversation with Pastor Daniel in Maceió. I had been stubborn. God didn't want me to stay in Liverpool, but I was insisting. I didn't listen. But I couldn't avoid it any more. It was time to accept. I decided it was time to seek another challenge for myself, another purpose. My time at Liverpool had come to an end.

It had been a beautiful story that I wanted to finish the right way. We are very grateful for everything we experienced in England; all of our dreams, mine and my family's, were fulfilled. We experienced the greatest joys and triumphs; it was all so intense. And we didn't want to leave with any bitterness, anger or resentment.

If it was difficult for them to say, well then I would say it: 'I'm not staying. I'll go.' If deep in their hearts they weren't sure about extending my contract, if they didn't know what to do, then for the good of everyone I would make the decision to leave.

And so we arrived at 3 March 2023. I wrote the message to Klopp on my own, on my cell phone, and let my heart guide my fingers.

Then I went to training.

After the session, I went to the Boss's office and asked his assistant if he was available. When I walked into the room, Klopp was sitting behind his desk, drinking a cup of coffee.

He looked at me and said, 'I think I know what you want to talk about.' I'm not sure if he knew. Maybe he thought I was going to complain about not getting many minutes. Maybe he knew the topic could be my departure. I had my phone in my hand. I opened the note titled 'Meeting'. But I didn't even need to read it. I had practised my speech so many times that I had memorized it. It felt like an eternity, but it only took a few seconds for it to leave my mouth. Our conversation didn't last longer than five minutes.

'There are things that are not in my hands. I don't have control over everything,' the Boss said. He accepted the decision very quickly. One of my fears was that he would insist on me staying. I had already made the decision guided by God and didn't want to backtrack now. It had been hard enough getting this far. He had fought to keep my friend Philippe Coutinho a few years back; I didn't want the same to happen with me. Now, having finally accepted the inevitable, I took the step I had never wanted to take.

But no, Klopp didn't insist. At that moment, it seemed like he already knew, or had come to terms with the idea. There would be no extension. It was over. I praised the Boss a lot, said he was the best coach I had ever worked with, and thanked him greatly for the opportunity he had given me at Liverpool. I think he felt awkward and it was the most emotional moment of the conversation.

Right afterwards, he said he didn't want to say goodbye

yet. After all, there were still three months left in the season. That's what I wanted to convey as well. The need to keep going and fighting until the end was in the message I had written on my phone. For all that we were parting, our mindset was still the same. 'Let's wait a bit, Bobby. We'll bid farewell later.'

There was football to play. We shook hands and I left the room.

Chapter 20

I'll Never Walk Alone

After the meeting with Klopp, the first person I ran into was Virgil van Dijk, in the gym. I told him what had happened and he was surprised, asking me why I had made the decision. I replied straight away: 'Because the club doesn't want me to stay.' After him, I talked to the Brazilian players on the team and with the captain, Jordan Henderson. Everyone was saddened, but they understood; there was no need to try to convince me to stay.

I don't believe that two options were presented to me: stay or go. Throughout, I had only one option, and, at some point, one side or the other was going to have to say so explicitly. In the end, it had to be me who took the initiative. But it doesn't matter. I don't hold grudges. Klopp was definitely not to blame for anything; he wasn't the villain. There are no villains in this story. I can't explain it, but it felt like, at that exact moment when I left the coach's office, a weight had been lifted off my shoulders. I felt free, I felt lighter; a sense of peace came over me.

From the moment I decided to leave, all I wanted was to leave well, with my head held high, and help the club achieve its goals. We were still in the Champions League, despite the 5–2 loss to Real Madrid at Anfield. And we were still fighting for the top positions in the Premier League table to secure qualification for the 2023–24 Champions League.

The first game after the announcement of my departure was against our bitter rivals Manchester United at Anfield. We needed to win to keep our hopes of finishing in the top four alive. And we did so in style! The 7–0 victory was the largest over our historic rivals in Liverpool's history. It was an epic afternoon, a match to be remembered by all who were at Anfield or watched from anywhere around the world. We had already achieved other big results; we weren't the kind of team an opponent could let their guard down against and lose intensity once a win was secure. We never stopped, we always wanted more. We were the team that scored one goal, then went for the second, the third, the fourth, the fifth ... even the seventh. That was the mindset of our Liverpool.

I came on towards the end of the game, with the rout already secured. I played a part in the sixth goal, as a United defender kicked the ball into my legs and it fell to Salah to score. And I had the joy of scoring the seventh. In all those years, this was the moment I felt most affection from my teammates, most loved. I had announced my departure a few days earlier, and that created an atmosphere of great emotion between me and the guys. Everyone celebrated massively, as if it were a farewell, as if it were my last goal for Liverpool. Besides, of course, adding to the humiliation of United and a much-needed victory.

I had never seen them celebrate a goal of mine so much; it was truly special. In the dressing room I received hugs from everyone. It was all: 'You're a legend, Bobby! ... I can't believe you're leaving!'

On top of all that, it was also the game's seventh goal I had scored, which held a special meaning for me. The Bible says that seven is the number of perfection. The game ended 7-0, a historic scoreline, and I scored the seventh, the goal of perfection. God had set me free again to be the footballer I was. No more barriers, no more anxieties; I just needed to follow His plan. Two days later, on 7 March, quite fittingly, our daughter Sophia was born.

After that epic moment against United, the rollercoaster continued. We were eliminated by Real Madrid in the Champions League – the fourth time in six years that our European title dream was halted by them. We suffered a ruthless thrashing from Manchester City. And I even – inadvertently, of course – helped City in their fight for the

Premier League by scoring a goal in our draw against the then league leaders Arsenal at Anfield, after we were 0–2 down. It was my 11th goal in 18 games against Arsenal, more than against anyone else, and it hurt their title push. Nothing personal.

And then I had another injury that kept me out for another month.

During the recovery period, the club organized one of those trips for players which Klopp had always encouraged as a way to create a more united group. The players all went to Barcelona for a farewell party for me, James Milner, Alex Oxlade-Chamberlain and Naby Keïta, who would also be leaving the club. The guys went right after a game against Brentford – there were nine days without Premier League matches afterwards. I chose to go only on Monday. We spent some really great hours at the hotel near the beach in Barcelona. I didn't expect to receive that tribute and was moved by the words I heard. Then came the final three matches, all emotional, all forever etched in my memory.

Curiously, I didn't even step onto the field in the first of those. I wasn't fully recovered and available yet. It was a game in Leicester, which we won 3–0 – our seventh consecutive victory in the league, still giving us a chance of finishing in the top four – and at the end of the match our fans serenaded me for over 15 minutes: '*Sí, Señor!*' My teammates joined in, brought me to them, and participated in that incredible moment. Alisson lifted me up. I hadn't even played! But they never left me alone for a minute. It was unexpected, touching. I felt it deep in my heart. Describing these kinds of moments is very difficult. Having to put those feelings into words is unfair, an impossible task that simplifies something complex and layered. It was one of the most beautiful tributes I've ever received – and, I repeat, it was absolutely unexpected, as I wasn't even in kit, and that wasn't our ground. The fans who made that night so special for me in Leicester will be forever cherished in my heart.

Next came the match against Aston Villa, my last at Anfield. On a day of tributes, my mother was at the stadium, along with my father and sister, and she said she cried while hugging a child who was wearing the number 9 shirt with her son's name on it. The child probably didn't understand much or have any idea who that emotional lady was embracing him, but it meant the world to her, and to her that kid represented the entire Liverpool fanbase. It was like this was her chance to hug them all, to offer thanks for how they had treated her family, who they had taken to their hearts.

The hours leading up to the game in the dressing room were very emotional. I exchanged messages with my wife, who sent me videos of beautiful moments being shared on social media. She also sent me a text from Captain

Henderson published in the matchday programme for that game against Villa. This is what it said:

> I think I can speak for all of the players when I say that to have had the opportunity to play alongside this guy has been a privilege. He's unique. There's no reference point when it comes to comparing Bobby. There's never been anyone quite like him and I doubt there ever will be again. To be that talented, have that much skill and then to work as hard and smart as he does, is remarkable.
>
> Humility in professional football is just as important as humility in life. The way Bobby plays, the selflessness of it, is what makes him so, so special.
>
> To have that much magic and ability and still sacrifice yourself for your team . . . honestly, for any young player wanting to be a forward, he is the benchmark. He's not afraid to express himself and do all the tricks but at the same time makes sure he earns that right by doing the non-spectacular things also. His status as an all-time Liverpool great is secured.
>
> His name will be sung at Anfield for decades, I'm sure, in the same way fans still celebrate players like Sir Kenny Dalglish and Ian Rush.
>
> Probably the biggest compliment I can pay Bobby is that he is an even better person than he is a football

player. The man is full of love and joy. Whenever I hear his name I will always smile. That's the impact he's had on all of us lucky enough to know him and be able to call him a friend.

I cried a lot when I read those words. I'm getting emotional now as I write them out again. It was one of the most beautiful and sensitive things anyone has ever said about me. Henderson, our great captain, is a friend for life.

The time had come, and around the stadium you could see the number 9 jersey everywhere. There were Brazilian flags, and a simply wonderful mural was painted on the side of a house on Rockfield Road in my honour. I was shocked by its size and detail, so I quickly grabbed my phone and recorded it from the bus window to keep that image with me.

This was the last time. *Everything* was the last time: a final glimpse, a final chance to live all that had been part of me. Stepping off the bus, arriving in the dressing room, putting on the kit. I wasn't very superstitious, but, on that day, knowing I was leaving and aware of the tradition, I touched the 'This is Anfield' sign which hangs above the tunnel exit from the dressing room to the field. I wasn't one of those players who did it habitually, before every game, but that day was different.

Again, I started on the bench and came on with the team

losing, about 15 minutes before the end of the game. After a pass from Salah in the penalty area, I threw myself at the ball to score the equalizer. It was a technically tricky move, a goal of determination – and it hurt. Initially, I didn't think about the fact that it would be my last goal at Anfield. I was only concerned about the victory; we needed the result to continue fighting for the Champions League place.

There had been so many memorable celebrations in that stadium: eye covering, capoeira moves, gunslinger shots. But at that moment there was none. I just picked up the ball from the back of the net and took it to the centre of the field to attempt a comeback. I might have been the only one concerned about the comeback, perhaps. Along the way, I knelt down, pointing my fingers to the sky, thanking the Lord. Then I turned toward the Kop and made a heart symbol with both hands. And right after that, the referee blew the whistle and the game ended.

In moments, everything faded. What followed overwhelmed me. Right after the final whistle, the tributes began. When I hugged my friend Alisson, I couldn't hold back the tears. My great brother in Christ, one of the most special people I've met to this day, carried me across Anfield's turf in the same way he carried me onto the path of the Lord, onto the right path. The eight-year film of my time in Liverpool flashed through my mind, and I was floored by the love emanating from the field and the stands.

Still, the draw had been disappointing and practically eliminated our chances of finishing the league in fourth place. When I met Larissa after leaving the field, in the tunnel to the dressing room, I was sulking and upset that I hadn't been able to help Liverpool achieve its goal. And she opened my eyes: 'Patience; this time it didn't work out, it doesn't depend solely on you. But it's your last game here. Look at what they're doing around you, all the love you're receiving.'

I wasn't the only one bidding farewell to Anfield on 20 May 2023. It was also the last game for three teammates who'd stood by my side through thick and thin, guys with whom I shared glory and laughter at Liverpool: Milner, Keïta and Oxlade-Chamberlain. Our teammates formed a guard of honour on the field and we were called one by one to receive from the hands of Sir Kenny Dalglish, Liverpool's greatest ever player, two frames displaying the trophies won in red, and some of the memorable photos from the past years and the tribute in Barcelona. When my name was called – even before that – Anfield was already singing 'Sí, Señor' at the top of its lungs.

After the tribute, the first embrace on the field was with Jürgen Klopp. The coach spoke beautiful words about me at that moment of farewell: 'I will forever be grateful for everything he did for us, for me. He will forever remain one of Liverpool's greats. What more can you wish for in a footballer's life?'

The next day, there would be another farewell party at Anfield, but this time without the fans. We wanted to say goodbye to everyone – families, friends, everyone who was part of that beautiful journey in the north-west. Liverpool were very accommodating and lent us the stadium for a private celebration. It's not something common. It's rare, something maybe only a few legends of the club, like Steven Gerrard, have had the opportunity to do. They arranged everything, did it all for me. And everyone they called came, which just doesn't happen – 98 per cent attendance, they told me. No one wanted to miss it; they said they had never seen anything like it. Everyone wanted to hug Bobby Firmino. I felt loved, respected, touched. It was our private party, but the club's guys, led by Ray Houghton, took care of everything. They were very kind. They provided a bus to collect our guests and friends, picked us up from home, and even allowed all the trophies I had won to be there for us to take pictures with. It was another extremely special day that left us humbled. It showed how the club was also grateful and respected the beautiful history we had built together. Not only were my teammates there, but all the club staff, executives and the scouts who recommended my signing: Michael Edwards, David Fallows, Barry Hunter, Andy Sayer and Fernando Troiani. Everyone showed up.

Klopp and almost all the players took to the stage and said beautiful things about me and those glorious years into the microphone. Henderson sang, leading another round of '*Sí, Señor*'. My four daughters, my entire family, and so many friends were there. I was moved once again. I also took to the stage and read my speech in English – when videos of it were posted on the internet, it was probably the first time most fans had seen me speaking in English. I've still got the full speech written down, from the heart. It went like this:

Dear teammates, dear colleagues outside the squad, dear manager, dear friends, dear children, dear Liverpool family,

Eight years of Liverpool are coming to an end for my family and me in a few days. Naturally, I already knew about Liverpool FC when I arrived here from Germany eight years ago. And yet, I had no idea! I had no idea how much passion there is in this club. And what a huge part this club plays in the lives of so many people around the world. I didn't know how positively crazy and how passionate the people who work at this club are. And how much this club and this stadium means to them.

And the truth is: I never would have dreamed that it was possible to achieve what we have achieved together. And never, never, never would I have imagined feeling so at home here. As important as the trophies we have won together are, at the end of the day football is just a game. And the title that one is currently fighting for will always be the most important.

It was the people that made Liverpool my home, not the sporting successes. It was not just any people, it was you, you who are here tonight. And for that I would like to thank you from the bottom of my heart. And you can see how much this means to me – how much you mean to me – just by the fact that I'm doing something that is actually one of my least favourite things to do. To speak publicly here in front of all of you.

Roberto – Bobby – Firmino and Liverpool was not a sure thing, not an overnight success ... If there is one experience I would like to pass on and share with every young player who arrives in this club, it is this. It is my story, the story of a young footballer with:

- a dream
- a chance
- mistakes
- setbacks
- defiance and anger
- even more mistakes
- even more setbacks, and then getting motivated again and again by the trust I received from my teammates, our manager and the people at the club who believed in me.

But you wouldn't have accepted my invitation tonight, and there's no way that Liverpool would have let me invite you to this stadium, if it wasn't for one person: my wife Larissa. Without you, there would be no Bobby Firmino. Without you, not only would there be no Bobby Firmino, as an athlete, but also there would be no Bobby Firmino as a person, a husband and a father. Without her and our wonderful family, no one would look back on my time at Liverpool and say goodbye the way you are doing tonight. *Muito obrigado meu amor!*

My story also cannot be told without talking about our manager. The confidence, the guidance, the motivation and passion I have received from you is unparalleled in quality and quantity. And how much has been said and written about this man ... How extraordinary he is, how brilliant he is, etc, etc ... But I have found out your secret ... You too have a Larissa by your side! *Obrigado treinador!*

Those who are familiar with my football know that I am not a solo artist. I can only function as part of a team, and it has been a pleasure and a tremendous honour over the last eight years to be on the pitch with some of the best footballers in the world – but, above all, with some of the finest people on this planet. Everything we have ever achieved has only been possible because of this incredible community. Dear teammates, thank you for this wonderful time, for your support and for allowing us to shape an era together in this extraordinary club.

This team is surrounded by the best, the warmest, the craziest, the funniest, the most detail-obsessed and the coolest people from every department imaginable. Without you not a single thing in this club would work. Thank you for doing what you do and being who you are!

I would also like to thank all my friends who are here tonight and who have nothing to do with football. You have helped us to feel at home here just like a normal family.

Wherever the road may take my family and me, we will miss you! But above all, we will keep you all in our hearts. Forever! It has been the honour of my life so far to have been part of this Liverpool family. You will never walk alone!

My final year had been confused and contradictory. I had mixed emotions. For a while, the truth is we felt somewhat sidelined by the club. My family and I were saddened and frustrated by a departure that, deep in our hearts, we didn't want to happen. But the final days were wonderful, and we felt loved and respected again. We held onto all we had done together; nothing could break that. We understood that

God's will was speaking loudly, and I reiterate, there are no villains. It's not a sad story. It's an incredibly happy story; the chapter of 'Firmino at Liverpool' had come to an end.

There was still one more game to play for the final round. We played in Southampton in a thrilling match that ended in a 4–4 draw. We practically had no chances left and, indeed, we ended up without a spot in the Champions League. In my last ever game for Liverpool, I scored. A pass into the area from another great friend, Fabinho, found me and, for the last time, I struck the ball right-footed into the net. It was my 111th goal.

Life takes many twists and turns. One month after the farewell, nearly four months after the announcement of my departure, the offer to play in the Saudi Arabian football league for Al-Ahli came to me through my representatives. A few weeks later, I received news that Fabinho would also leave Liverpool to live in Jeddah, in the same city and country where I would begin the new phase of my career. On that sunny afternoon in Southampton, we had no idea about the plan God had prepared for us. Unfortunately, Fabinho couldn't bid farewell to our fans in the way he deserved, as the deal was finalized during the summer transfer window. The same happened to Henderson.

Leaving home – and it was home – was very tough. Alisson and Natália helped us load our bags into the cars. Larissa cried a lot. We explained to the kids that those toys that had been part of their lives would have to be left behind and a new phase was about to begin. We returned to Maceió, to reconnect with close family and friends, and, of course, the Christian community that shares our faith. Then came the move to a place with different customs and culture, trying to open its doors to the world; a place where football still needs to develop but where there's a passion for the game. In my first official match, I donned an all-green jersey, just like the last one with Liverpool. I scored three goals in Al-Ahli's victory, my first hat-trick in so many years. And the story goes on.

I wonder if I'll ever find another place like Anfield, with the same atmosphere, the same feeling; if I'll ever find fans as amazing as those of Liverpool Football Club. I love the club, love the city, love the fans, and I will miss those wonderful days, but I will always have the memories we made together. What we built there was beautiful and it will remain in my life forever. I never dreamed it would be possible to achieve what we did. It was the honour of my life to be a part of Liverpool, and I will forever be a Red.